www.ingramcontent.com/pod-product-compliance
Lightning Source LLC
Chambersburg PA
CBHW081216230426

43666CB00015B/2756

זְמַן לִקְרֹא
TIME TO READ HEBREW
VOLUMES ONE & TWO

TEACHER GUIDE

Hillary Zana and Dina Maiben
with Orna Ariel Lenchner

A.R.E Publishing
an imprint of Behrman House, Inc.
Springfield, New Jersey

Published by:
A.R.E Publishing
an imprint of Behrman House, Inc.
Springfield, New Jersey

© A.R.E. Publishing, Inc. 2002
ISBN 13: 978-0-86705-076-9

All rights reserved. No part of this work covered by the copyrights hereon may be reproduced or copied in any form or by any means — graphic, electronic, or mechanical, including photocopying, recording, taping, or information retrieval systems — without the written permission of the copyright owner.

Printed in the United States of America

ACKNOWLEDGEMENTS

Grateful thanks to:

Those who served on our Peer Review Committee and offered many valuable comments and suggestions on the program prior to publication: Lori Abramson, Director of Education, Temple Sinai, Oakland, California; Ophira Druch, Assistant Educator, Temple Sinai, Oakland, California; Vanessa Ehrlich, Director of Education, Lakeside Congregation, Highland Park, Illinois; Ronald Leff, Director of Education, Congregation Emanuel, Denver, Colorado; Rabbi Barry Lutz, Director of Education, Ahavat Shalom, Northridge, California; Michael Raileanu, Religious School Director, Sinai Temple, Los Angeles, California; Dr. Barbara Rosoff, Master Teacher for the Teacher Professional Development Program of the Central Agency for Jewish Education of Broward County, Florida; Leslie Smith, Associate Director, California Writing Project, University of California Santa Cruz; Cantor Arlyne Unger, Cantor and Educational Director, Beth Tikvah B'nai Jeshurun, Erdenheim, Pennsylvania; Ephrat Yakobi, Hebrew Coordinator, Temple Ahavat Shalom, Northridge, California; Rabbi Bernard Zlotowitz, Senior Scholar, Union of American Hebrew Congregations; Orly Zvi, Hebrew Language Curriculum Coordinator and Ulpan Director, Day School and Religious School of Valley Beth Shalom, Encino, California. Special thanks also to members of the faculty of the Temple Shaari Emeth Religious School in Manalapan, New Jersey; Hana Alter, Barbara Cautin, Lisa Greenberg, Joanna Livne, and Marsha Zagoren, who field tested drafts of these materials with their students and provided valuable feedback on the project as a whole.

Marji Gold-Vukson, author and consultant, for her analysis of the workbooks for age appropriate language.

Professor Rivka Dori, Hebrew Language Educator and Coordinator of Hebrew Programming at Hebrew Union College-Jewish Institute of Religion in Los Angeles, who has consulted with us since the initial conception of the זְמַן לִקְרֹא Program almost two decades ago. We are grateful for her very careful and perceptive reading of every draft of these workbooks, and for her help, support, and encouragement throughout the development and publication of the entire A.R.E. Hebrew System. Any errors in this Teacher Guide and in the Workbooks are not hers, and will be corrected in future editions.

Our editors, Rabbi Raymond A. Zwerin and Audrey Friedman Marcus, Senior Editors at A.R.E. Publishing, are true visionaries. For more than a quarter of a century, they have dedicated themselves to creating materials for Jewish education that meet the highest standards of excellence. We owe a debt of gratitude to them for their unwavering faith in this program from its inception all the way through this new edition, for their expert cultivation of the creative team, and the courage to support innovation. The trust they place in their authors and their willingness to listen are rare gifts. We take this opportunity to welcome our new publisher, Steve Brodsky, who assumed the helm of leadership in the middle of this revision. His integrity and passion for Jewish education, his warmth and support, and his ability to think outside the box ensure the continuation of A.R.E. Publishing's long tradition of excellence.

Finally, very special thanks are due to our families, who willingly supported us and endured our interminable late night phone calls. Without their love and devotion, the new זְמַן לִקְרֹא would not have come into being.

CONTENTS

Introduction	7	Lesson 6	57
Overview	7	Lesson 7	64
Goals of the Program	7	Lesson 8	70
Unique Nature of the Program	7	Lesson 9	75
Sequence Chart	9	Lesson 10	83
A Note about Pronunciation and Spelling	10	Lesson 11	88
		Lesson 12	96
Type Styles and Letter Formation	11	Lesson 13	100
Components of the Program	11	Lesson 14	107
Letter Formation Chart	13	Lesson 15	111
The Seven Lesson Steps	14	Lesson 16	119
Research on Hebrew Reading	17	Lesson 17	124
Classroom Interaction	20	Lesson 18	129
Approaches to Teaching	21	Lesson 19	134
Remediation	23	Lesson 20	137
Mnemonics Chart	24	Games and Other Activities	141
Additional Uses of the Program	24	Using זְמַן לָשִׁיר in the Classroom	152
Bibliography	26	זְמַן לָשִׁיר Vocabulary Chart	160
Lesson 1	27	Class Evaluation Forms	161
Lesson 2	35	Placement Test	163
Lesson 3	40	Dictionary	165
Lesson 4	45	Cognate Cards	167
Lesson 5	50	Hebrew Letter and Vowel Cards	175

INTRODUCTION

Overview

You are about to implement a unique program for teaching Hebrew "decoding" (mechanical reading) through Jewish concepts. This program is designed for children in Grades 3 or 4 who receive at least one hour of Hebrew language instruction each week. It is appropriate for supplementary Hebrew school students as a beginning Hebrew reading program, as a refresher course, and in remedial settings. It consists of 20 lessons, 10 in each of two Workbooks.

זְמַן לִקְרֹא *Time to Read Hebrew*, is a Hebrew primer. It is the second component of the A.R.E. Hebrew System, which begins with the Hebrew reading readiness book, קָדִימָה! *Get Ready for Hebrew!* The A.R.E. Hebrew System continues in the following years with the זְמַן לִתְפִילָה *Time for Prayer* Program. Although זְמַן לִקְרֹא *Time to Read Hebrew* can stand alone, it works best when used as part of the entire system.

Goals of the Program

The primary goal of זְמַן לִקְרֹא is to enable students to acquire skills necessary to decode Hebrew accurately and with some fluency. Upon completion of the 20 lessons, students should have the skills to decode almost any vocalized text in modern, biblical, or *Siddur* Hebrew. More advanced reading skills and those specific to reading *Siddur* Hebrew are introduced later in the זְמַן לִתְפִילָה series. זְמַן לִקְרֹא introduces each letter and vowel through a set of Hebrew "Key Words," many of which represent basic Jewish vocabulary. In addition to these Key Words, a core vocabulary of approximately 60 words is offered, along with several basic sentence structures. These items may be taught at the teacher's option. Although this supplemental vocabulary component is optional, making use of it can greatly enrich the program.

Unique Nature of the Program

The following ten characteristics and their interrelationships are what make this program the most effective and pedagogically sound Hebrew primer available.

1. זְמַן לִקְרֹא is a highly structured program based on a solid foundation of **educational research**.
2. New consonants and vowels are taught through the use of **Key Words**, which are Jewish concept words.
3. Hebrew reading is placed within a **language framework**.
4. **Confusing consonants and vowels** are separated.
5. **Easy and common concepts** are taught first.
6. **Difficult concepts** are taught directly.
7. Hebrew decoding is presented as a **bridge to** *Siddur* reading.
8. **Active learning strategies** are integrated into the program.
9. **A variety of materials and components** is available to teach, evaluate, and reinforce.
10. The program is **effective with all learners** — the highly skilled, as well as slow learners and the learning disabled.

Following is a full discussion of each of these ten characteristics:

1. **Research Based**

    All the central features of זְמַן לִקְרֹא are based on the findings of research into language acquisition and Hebrew reading instruction. Confusing letters (such as ד and ר) are separated, those that represent identical sounds are generally presented together (e.g., ב and ו), and reading drills focus on the vowels. Further, the entire program has been built around a framework of Hebrew language because educational research has shown that such strategies and approaches foster success in learning to read Hebrew. For a more complete discussion of the research on which זְמַן לִקְרֹא is based, see the section entitled "Research on Hebrew Reading," below.

2. Key Words

The program introduces new consonants and vowels through Key Words. The Key Words are usually Jewish concept words that are already part of the vocabulary of most children, e.g., מַצָּה, מִצְוָה, חַלָּה, שַׁבָּת. These concept words are often grouped into topics, such as Israel, holidays, the classroom, and the home.

After students are introduced to the whole Key Word, they are encouraged by the teacher to break the word into its component sounds. This emphasis on phoneme analysis helps students understand the relationship between letters and sounds in Hebrew. (For a complete explanation, see Bryant and Bradley, 1985.)

The chart on the next page outlines the sequence in which the Key Words, new letters, new vowels, and vocabulary are introduced.

3. Language Framework

Hebrew reading is taught within a language framework. In addition to the Key Words discussed above, real Hebrew words are used for decoding practice as soon as possible. This differs from the common practice of teaching phonics through nonsense words. It also ensures that students will not be exposed to Hebraically impossible combinations, an error often found in Diaspora Hebrew primers. זְמַן לִקְרֹא also contains supplemental vocabulary, an introduction to root words, and cognates (words that are the same in Hebrew and English). If desired, the teacher can incorporate the Hebrew vocabulary component as an integral part of the program. As students learn new consonants and vowels, they are taught new Hebrew words formed from them. Varied written exercises and short conversations reinforce this vocabulary.

A list of the vocabulary included in the Workbooks is included in the chart on page 9 of this Teacher Guide.

4. Confusing Consonants and Vowels

The Hebrew letters are not introduced in *alef-bet* order. The order in which letters are introduced is planned specifically so that confusing consonants and vowels are taught separately (e.g., שׁ/שׂ, ר/ד, ב/ב, ו/וֹ, ◌/◌). This principle has been well documented in research literature (Carnine, 1979; Feitelson, 1981), but it is often violated in other Hebrew textbooks.

5. Easy and Common Concepts

Easy and/or common concepts are taught first. For example, easily pronounced and common vowel sounds (the *Kamatz* and *Patach*) are taught first, while the more complex combinations, such as the final position of ◌ָה and ◌ִי are introduced later on in Lessons 15 and 18.

6. Difficult Concepts

Difficult concepts are taught directly. For example, there are separate Key Words for teaching each of the three positions of the *Shva* (Lessons 9, 14, 19), and the *Kamatz Katan* (Lesson 19). Virtually every idiosyncrasy of Hebrew decoding is explained.

7. A Bridge To Siddur Reading

זְמַן לִקְרֹא creates an effective bridge between basic Hebrew decoding and the mastery of *Siddur* text. Many of the words incorporated into the reading drills are drawn from prayer texts. In addition, the final pages in lessons 5 through 17 are entitled "Prepare for Prayer." Through these pages, students are introduced to words and phrases, as well as several Hebrew root words, that are commonly found in the *Siddur*.

8. Active Learning Strategies

Whenever possible, new learning actively involves the learner. This is especially important for students who learn Hebrew in a supplementary school setting after a long day engaged in secular studies. Active learning is generally a most effective way to learn and to teach. For example, lessons begin by asking students to evoke the Key Words rather than simply presenting the words to the class and explaining what they mean. The exercises rely heavily on cognates, words that are used in both English and Hebrew (e.g., pizza, banana, telephone). In

Sequence Chart

Additional Vocabulary	Key Words	New Vowels	New Letters	Lesson #
-	שַׁבָּת	ַ ָ	שׁ ב ת	1
-	דָג	-	ד נ	2
-	אַבָּא, אִמָּא	ִ	א מ	3
חַ__	מַצָּה, הַגָּדָה	-	צ ה	4
מִי?, בַּיִת, בַּ__, בַּבַּיִת	אֲנִי, יָד	ֲ	נ י	5
מַה?	קָדוֹשׁ, יַיִן	וֹ וִי	ק ו	6
רַבִּי, מַיִם, גִיר	פּוּרִים	-	פ ר ם	7
אַתָּה, תַּחַת, חָתוּל	חַלָּה	-	ח ל ך	8
אֶת, מִשְׁפָּחָה, בַּר-מִצְוָה, בַּת-מִצְוָה	מִצְוָה, הַבְדָּלָה	silent medial ְ	ו ב	9
בְּכִתָּה, עַל, עַל-יַד	עִבְרִית, כִּתָּה	-	כּ ע	10
דֶגֶל, יַלְדָה, יֶלֶד, מָגֵן דָוִד, מַחְבֶּרֶת	פֶּסַח, יִשְׂרָאֵל	ֶ ֵ	שׂ ס	11
כֶּלֶב	סֵפֶר, אָלֶף	-	פ ף	12
מוֹרֶה/מוֹרָה, תּוֹרָה, לוֹמֵד/לוֹמֶדֶת, לֹא, כֵּן	שָׁלוֹם, בֹּקֶר טוֹב	וֹ ֹ	ט	13
צְדָקָה, אוֹהֵב/אוֹהֶבֶת, עִם, וְ__	סְלִיחָה, בְּבַקָּשָׁה	initial voiced ְ	-	14
כִּסֵא, עִפָּרוֹן, לוּחַ, גָדוֹל, קָטָן, נֵר, זְבְרָה	מַזָּל טוֹב, חַג שָׂמֵחַ, בֵּית-כְּנֶסֶת	ַחַ ֵי ֵה ֵא	ז	15
אֵיפֹה?, בֵּית-סֵפֶר	עֵץ חַיִים, מִצְוֹת	וֹ (vo)	ץ	16
-	בְּרָכָה, שֻׁלְחָן	ֻ	כ	17
-	מֶלֶךְ, חַי	ַי ֵי	ךָ	18
-	בְּכָל נַפְשְׁךָ	ָ = וֹ, ָ	-	19
-	מֹשֶׁה, גוֹי	וֹ שׁ "double-duty dot"	-	20

this Teacher Guide, various strategies are provided that enable teachers to help students figure things out for themselves (based on their knowledge of English and whatever Hebrew they have learned).

9. A Variety of Materials and Components

A variety of materials is used to teach and to reinforce. In addition to sounding out Reading Pages and completing worksheets, students learn through the use of large letters that can be manipulated, as well as through games, chalkboard activities, and so forth. Students can be evaluated continually by using the Lesson Evaluations at the end of each Workbook, or by using the Placement Test found on page 163 of this guide. The basic program can be supplemented with the זְמַן לִקְרֹא *Activity Book*, Key Word and Vocabulary Poster Cards, and a creative song curriculum entitled זְמַן לָשִׁיר *Time to Sing Hebrew*.

10. Effective with All Learners

Not only is זְמַן לִקְרֹא an excellent program for highly skilled students, it is also appropriate for slow learners or children who are mildly learning disabled. For the latter students it can be used effectively in either a regular classroom or in a remedial setting. For these students, be sure to break lessons into two parts as explained later in this Teacher Guide.

A Note about Pronunciation and Spelling

Because Hebrew pronunciation is rather controversial, a note about its presentation is necessary here. זְמַן לִקְרֹא is based on the notion that all Hebrew pronunciations are valid, and seeks to facilitate the pronunciation of the community with which the Jewish school is affiliated.

It is a fundamental tenet of linguists that languages change as they are used. In fact, one of the best signs that Modern Hebrew is truly a living language is its constant state of change. Linguistic change can be observed in all aspects of a language: pronunciation, vocabulary, and grammar. These changes are readily apparent in the development of new words, in the gradual adaptation of existing word meanings, and even in the very slow transformation of grammatical forms. However, the aspect of language most prone to change is the area of pronunciation. Changes in pronunciation generally occur to facilitate the rapid speech of conversation, a pace that is much faster than either oration or dramatic reading.

While linguistic change is an inevitable feature of all living languages, there are certain conditions that tend to retard the rate of change within a given language. The first of these conditions is the development of writing. Those languages that have a form of written expression tend to change much more slowly than those that are purely oral. And of all the things that can slow the process of linguistic change, the thing that slows it the most is the use of a language for religious purposes. Because religions tend to preserve traditions, the use of a special language for religious expression tends to fossilize all aspects of that language, even its pronunciation. This is certainly the case of Hebrew, which survived for some 1700 years as לְשׁוֹן הַקֹּדֶשׁ (literally, "the sacred tongue"). For nearly two millenia, Hebrew has been the quintessential literary and liturgical language.

In the course of 17 centuries, all the Jewish communities in the Diaspora developed their own traditions regarding the pronunciation of vocalized Hebrew for use in reading the essential Hebrew texts, such as the Bible and prayer book. The people who inherited these traditions of pronunciation often developed strong emotional reactions to their own traditions of pronunciation. With the rebirth of Hebrew as a modern language, emotions became highly charged. Partly as a matter of cultural pride, Sephardic speakers strongly advocated the adoption of Sephardic pronunciation as the standard by claiming that Sephardic Hebrew is closer to the original pronunciation of the language. By contrast, many of the Ashkenazic pioneers in Israel, and the later refugees of war torn Europe, decried the use of the Ashkenazic pronunciation because of its negative association with life in the ghetto and *shtetl*.

Gradually, compromises began to emerge, through both natural linguistic development and the intervention of the Hebrew Language Committee (composed of the leading Hebrew scholars and writers). For example, the issue of creating a standardized pronunciation was raised at the first convention of the Hebrew Teachers' Association in 1903, but was unresolved because various members of the Hebrew Language Committee disagreed about certain key aspects of Sephardic pronunciation. Twenty years later, the Hebrew Language Committee officially ruled on a standard pronunciation of several key letters and vowels, but in several cases opted against a pure Sephardic pronunciation (e.g., צ as the Ashkenazic "tz" instead of the Sephardic "s"). Even in cases where the Committee ruled in favor of a Sephardic pronunciation, these rulings were useless in the face of the speech patterns that were naturally beginning to emerge within the real community of Hebrew language speakers.

One salient example of a linguistic compromise that developed naturally is in the pronunciation of ֵ (Tserey) and the ֶ (Segol). While the classical Hebrew grammar of most communities makes no real qualitative distinction between the pronunciations of ֵ (Tserey Chaser) and the ֵי (Tserey Maley) or between ֶ (Segol Chaser) and the ֶי (Segol Maley), a distinction began to develop in modern Hebrew pronunciation in Israel. Thus, most Israelis pronounce the ֵ and ֶ as the Sephardic "eh," but differentiate ֵי by pronouncing it as the classical Ashkenazic "ay." In recent years, there has been a very deliberate attempt by the Academy for the Hebrew Language (which succeeded the Hebrew Language Committee) to promote a true Sephardic pronunciation. At present, the Ministry of Education has been training language teachers to teach the pronunciation of all four of these vowels (ֶ, ֶי, ֵ, and ֵי,) as the pure Sephardic "eh," despite the already established speech patterns of Israeli students. (For a more complete discussion of Hebrew pronunciations and the development of the Hebrew language, see the *Encyclopaedia Judaica*, 13: 1120-1145 and 16: 1560-1662).

זְמַן לִקְרֹא allows for great flexibility in teaching Hebrew pronunciation, in recognition that pronunciation can vary from one congregation or community to another. So, the ֵ can be pronouced identical to the ֶ, as an English short "eh" as in "bed," which is in accord with traditional Israeli pronunciation, or the ֵ can be pronounced identically with the ֵי. The *Tserey Maley* (ֵי) is presented as "ay" as in "hay," despite the current directive of Israel's Ministry of Education to say even this phoneme as "eh." The *Tav* with and without a *Dagesh* (תּ, ת) is presented as "t." Finally, only the *Bet*, *Pey*, *Kaf*, and beginning in lesson 8, the *Tav*, appear with a *Dagesh*, and then only when grammatically appropriate. The *Tav* with a *Dagesh* (תּ) is not presented at the same time as the *Tav* without a *Dagesh* (ת) in Lesson 1 so that learners will not confuse it with ב. All other letters containing the *Dagesh* will be presented when students begin their study of prayer in the זְמַן לִתְפִּלָה series.

Type Styles and Letter Formation

Two styles of Hebrew type — *Siddur* and stylized stick figure — are used throughout the Workbooks. Students will need to be familiar with the *Siddur* style to read most Hebrew texts. However, they will occasionally encounter less formal styles of print. Therefore, a second type style is used to help students generalize the unique features of Hebrew letters. The stick figure style used herein is very close to the style students are asked to use when they write in the Workbooks. In this program students will write only block letters so as to reinforce the primary goal of Hebrew decoding. For script writing exercises, see the זְמַן לִקְרֹא *Activity Book*. A Letter Formation Chart, which also includes the names of letters, follows on page 13.

Components of the Program

The materials pertaining to this program include: the Workbooks, Volumes One and Two; this Teacher Guide; the זְמַן לִקְרֹא *Activity Book*; the music program זְמַן לָשִׁיר *Time to Sing Hebrew*; *Key Word Poster Cards* and *Vocabulary*

Poster Cards; and felt or magnetic letters (and board). In addition, you will find information and suggestions in the Hebrew Materials section of the A.R.E. web site. There are also some optional support materials, which you may find helpful. Each of these components is described below.

Workbooks

The Workbooks (Volumes One and Two) are the core of the program. Each Workbook contains 10 lessons which consist of three major components:

1. A Key Word/Phonics Introduction Page.
2. One or two Reading Pages.
3. Worksheets containing exercises to reinforce phonetic decoding and vocabulary. (These follow the Reading Pages.)
4. Prepare for Prayer Pages (Lessons 5-17) or Text Reading (Lessons 18 and 19).
5. A ten-word Evaluation for each lesson is found in the back of each Workbook.
6. There is also a dictionary at the back of each Workbook.

This Teacher Guide

In addition to a discussion of the rationale and structure of the זְמַן לִקְרֹא program, this Teacher Guide provides lesson-by-lesson and step-by-step instruction on how to teach the program. It specifies which new material is to be taught in each lesson, and also provides ideas for introducing new material, suggestions for reinforcement, and a section called "Games and Other Activites" (page 141).

Additionally, you will find two Class Evaluation forms on pages 161 and 162, one for each Workbook. After you have finished evaluating a student, record the score first in the student Workbook, and then on the Class Evaluation form. The use of these forms will give you a picture of individual student performances as well as overall classroom performance.

Use the Placement Test on page 163 to determine the lesson at which to begin a new student who has had some previous Hebrew instruction. It can also be used as a test at the end of the program to identify specific problems and to determine exactly which lesson should be used for remediation.

A list of the Key Words, New Letters, New Vowels, and Vocabulary is on page 9. Additionally, a dictionary which contains all of the words in both Volumes One and Two is included on page 165.

On page 167 is a list of cognates (words used in both Hebrew and English, such as "guitar"). This is followed by a set of pictures of these cognates which may be used for games. There is also a complete set of Hebrew consonants and vowels for use in games and as flash cards.

זְמַן לִקְרֹא *Activity Book* (for Volumes One and Two)

This supplementary resource for students provides additional worksheets and reading practice; vocabulary review sheets; games; hints and mnemonics for remembering the sounds of letters; passages to read from *Tanach*, *Siddur*, and *Haggadah*; and instructions and practice for writing script. It is available from A.R.E. Publishing, Inc.

זְמַן לָשִׁיר *Time to Sing Hebrew*

This innovative song curriculum can be integrated throughout the A.R.E. Hebrew System. Based on vocabulary from זְמַן לִקְרֹא, קָדִימָה!, and זְמַן לִתְפִילָה, it introduces students to simple sentence structures through a set of 14 delightful, easy to sing songs that were composed especially for this program by Fran Avni. A cassette tape and songbook that presents sheet music, lyrics, and chords for all of the songs are available from A.R.E. Publishing, Inc.

Felt or Magnetic Letters (and Board)

New consonants and vowels are introduced and reinforced through the use of large felt or magnetic letters. Letters should measure at least 1½" and need to be seen from all parts of the room. The ability to manipulate these letters and create new combinations with ease makes their use an essential part of the program.

Ready-made felt letters are available from A.R.E. Publishing, Inc. You will need to purchase two sets of these, as well as a felt board (or piece of non-synthetic felt). Keep letters that have already been learned in a separate plastic bag.

Letter Formation Chart

Ayin	ע	Yud	י	Alef	א
Pey	פ	Kaf	כ	Bet	ב
Final Fey	ף	Final Chaf	ך	Gimel	ג
Tsadi	צ	Lamed	ל	Dalet	ד
Final Tsadi	ץ	Mem	מ	Hey	ה
Koof	ק	Final Mem	ם	Vav	ו
Resh	ר	Nun	נ	Zayin	ז
Shin/Sin	ש	Final Nun	ן	Chet	ח
Tav	ת	Samech	ס	Tet	ט

For magnetic letters, apply a magnetic strip to the back of Hebrew letters mounted on card stock. Purchase the strips at arts and crafts or school supply stores. Use them on a magnetic board or magnetic chalkboard.

Additional Components

The following components maximize the effectiveness of זְמַן לִקְרֹא.

Flash Cards – זְמַן לִקְרֹא *Key Word Poster Cards* and זְמַן לִקְרֹא *Vocabulary Poster Cards* can be obtained from A.R.E. Publishing, Inc. These Poster Cards are flash cards that are large enough to be seen by the entire class. Not only are they useful for group drill and games, they make excellent labels for bulletin boards. A.R.E. Publishing, Inc. also produces *Kadimah Cards*, special folded cards of each Hebrew letter with a picture of a Key Word that begins with that letter. Although designed for use with the reading readiness program, these cards are very useful for review with students using זְמַן לִקְרֹא.

A set of small felt letters – A smaller version of the large letters is excellent for individual work with students who need remediation. These letters, available from A.R.E. Publishing, Inc., can be used for a variety of activities.

Hebrew foam letters – Small foam letters provide valuable tactile experience. They are ideal for use by students at their desks, and are available from A.R.E. Publishing.

The Internet Connection

The A.R.E. web site (www.arepublish.com) contains a special Hebrew Materials section. There you will find translations of all the real Hebrew words included on the Reading Pages, as well as other information and resources of interest to users of the A.R.E. Hebrew System. Periodic updates of the information in this section will allow teachers to remain on the cutting edge.

Optional Support Materials

The following support materials can be made by you, a teen classroom assistant, or an exceptional student who needs additional work. Each will enrich the program.

Hebrew/English letter cards – Make a set of letter cards using the Hebrew Letter and Vowel Cards at the back of this book. Write the English sound on the back of each card.

Picture file for vocabulary development – Create a file of pictures that correspond to the vocabulary taught in the program, as well as any other oral vocabulary you wish to teach.

Games and reinforcement activities – For many creative suggestions to enliven your classroom, see "Games and Other Activities" on page 141 in this Teacher Guide.

The Seven Lesson Steps

Before you begin any lesson, have all the materials ready and at easy access. It is recommended that the order of every lesson follows the Seven Lesson Steps below. (The **Oral Language Lesson** which preceeds the seven steps is optional, and is described below.)

1. **Review** recently learned consonants, vowels, and Key Words (and vocabulary if you are teaching that component).
2. Evoke the new **Key Word(s)**.
3. Introduce new **letters and vowels**.
4. Read from the **Reading Page(s)** with students.
5. Supervise students as they complete the **worksheets**.
6. Complete the **Prepare for Prayer Page** (Lessons 5-17) or the **Text Reading** page (Lessons 18-19).
7. **Evaluate**, then **remediate** trouble spots.

As stated above, the Oral Language Lesson is optional and, in each lesson, precedes the Seven Lesson Steps.

In a natural setting, children first acquire aural comprehension and then speech. Subsequently, they learn to read words that they already know. Knowing the vocabulary presented in the text makes reading easier and more enjoyable. If you have chosen to use the vocabulary component of the program, begin each session with a review of words previously taught. Then teach the new vocabulary of the current lesson. Make sure that you have introduced the new vocabulary word or words before students encounter them in their Workbooks. For each lesson, there are specific suggestions for introducing new vocabulary. Ideas in "Games and Other Activities" on page 141 in this Teacher Guide can be adapted for use in teaching vocabulary.

A full description of the Seven Lesson Steps follows:

1. Review

Review the Jewish concepts students have learned through the Key Word(s). Next, practice consonants and vowels that were learned in the last few lessons. Then, using flash cards, felt or magnetic letters, review consonants and vowels learned in the previous lesson. Finally, if you have recently introduced the second member of a pair of look-alike letters (e.g., the *Shin* and the *Sin*), practice reading these together.

Initially, don't emphasize the names of letters or vowels, and wait until Lesson 15 before you teach a Hebrew alphabet song.

2. Evoke Each New Key Word

Engage children in spirited interactions by giving them clues which will enable them to guess the new Key Word. Many of the Key Words will be familiar to the students. For each lesson, this Teacher Guide provides sample questions to ask the students that will help to evoke from them each Key Word. Be sensitive to the fact that some children may not be familiar even with the most common Jewish concepts, such as Shabbat. Have the more informed students share their knowledge without embarrassing others. Make sure all students understand the meaning of the Key Word before you proceed to the next step.

3. Introduce the New Letters and Vowels

One of the unique characteristics of alphabetic systems, such as English and Hebrew (as opposed to Chinese), is that the writing system represents phonemes (the smallest sound units). But it is difficult for some children to realize that you can break words into sounds and that each of these sounds has a corresponding letter or letters. In Hebrew, each letter or vowel has only one corresponding sound. Ask students to break a word into its different sounds, for example, SH-A-B-A-T or P-U-R-I-M. Ask students what the first sound is, then the next one, and so forth. (Learning disabled individuals often have difficulty with this kind of task, and especially benefit from this exercise.)

After you have broken the word into its component sounds, show the visual symbol (consonant or vowel) that goes with each respective sound. You can do this using the large felt or magnetic letters. The following simple guidelines will help you with this step.

a. Teach one consonant at a time. Make sure all students know it before introducing a new one.
b. When teaching more than one new letter in a lesson, remove the letter you have just taught from the felt or magnetic board, and do not bring it back until the second letter is learned.
c. Never introduce confusing letter pairs in the same lesson. If you are teaching the second member of a look-alike pair (for example, in Lesson 11, when you teach the שׂ, avoid the old letter at first, i.e., the שׁ).
d. Allow students every possible opportunity to apply what they already know, and to figure things out for themselves. For example, in Lesson 1, have students figure out that the ָ (*Kamatz*) and the ַ (*Patach*) make the same sound. Later, in Lesson 5, have them figure out that the ֲ (*Chataph-Patach*) has the same sound, too.
e. Reinforce and practice at each step.
f. When all components of the new Key Word have been taught, form that word on the felt or magnetic board. Show the appropriate Key Word Poster Card. This completes the process of breaking the whole word into its component sounds, forming each sound, and then putting the parts back together.

4. Read from the Reading Page(s)

The Reading Pages have been carefully structured according to several principles:
a. Reading drills focus on the vowels. When a new vowel is introduced, it is drilled with all of the consonants that have been introduced. This conforms to the findings of the research into Hebrew reading acquisition.
b. Short letter-vowel combinations appear first,

followed by longer combinations, and then by actual Hebrew words. Thus, when students read in a complete column from top to bottom, they confront words of increasing difficulty. From Lesson 8 on, all of the words on the Reading Pages are real Hebrew words. Even before that point, real Hebrew words are used as much as possible.

c. In each lesson, the Reading Pages begin by offering practice in the new letters and vowels. This is followed by letter-vowel combinations that review what was learned in the most recent lessons.

d. When the second of a pair of confusing letters or vowels is introduced in a lesson, the first of that pair is not shown with its look-alike for several numbered lines. In this way, students can master the new before going back to the old. Later in the lesson, those previously taught look-alikes do appear together.

e. There is often a relationship between the numbered lines. The same few letters will appear, but in combinations in which the blending gets increasingly more challenging (see pages 9 and 15 of Volume One for examples of this).

Use the Reading Pages to practice the new consonants and vowels in different combinations. First have students read the numbered lines, and then have them read the columns from top to bottom. Begin with group responses, progress to individual responses in seated order, and then go to individual responses at random. Consult "Games and Other Activities" on page 141 in this Teacher Guide for suggestions that will enrich the reading sessions.

f. Words derived from the same root are introduced to develop a feel for Hebrew's unique root system. Hebrew root words are introduced more formally in the Prepare for Prayer Pages that accompany Lessons 9, 10, 11, 13, and 14.

g. At the bottom of the Reading Pages for Lessons 1 through 14, you will find several words in a box. These are either Jewish concept words or useful words that you may want to teach your students. In Lessons 15 through 20, the boxes contain meaningful phrases, all of which are commonly available set to music. You might wish to integrate these songs into your school's music curriculum once students can read the text.

5. Supervise Students as They Complete the Worksheets

Most of the worksheets can be completed independently. However, you may find that some require extra explanation. Share this explanation right after students have finished reading from the Reading Page. In the Workbook dictionary, have students fill in the English definition of the new vocabulary for that particular lesson (if you are teaching vocabulary). In the dictionary, the numbers in parentheses refer to the lesson in which the word is introduced.

Some of your better students will be ready for the evaluation even before they have completed the written work. Evaluate these students whenever they are ready.

6. Complete the Prepare for Prayer Page

Lessons 5 through 17 end with a page designed to serve as a bridge between general Hebrew decoding and text reading in the *Siddur*. These pages are entitled "Prepare for Prayer." Some of the pages contain games that utilize the kinds of words found in the *Siddur*. Others introduce students to proper phraseology through common *Siddur* phrases. Many introduce students to the elegant system of Hebrew root words through examples of root words found in the *Siddur* and Bible. These activities lay the groundwork for full text reading, to which students are introduced in Lessons 18 and 19.

7. Evaluate and Remediate

One of the unique characteristics of this program is the built-in evaluation. The program is designed for the purpose of achieving mastery. You are not evaluating for grading purposes! You are evaluating to see what students really know. It is therefore important to organize your time so that you can evaluate each child individually. Their initial nervousness will slowly disappear as students come to realize that they can master Hebrew decoding, and that you will help them if they are having difficulty. It is best not to evaluate new material during the same session in which it is introduced. Rather, it is preferable to evaluate material that was learned in previous sessions.

Note that during the evaluation, the student

should read from a clean copy. If the student's Workbook is clean, use that. Otherwise, you can use your own Workbook or a separate laminated evaluation sheet. Record the student's responses on a clean photocopy of the page, rather than in the student's Workbook. That way you will have an ongoing record of each student's progress. Do not let the student see what you are writing. Accept self-corrections, but do not give feedback until the student has read all ten words. Write down any mistakes that the student makes on the photocopied sheet. You should write these notes phonetically, preferably in Hebrew script (see examples on pages 34, 63, and 82 in this Teacher Guide). A score itself will not tell you how to help the child, but from this written record of the evaluation, you will be able to plan your remediation strategy.

If a student is having difficulty with the first three words, discontinue the evaluation. Try to pinpoint the problem and have him or her practice the trouble spot with a classroom aide or the Resource Room teacher. You should use the appropriate Reading Pages as the basis for remediation. Do not have the child just memorize the test words.

The evaluation can also reveal areas that need further teaching and reinforcement. If you see that a considerable number of children are having difficulty with the same concept, a classroom or a small group review might be called for. Start by using the Reading Pages and progress to other teaching activities (see "Games and Other Activities" on page 141 of this Teacher Guide). The game *Connect-4* is a good one to fall back on. For further ideas about remediation, refer to individual lessons.

Time permitting, it is best to teach each lesson over the course of two sessions. In the first session, complete Steps 1 through 4 and begin Step 5 (the worksheets). In the second session, review the materials, and complete Step 6. You can start evaluating the better students first, while others continue to complete the worksheets. Those who were evaluated and have completed their work can help other students who need further practice, or they can play an individual or group game.

A Note about Homework

Whether or not you assign homework is a decision to be made by your school administration. If your students will be completing this program in one lesson a week, homework is strongly advised. It will help them remember the Hebrew reading skills and vocabulary they learn in school. In addition, you may need to assign homework in order to be able to complete all 20 lessons within one year. The worksheets are generally self-explanatory and lend themselves to independent work. If there is a parent or sibling at home who reads Hebrew, you can assign students to review a Reading Page.

If you send the Workbooks home, make sure that you have a backup plan in case students forget to bring their books to class in the following session. For example, you can keep several unused copies of the text at school and ask students who forget their Workbooks to write their answers on notebook paper.

Research on Hebrew Reading

No matter what the ultimate goal of the Hebrew curriculum, learning to decode the letters and vowels is a necessary first step. Unlike English, Hebrew utilizes a highly consistent phonetic system, making phonics the logical method of choice for introducing students to the process of Hebrew decoding. זְמָן לִקְרֹא *Time to Read Hebrew*, is a phonics program that is designed to teach students how to decode Hebrew. Because זְמָן לִקְרֹא is the only Hebrew primer based on research in Hebrew reading and second language acquisition available today, an understanding of this research will greatly help any teacher implement the program successfully.

Reading, Language, and Script

The first cross-national investigation of reading was conducted by William S. Gray in 1956. He identified a great number of similarities in mature readers of a wide range of languages. For example, eye movements during reading follow a universal pattern of quick sideways motions known as *saccadic movements*, which alternate with short pauses known as *fixations*. Occasionally, the eyes backtrack along the line of print, fixate, and then move forward again. These are known as *regressions*. It is only during fixations that the reader can actually see the print, while regressions are usually a means of verifying or correcting what one has already seen.

Although Gray concluded that the process of reading is essentially the same in all languages, he did note that mature readers of both Hebrew and Arabic make longer fixations and more frequent regressions than readers of European languages. Subsequent investigations have pointed to the manner in which Semitic languages build words and the idiosyncrasies of their scripts as likely explanations for the need to look longer and verify more frequently. For the purposes of this brief review, three crucial aspects of the Hebrew language and its writing system will be examined here: the nature of Hebrew word building, the visual complexities of the script, and the difficulties created by the vocalization system. For a more complete analysis of Hebrew orthography and its implications for reading, see the works of Feitelson, Lenchner and Dori, Maiben, and Share and Levin that are cited in the bibliography.

The central linguistic aspect that can influence how beginning readers learn Hebrew is in the area of word building. Hebrew, like Arabic, derives much of its vocabulary from roots of three consonants which are inflected with prefixes, suffixes, infixes, or changes in the vowel patterns to create a wide variety of words. While such a system lends a mathematical elegance to the language, it can also create substantial difficulties in reading. Because words tend to be of a similar length, and slight alterations create significant variations in meaning, readers must pay close attention to minute visual cues in order to identify individual words correctly. Similarly, Hebrew script is filled with idiosyncrasies that can exert a profound influence on the learner's success in learning to read. Consider the number of letter pairs that are visually similar. Distinguishing a ך from a ר requires the reader to pay close attention to a single tiny difference in shape. The vowels are also problematic, as they are much smaller than the letters, and are tucked away below, above, or within the line of print. Vowels account for more reading errors than consonants in all languages, possibly because vowels tend to have multiple pronunciations, but they are a particular source of trouble in Hebrew. Feitelson (1981) reports one investigation in which vowels accounted for 38% of all errors made on an oral Hebrew reading test at the end of first grade.

Although the overall process of reading is fairly universal, the variations inherent in a specific language and script can create subtle differences in the interplay of the skills associated with reading. For example, the research on English reading points to phonological awareness (the ability to extrapolate sounds from syllables and syllables from words) as an early predictor of reading success. While phonological awareness also plays a significant role in Hebrew decoding, it has been shown to be far less important than visual skills as a predictor of Hebrew reading success (Share and Levin, 1999). Clearly, the approaches to English reading often used for instruction in North American settings, which emphasize global reading or glancing at individual words in order to comprehend the text with minimal attention to the visual information, are ineffective for Hebrew decoding. For this reason, זְמַן לִקְרֹא is based on investigations of Hebrew decoding, and the research here suggests very specific instructional approaches.

Hebrew Decoding: Planning for Success

First, beginning Hebrew readers must be taught to attend to and fully process every visual cue. This strategy should be emphasized from the outset, and students should be told explicitly that the way one reads Hebrew is absolutely different from the way one reads any European language. Second, because Hebrew has so many letters that look so similar, everything possible must be done to reduce the likelihood that learners will confuse them. Finally, the phonics program must pay special attention to the vowels, employing drill patterns that will best foster mastery of these troublesome symbols.

Israeli researcher Dina Feitelson has long

pointed to the pivotal role that instructional sequences play in the introduction of individual letters and vowels. In her research with Israeli school children, three different sequences were examined for introducing "look alike" letters. With some groups, the letters were introduced concurrently (at the same time). In other groups, the letters were introduced sequentially with confusing items presented one right after the other, and, finally, in some groups these items were introduced sequentially with confusing letters separated by strings of neutral symbols. While logic may dictate that concurrent introduction should be the most effective approach, as it allows the teacher to draw specific comparisons and contrasts between similar items, classroom experimentation revealed a different finding. In every case, both concurrent and sequential introduction where two confusing items were presented one right after the other actually led to an increase in confusion, while the students who were given ample time with one item before the second was introduced were far more capable of making the fine distinctions necessary. Here the research strongly suggests that learners must fully master one member of the pair before being able to attend to the subtle differences presented by the other.

Comparable experiments were conducted with the introduction of different symbols that represent similar sounds (such as ז, ס, and צ, or ב and כ), as well as those that represent identical sounds (such as ח, ת, and ט, or ש and ש). In the case of similar sounding letters, sequential introduction with strings of neutral sounds separating each item was found to decrease the likelihood of confusion, while both other approaches led to greater confusion. By contrast, concurrent introduction was found to be the most advantageous approach for different symbols that make identical sounds. In this case, both kinds of sequential instruction led some students to remember one symbol, but not the other. Nevertheless, because Hebrew makes such great demands on the reader's visual system, it is of particular importance that visually similar letters are not introduced together or one after the other, because once this confusion sets in it can plague the reader literally for years. And if this is true for Israeli learners who live in a fully Hebrew environment, it is an even greater concern for students in the Diaspora whose exposure to Hebrew is often a very part-time enterprise.

Consideration must also be given to the manner in which vowels are presented and drilled. Here again, some vowel pairs are visually similar (such as ֶ and ְ); there are sets of different symbols that make the same sound (such as ַ, ָ, and ֲ); and some make similar sounds (such as ֶ and ֵ). Whenever possible, these should be introduced through the same kinds of sequences employed for letters, with concurrent instruction for different vowels that represent the same sound, and sequential introduction with strings of neutral symbols separating those that either look or sound similar.

Feitelson also reports that the drill patterns influence successful mastery of the vowels, and that the most effective approach lies in structuring reading drills around single vowels rather than consonants. As students acquire a vowel it should then be drilled with all of the consonants that they have already learned (e.g., בָּ, שָׁ, תָ, etc.), instead of the more common pattern of drilling single consonants with different vowels (e.g., בַּ, בּוֹ, בָּ, בּוּ, בֶּ, etc.).

זְמָן לִקְרֹא incorporates all of these research findings into its structure. For example, neither visually confusing letters nor those that represent similar sounds are introduced together. In fact, similar items are separated by at least three lessons. By the same token, items that represent the same sound are usually introduced together to facilitate mastery.

Reading and Language

A final consideration is the relationship between reading and language. This is a crucial consideration if the curriculum in the years following the primer contains a Hebrew language track, but it is important even in settings that place an emphasis only on prayer recitation. Reading, after all, is fundamentally a language skill. While there is no evidence that the acquisition of language skills detracts from a student's ability to master phonics, there is considerable evidence to indicate that learning some language can actually enhance a learner's decoding skills. Frank Vellutino and his colleagues found that learning Hebrew as a language actually improved scores on a test of visual memory, an important finding considering how crucial visual skills are to successful Hebrew decoding. Similarly, Lenchner and Dori note that oral Hebrew vocabulary instruction is particularly helpful for students who are weak in visual processing since it enables them to bring their stronger auditory skills to the task of decoding. Here again, the research strongly suggests that students benefit greatly from phonics programs that teach reading within a language framework.

Minimally, a language framework dictates that reading drills be restricted to the use of actual Hebrew words once students have mastered enough letters and vowels to produce ample words for practice. Even before that point, the individual syllables and clusters should be composed of combinations that actually exist in Hebrew, given the limited number of phonetic items that have been introduced. This is important because these drills predispose the learner to attend to key syllabic patterns. It is both ineffective and inefficient to introduce students to combinations that they will never encounter in a real text.

On a second level, a language framework provides the structure for introducing each phonetic item through an authentic Hebrew word. In זְמַן לִקְרֹא these "Key Words" are derived from the general vocabulary of Jewish life, including holiday terms, greetings, ritual items, and so on. Not only does this approach give students a feel for Hebrew as an authentic spoken language, it also provides them with a means of checking an individual symbol they may not recognize immediately against a known entity.

On a yet more sophisticated level, the language framework of זְמַן לִקְרֹא incorporates additional vocabulary and basic sentence structures into the primer, allowing students to practice their skills with increasingly larger pieces of text. This naturally lends a reading comprehension component to the curriculum. In any case, if the goal of phonics instruction is to prepare students for reading Hebrew texts, it is only natural that the items they practice should relate in some way to the materials they will eventually encounter. This is one of the key features that separates זְמַן לִקְרֹא from the programs that transliterate English words into Hebrew, or that associate English words with Hebrew letter sounds. The latter kinds of programs are actually antithetical to this overall goal of a language framework and, in many ways, negate the benefits that even minimal language instruction provides. By contrast, Hebrew-English cognates (words that are the same in both languages), although somewhat difficult to read, allow students to bring their language skills to the task of Hebrew decoding while also practicing their decoding skills through legitimate Hebrew vocabulary. Thus, teaching that ט is for טַלִית is the preferred association; ט is for טֶלֶפוֹן is satisfactory; but ט is for "turtle" is unacceptable at any stage.

Great care has been taken to ensure that זְמַן לִקְרֹא conforms to as much of the criteria established by research as possible. It makes use of the instructional sequences and drill patterns that research has demonstrated to be most effective for fostering the mastery of Hebrew decoding skills. זְמַן לִקְרֹא also uses direct instructional techniques to address critical and difficult concepts. Thus students are told directly that they need to pay attention to even tiny markings. And, finally, זְמַן לִקְרֹא is set within a language framework that affords great flexibility in teaching pure decoding, Hebrew language, or a combination of both.

Classroom Interaction

The seating arrangement has a bearing on the classroom environment. It is wise to place a student who is having difficulty in the front of the class, next to a more highly skilled student. Separate students who have difficulties with each other as needed.

As you teach, maintain a rapid pace, and try to switch activities approximately every 20 minutes. After a full day of school, children are tired and easily distracted. Active learning strategies are also an effective approach for teaching Hebrew as they engage the learner in the process of mastering the required skills and concepts. Finally, use class time efficiently, spending as little time as possible on administrative issues.

Asking good questions that generate enthusiastic responses is an art. It seems that there are always some students who are eager to respond to every question you ask. However, you want to make sure that all students are involved. Here are some suggestions for increasing student attention and involvement.

1. When practicing a Reading Page, ask first for group responses. Start with the entire group, then have boys or girls only respond, then one row only, then pairs of students. Then progress to individual responses.

Ask individual students to decode, calling first on more able students before calling on less able ones. This gives the slower learners an opportunity to see the skill modeled a few additional times before being asked to perform. This can greatly assist both stronger and weaker students. Gradually begin to call on students more "at random." (This strategy provides an excellent opportunity to interact with students who are having difficulty and to choose a particularly challenging word for your advanced students.)

2. Identify students who are having difficulty (based on their reading evaluations and responses in class) and provide them with extra opportunities to respond to your questions.

3. Make sure you activate students who tend not to participate. For students who are more introverted, and those who may be having difficulty, it is essential that they be given the opportunity to be successful. While you might not call on such students to make the first responses, do engage them more often than students whom you know have grasped the material. One effective strategy is to allow students who do not readily volunteer to provide information that you are sure they know. For example, you might not ask them to tell you what sound the new vowel makes, but you might ask them what sound the doctor tells you to make when you open your mouth so that he or she can look at your throat.

4. Ask questions that are open-ended and require thinking.

5. Give students time to think through their answers before they are expected to respond. A wait-time of at least three seconds is strongly advised. This is especially true when you ask open-ended questions.

6. If a student gives an incorrect answer, do not ask another student to help, as this often embarrasses both students. Instead, you could respond by saying something like, "That's the answer to a different question." Or you might provide hints and clues that will guide the student to the correct answer.

Approaches To Teaching

Teachers, both new and experienced, often struggle with the following problems:
- How can I use the short amount of time I have in the most efficient manner?
- How can I know that everyone has learned the new material?
- How can I give each child individual attention if I have 20 students in my class?
- How do I keep my more skilled students challenged while making sure that my less skilled students are keeping up?

Using different teaching approaches might solve these problems. Three suggested approaches are: frontal teaching, total individualization, and group work. Each is explained below.

Frontal Teaching

In frontal teaching, a teacher stands in front of the entire class and conducts a leasson. This is an efficient way of presenting new material as long as the entire class is on the same reading level. It is also efficient for oral language instruction, since it allows students to hear the teacher model correct pronunciation first and then to interact in Hebrew with other students.

The major disadvantage of frontal teaching is that it does not let the teacher attend to children with different needs, e.g., the very bright, the slow child, or the learning disabled. Children learn at different rates and through different methods of instruction. For example, while some gifted children could advance in the program with minimal teacher instruction, others (in particular, the learning disabled) do not learn well at all through frontal instruction in a large classroom.

Total Individualization

In a totally individualized setting, such as a Resource Room, students work and progress at their own rate. The program can be modified to meet their special needs. This approach is most appropriate when there are students of different ages or levels in one class, or in remedial settings. When individualizing, use the worksheets in the Workbook, but also prepare in advance a variety of additional activities. In this way students do not have to wait around for additional instructions (for ideas, see "Games and other Activities" on page 141 in this Teacher Guide). Another exceptional resource is the זְמַן לִקְרֹא *Activity Book* (for Volumes One and Two), which contains additional activities that drill specific skills taught in each lesson of זְמַן לִקְרֹא *Time to Read Hebrew*.

It is very difficult to monitor a totally individualized program in a large classroom, especially if the teacher does not have an assistant. However, occasionally, a student will need such a structure (e.g., a new student who enters after the beginning of the school year and needs to catch up to the class or a learning disabled child who is mainstreamed in a large regular classroom).

Group Work

Group work combines elements of frontal teaching and total individualization. This approach is highly recommended for classes that have a teaching assistant. To implement this approach, divide the class into three groups after the first few lessons. It is important that these groups be heterogeneous, meaning that they be as diverse as possible. The reason for this is that students are often very sensitive to the ways that their teachers divide them into groups. When students are placed in groups according to their abilities, the less able students inevitably suffer, partly because they perceive themselves negatively, and partly because teachers frequently treat top students in ways that promote success and do not communicate the same kinds of expectations to weaker students. The effects of such self-fulfilling prophecies have been well documented in educational literature (see Brophy and Good, 1970). Additionally, weak students do not get the benefit of being exposed to stronger peers who can act as models for the skills being taught. By thoroughly mixing the students in each group, the teacher can gain all the benefits of peer tutoring without creating the hierarchy between peers that makes some students feel uncomfortable.

There are a couple of circumstances in which homogenous grouping is quite effective without creating negative feelings for the students. An example might be if you have several students from different groups who all need additional work in a single specific skill (such as syllabification or identifying the וֹ). Logic dictates that these students can be brought together for a quick refresher course on a very short-term basis. Another example of using homogenous groupings effectively is a cooperative learning strategy known as the "Jigsaw Method" (see page 150 in this Teacher Guide).

During a typical session, each group might participate in several types of learning activities: a large group introduction; small group reading practice; completion of games, activities, or worksheets (either independently, with partners, or in small groups); and individualized evaluation/remediation.

Start the class with a frontal lesson, then break students into groups for reading practice and specific learning tasks. Bring all groups together and conclude with an activity involving the whole class. Each of these steps is discussed in more detail below.

1. Begin the lesson near the chalkboard, felt, or magnetic board. Here you review previous

lessons, evoke the new Key Word(s), have students break the Key Word(s) into sounds, and introduce the new consonants and vowels.

2. Then, break the class into small reading groups. If you have an assistant who reads Hebrew fluently and is familiar with this program, you can supervise one reading group while the assistant works with a second group. Any additional groups can be doing independent work or partner activities. Switch groups so that you and/or your assistant can listen to every student's reading. Have students read from Reading Pages and do other reading activities that require supervision (e.g., play *Connect-4*, spell words formed from the new word, etc.). After students have read and demonstrated fluency, you and the assistant should explain the instructions for doing the worksheets in the student Workbooks.

3. Students begin work on their independent activities. These can be completed individually or with partners. You and the assistant should monitor these activities, and gradually the assistant should take over so you are free to begin evaluating students.

4. As students complete their worksheets, they can be evaluated on the material using the evaluations found at the end of each Workbook. If students complete their work and need to wait their turn for evaluation, they can play a Hebrew game or practice reading to a partner.

Remediation

After you evaluate a student, remediate any problem areas before you proceed to the next lesson. It is often difficult to find time to remediate. Here are some suggestions:

1. If your school has a Resource Room or a pull-out program for students who need one-on-one assistance, refer students who need remediation to that program.

2. If you have a student assistant, ask him or her to spend a few minutes re-teaching a specific skill or concept to a student who needs help.

3. If your students are working in groups, set aside some time to work with individuals.

4. After you have carefully diagnosed a problem, assign the child a student tutor and give specific instructions regarding which Reading Pages to read, and what letters and/or vowels to review. (Let students take turns being tutors.) An alternative is to obtain a tutor from a higher grade. Make sure that this student is familiar with the program and does not try to teach new material. It is best to use a student who has been in the program previously.

5. If the student has a relative or friend who is fluent in Hebrew, send home the appropriate Reading Pages. If no such person is available, send home Hebrew/English letter flash cards.

Specific Suggestions for Specific Problems

Problem 1: The student forgets (or confuses) consonant and vowel sounds.

Solutions:
a. Send home Hebrew/English letter flash cards.
b. Use pages from the זְמַן לִקְרֹא *Activity Book* (for Volumes One and Two) that review only the letter sounds causing trouble.
c. Use mnemonics (memory helpers). Some useful ones can be found in the chart on the next page.

Mnemonics are particularly useful for auditory learners, but may actually be distracting for some visual learners. You may want to tell students to use mnemonics if they help reinforce their memory, and to ignore them if they do not help. The following mnemonics **do not** work for children, but may help adults:

שׁ you *sh*ake with the right (as opposed to שׂ)
שׂ "a שׂ (*sin*) isn't right!"

Using the following mnemonic for the vowel וּ is not recommended: when a ball hits you in the stomach, you say "**oo**." This hint is likely to confuse both children and adults, rather than helping them distinguish between the sounds of the ‏וּ‎ and the ‏וֹ‎. Logically, a ball hitting you in the stomach might just as easily make you say "oh," and a ball hitting you on your head could result in you exclaiming "oo." Avoid this mnemonic!

Mnemonics Chart

ב	has a *b*alloon or a *b*elly button
ג	is *g*oing for a walk and has two legs
ד	is a *d*oor with a hinge
ה	has a *h*ole
ז	is *z*igzagged
ט	is open on the *t*op (as opposed to מ)
כ	a person *c*oughing up *c*andy
כ	and ה are the same turned around
מ	*M*oses on the *m*ountain
ס	a *s*mile
פ	*p*ut the dot in
פ	and now *f*orget the dot
ר	is *r*ounded
ת ת	have a *t*oe (as opposed to ח and ה and initially the ב)
ְ	the doctor uses a tongue depressor that looks like this (show one) and tells you to open your mouth and say "*ah*"
וֹ	the ball goes *o*ver the net
ֶ ֵ	make the sound of "*eh*" as in *e*gg
ֵ	is a b*ea*d

Problem 2: Blending

The student can identify the sounds of the consonants and vowels in isolation, but cannot put them together correctly (e.g., they add a sound, usually an "ah" sound); they read words with a middle *Shva* as if the *Shva* has an "eh" sound; or, they break syllables in the wrong place.

Solutions:
a. Begin by asking the student to find (rather than utter) a specific word on a specific line.
b. Have student practice orally adding a consonant to the end of words. For example:

בַּת = ת + בַּ

c. If the student has difficulty with consonant-vowel-consonant combinations, work on this, using the letters and vowels that the child knows. Model a correct response (rather than try to explain), then just change a single letter in the combination. For example:

שָׁת בָּת תָּת תָּשׁ

d. When a student is ready for two syllable words, teach the student to break words into syllables (consonant + vowel, or consonant + vowel + consonant) and draw a thin pencil line between syllables.
e. Mark with a "highlighter" pen one syllable of a two syllable word and have student read syllables one at a time. Or, have two students alternate reading the syllables. (See instructions for syllable reading for the Lesson 9 Reading Page on page 77 of this Teacher Guide.)
f. Let the student first read the first few numbered lines, since the words on the initial lines of each Reading Page are easier to blend. Then have the student read by column from top to bottom for practice in more complex blending.

Problem 3: Slow and/or Inaccurate Reading

Solutions:
a. Practice and more practice!
b. Provide students with more individualized reading time, with either a teaching assistant or a peer tutor.
c. Use the Reading Games suggested on pages 142 and 143 in this Teacher Guide.

Additional Uses of the Program

Day School Settings

The program can be used as a quick course in basic Hebrew decoding skills for children who enter day school after their class has learned to read. Furthermore, the vocabulary component will give students a head start for whatever language text they will be using next. This program can be adapted for second graders by assisting them with some of the more demanding worksheets and the English reading.

Refresher Course

Some schools use the Reading Pages for reading review with students who transfer into the school, and who did not fully master Hebrew decoding in their previous schools. Since the pages are so carefully sequenced, you can readily identify weak spots in a student's Hebrew decoding. You can also use the Placement Test (page 163 in this Teacher Guide) to determine with which lesson the student should begin. If a student, for example, does well up through number 10 (תְּחוּל), and does poorly on the rest of the test, then start the student in Lesson 9 as reflected by the corresponding number in the shaded box on the Placement Test. If a student is just making isolated errors on a particular consonant or vowel sound, assign specific review materials.

Remedial Settings

This program has been successfully piloted in remedial settings in both supplementary and day schools. Its success in these settings lies in several of the program's characteristics: it is carefully structured to optimize learning efficiency, it challenges children to reason, it allows the teacher to monitor individual progress, and it provides opportunities for multisensory learning.

Adult Education

This program can also be used with adults. Besides teaching in an orderly fashion all of the skills which are needed for decoding, the Workbooks link the reading of Hebrew with knowledge of Hebrew concepts. If your school is building a strong family education component, you may want to offer a parallel Hebrew education course for the parents of the students who are completing זְמַן לִקְרֹא. This approach enables parents to master Hebrew reading skills at the same time as their children, allowing each to provide further assistance to the other at home.

AND NOW . . . IT'S TIME TO READ HEBREW!

Bibliography

Brophy, Jere E. and Thomas L. Good. "Teachers' Communication of Differential Expectations for Children's Classroom Performance: Some Behavioral Data." *Journal of Educational Psychology* 61 (1970).

Bryant, Peter, and Lynette Bradley. *Children's Reading Problems*. New York: Basil Blackwell, Inc., 1985.

Carnine, Douglas W. *Direct Instruction: Reading*. Columbus, OH: Charles Merrill, 1979.

Feitelson, Dina. "Relating Instructional Strategies To Language Idiosyncrasies in Hebrew." In *Orthography, Reading and Dyslexia*, James F. Kavanagh and Richard L. Venezky, eds. Baltimore, MD: University Park Press, 1981.

Gray, William S. *The Teaching of Reading and Writing: An International Survey*. Paris: UNESCO, 1956.

Lenchner, Orna and Rivka Dori. "Why Jonathan Can't Read." Part One, *Compass*, Spring 1983. Part Two, *Compass*, Summer 1983.

Maiben, Dina. "Issues in Hebrew Reading Instruction." In *The New Jewish Teachers Handbook*, Audrey Friedman Marcus and Raymond A. Zwerin, eds. Denver, CO: A.R.E. Publishing, Inc, 1994.

Roth, Cecil (ed.). *Encyclopaedia Judaica*. Jerusalem: Keter Publishing House, Ltd., 1972.

Share, David, and Iris Levin. "Learning to Read and Write in Hebrew." In *Learning to Read and Write: A Cross-Linguistic Perspective*, Margaret Harris and Giyoo Hatano, eds. Cambridge, England: Cambridge University Press, 1999.

Vellutino, Frank R., Robert M. Pruzek, Joseph A. Steger and Uriel Meshoulam. "Immediate Visual Recall in Poor and Normal Readers as a Function of Orthographic-Linguistic Familiarity." *Cortex* 9, 1973.

Vellutino, Frank R., Joseph A. Steger, Mitchell Kaman and Louis De Setto. "Visual Form Perception in Deficient and Normal Readers as a Function of Age and Orthographic-Linguistic Familiarity." *Cortex* 11, 1975.

LESSON 1

Key Word: שַׁבָּת (Shabbat)
New Letters: שׁ ב ת
New Vowels: ַ ָ

Before Beginning the Workbook

This lesson begins Volume One of זְמַן לִקְרֹא. Prior to beginning the first lesson in the Workbook, elicit from students Hebrew words they know: holidays (שַׁבָּת, פֶּסַח, פּוּרִים, חֲנֻכָּה); foods related to holidays (חֲרֹסֶת, מַצָּה, חַלָּה); religious artifacts (מְנוֹרָה, מְזוּזָה, מָגֵן דָּוִד); greetings or expressions (מַזָּל טוֹב, שָׁלוֹם).

Give them examples of words that are the same in both English and Hebrew. Explain that these words were borrowed from other languages because words for these things didn't exist in Hebrew. Have students guess what each word means. Give students the feeling that they already know many words. Here are some suggestions:

Foods and Drinks

banana	בָּנָנָה
pizza	פִּיצָה
hamburger	הַמְבּוּרְגֶר
milk shake	מִילְק שֵׁיק
coffee	קָפֶה
chocolate	שׁוֹקוֹלָד

Sports

tennis	טֶנִיס
football	פוּטְבּוֹל
ping-pong	פִּינְג פּוֹנְג
ski	סְקִי
baseball	בֵּיס בּוֹל
golf	גוֹלְף
karate	קָרָטֶה

Places

America	אָמֶרִיקָה
Canada	קָנָדָה
Africa	אַפְרִיקָה
Brazil	בְּרָזִיל
London	לוֹנְדוֹן
Paris	פָּרִיז

Home Appliances

mixer	מִיקְסֶר
telephone	טֶלֶפוֹן
television	טֶלֶוִיזְיָה
toaster	טוֹסְטֶר
radio	רַדְיוֹ
video	וִידֵאוֹ

After students realize that they know some words in Hebrew, talk about the Hebrew alphabet. Here again, they will find that they already know a lot. Ask:

"What do you know about the Hebrew alphabet?"

Write relevant responses on the chalkboard. Elaborate, and include in your discussion the following points:

1. The letters of the Hebrew alphabet are totally different from the letters of the English alphabet. Hebrew comes from a family of languages different from English.
2. Hebrew is written from right to left and, therefore, the Workbook opens from right to left.
3. The little dots and lines underneath, next to, and above letters are vowels.
4. Hebrew has no capital letters.
5. Hebrew has five final letters.

Following this introduction, pass out Volume One. Give students a chance to look through the Workbook, then have each write his/her name inside the front cover. Next, read aloud the Letter to Students found on page 1 of the Workbook. Do not require students to read the letter to themselves, nor call on anyone to read it aloud. As you read, point out how this letter summarizes much of the information that you presented in your introduction.

Oral Language Lesson (optional)

The Key Word (שַׁבָּת) is the only new word taught in Lesson 1. In subsequent lessons, however, new vocabulary other than Key Words may be included. You may elect to teach those words or not.

If you do plan to teach the additional vocabulary, it is recommended that you look at the Sequence Chart on page 9 and begin introducing these vocabulary words orally in an informal manner so that the students will have heard them by the time they see them in the Workbook. In this Teacher Guide, at the beginning of each lesson, you will find suggestions for introducing new vocabulary specific to that lesson. Consult the section "Spoken Language" on page 148 for general ideas.

The Seven Lesson Steps

1. Review (There is no review in Lesson 1.)

2. **Evoking the Key Word**

The word "evoking" is used instead of "introducing" because the students should guess the Key Word based on clues that you give them. For example, in this lesson you can ask:

"What is the name of the special day of the week?"

"Which is the day of rest?"

"Every week we have a Jewish holiday. What is it called?"

Continue describing Shabbat until it is evoked from the students (i.e., they come up with the word). In this way, they will feel that although starting to learn a novel alphabet and language, they really know something about the topic already. This also encourages active involvement in the lesson; students are not just passive recipients of information. Conduct a brief discussion about Shabbat, e.g., its customs and rituals, associated foods, and special Shabbat activities.

If there are students who do not know anything about Shabbat, it is important to encourage their participation and involvement without making them uncomfortable. You can compliment the entire group on their enthusiastic participation, so that everyone feels a part of the process.

Have a קַבָּלַת שַׁבָּת (Welcoming the Sabbath) ceremony in your class. Everyone will enjoy it, and the children with no background will learn something about Shabbat in a non-threatening manner.

If the time allotted to Hebrew is limited, perhaps the Judaica teacher would be willing to have the ceremony and discussion during his or her class time. If this is not possible, you may need to shorten this part of your lesson, omitting the ceremony and making your discussion very brief.

For this first lesson, you might want to keep the Workbooks closed until this point. Students will be so excited to have a new book that it may be too much of a distraction for them. In later lessons, you can use the pictures at the top of the first page of each lesson to help evoke the Key Word.

3. **Introducing New Letters and Vowels**
a. Sound of שׁ

Now that students have heard and can say the Key Word (שַׁבָּת), have them break it down into its component sounds. This is a very important part of your introduction to new letters. Notice the emphasis on the individual sounds of the word, and not on the syllables of the word.

שַׁבָּת has five sounds: **sh**, **ah**, **b**, **ah**, **t**. First ask:

"What is the first sound in שַׁבָּת?"

Some students may answer **shah** instead of just **sh**.

In that case, reinforce and say:

"Yes, it starts with **shah**, but **shah** is already two sounds. What is the first sound you hear in **shah**?"

Students will say **sh**. Then say:

"That's right. שַׁבָּת starts with a **sh** sound. In Hebrew this letter makes the **sh** sound."

Place the שׁ on the felt board. (See page 12 in this Teacher Guide for a discussion of using felt letters.) Say:

"So what is the sound of this letter?" (**sh**)

"Now, tell me what you notice about this letter.

How is this letter different from English letters?"

Encourage at least two or three responses from students. For example, in English the **sh** sound is composed of two letters, but in Hebrew it is only one. It is obviously a different alphabet; there is a dot on top of the letter. (DO NOT mention anything at all about the שׂ at this point. If anyone does, say, "We're not learning that one now.")

b. Sound of ַ and ָ

Ask:

"After **sh** what sound do you hear?"

"That's right, **ah** is the next sound."

Place the ַ (*Patach*) under the שׁ. Do not give the name of the vowel. That information might confuse students. It is not recommended to teach vowel names in this program, as the names will not necessarily serve as a memory aid.

Continue:

"So, if שַׁ is **shah**, how do you get the sound of **ah**?"

"Yes, the tiny line is pronounced **ah**. It is a very small line. It goes *under* the letter."

Next, give the mnemonic. Use a real tongue depressor. Say:

"At the doctor's office, a tongue depressor is put in your mouth and you say **ah**. This **ah** sound looks just like a tongue depressor."

Next, ask:

"Is **ah** a consonant or a vowel? Are vowels ever written under a letter in English?"

Notice that the emphasis here is on encouraging comparisons between English and Hebrew.

c. Sound of בּ

Ask:

"What sound do you hear in Shabbat after the שׁ sound?"

After a student answers correctly, take the שׁ off the felt board and replace it with a בּ. Say:

"This letter makes the **b** sound." (DO NOT tell them what sound the ב (*Vet*) makes, or even show them the letter. If anyone mentions it, say that we will learn that sound later in the year.) Place the *Patach* under the בּ and ask:

"What do you think this says now?" Or, to get students more actively involved, ask:

"Who can come up to the felt board and form the **bah** sound with the letters?"

In the word שַׁבָּת, however, there is a ָ under the בּ, so introduce this vowel by saying:

"Well, this בַּ says **bah** and this בָּ says **bah**, what can you tell me now about the ַ and the ָ?"

"Yes, they both make the same sound of **ah**."

Now, on the felt board, form שַׁבָּ. Ask:

"What does this say?"

"Correct. This says **shah bah**."

Before you teach the third letter of the word שַׁבָּת, work on the first two sounds. Here is a list of recommended combinations to use on the felt board:

שׁ   בָּ   בַּשׁ   בָּשׁ
שָׁ   בַּב   בַּשׁ   שַׁב

Students frequently have problems in the initial stages of decoding with consonant-vowel-consonant (C-V-C) combinations. They tend to add on an extra vowel (C-V-C-V). An English example of this is reading "Bob" as "Bob-ah." If you notice any students making this error, give them pairs like the following to decode:

בַּב   בַּ   שַׁ   שַׁשׁ   בַּ   בַּב

Additional pairs like these are found on page 6 of the Workbook.

When you are finished with this, teach the ת. Or, if students need more practice on the שׁ and the בּ, have them use the foam letters at their seats (see Introduction, page 14 in this Teacher Guide). Dictate the same words that you formed on the felt board.

d. Sound of ת

To introduce the last letter of the word Shabbat, form שַׁבָּ on the felt board and ask:

"What is this?"

"What sound is needed to have the word Shabbat?" Add on the ת and ask:

"What do you think this says now?"

"Yes, it says שַׁבָּת. Congratulations! You have learned to read your first word in Hebrew."

"So what does this letter ת say by itself? And if I put ַ underneath it?"

Put the following combinations on the felt board:

בַּת   שׁ
בַּב — שַׁ   ת — בַּ   תַּ   בַּת   תַּשׁ   ת
בַּשׁ   ב

Dear Student,

You are about to start a great adventure! This year, you are going to learn how to read Hebrew. By learning to read Hebrew you are taking your first big step toward fully being a part of the Jewish community.

Hebrew is the Jewish people's oldest language. It is the language of the Bible and Jewish prayer. It is also our newest language. Today in Israel, Hebrew is the language people speak. Hebrew has always held our people together, and when you learn Hebrew you link yourself to all Jews who have gone before you. As you begin to read Hebrew, you will learn some new Hebrew words and some words that are almost the same in Hebrew as they are in English.

Reading Hebrew can be a lot of fun. But Hebrew reading is a lot different from English reading. Here are some hints to help make Hebrew reading easier:

- English is read from left to right. We read Hebrew from right to left.
- Hebrew does not have capital letters, but there are five final letters in Hebrew. These are letter forms that are used only at the end of a word.
- In Hebrew, the name of the letter often tells you its sound. Learning the letter's name can help you remember the sound it makes.
- By reading every letter and every vowel, it is easy to sound out new Hebrew words.
- In Hebrew, the vowels are often tiny dots and dashes written under, over, or after the letters. People who know Hebrew can read without these markings.
- In Hebrew reading, tiny markings can be very important. You need to look closely at every letter and every vowel.
- When you chant Torah or pray in Hebrew, you will be reading out loud. So, it's a good idea to practice reading Hebrew out loud.

And now . . . it's
Time to Read Hebrew!

Lesson 1
KEY WORD:
שַׁבָּת

New Letters:

Shin ש

Bet ב

Tav ת

New Vowels:

Both of these vowels make an "ah" sound.
(The doctor says, "Open your mouth and say 'ah.'")

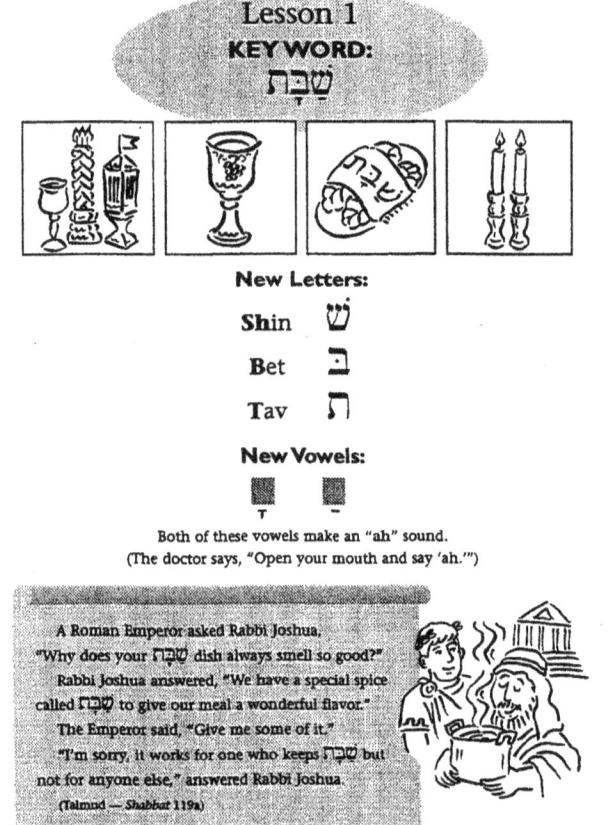

A Roman Emperor asked Rabbi Joshua, "Why does your שַׁבָּת dish always smell so good?"
Rabbi Joshua answered, "We have a special spice called שַׁבָּת to give our meal a wonderful flavor."
The Emperor said, "Give me some of it."
"I'm sorry, it works for one who keeps שַׁבָּת but not for anyone else," answered Rabbi Joshua.
(Talmud — *Shabbat* 119a)

Come back to the word שַׁבָּת and review. Say:

"You have learned to read your first Hebrew word, שַׁבָּת. How is this word different from words you read in English?" Do not tell the students; they should tell you. Possible student responses are: it is written from right to left, the vowels are little lines that are under the letters, little dots are also part of the letters.

e. Using the Introduction Page

Now, you are ready for students to open their Workbooks. In later lessons, you will move back and forth between your frontal lesson and the Introduction Page, as students will be familiar with the Workbook, and not distracted by it. For this lesson, ask students to note that the lesson number appears at the top of each page, including this one. Say:

"Find the Key Word and put your finger under it." Verify that everyone is actually doing this. Read the word chorally, then call on individuals to read it. Do not worry that you are repeating something they just learned; this is a word you want them to recognize immediately.

Next, move to the pictures. Ask:

"How are these pictures related to the Key Word?" Students should realize that שַׁבָּת symbols are depicted. Explain that each lesson's Key Words are defined through this strip of pictures on the Introduction Page. Many students will not recognize the הַבְדָלָה symbols, which you can briefly explain. הַבְדָלָה is a Key Word in Lesson 9, so whatever information you convey will be reinforced then. Ask students:

"Look at the pictures from right to left, in the Hebrew direction. Can you guess why the pictures appear in this order?"

"Right, this is the order in which we say the blessings on שַׁבָּת. First candles, then wine, then the חַלָּה, and finally on Saturday night, the הַבְדָלָה blessings mark the end of שַׁבָּת." Compliment the whole group on their knowledge, as the information they share is most probably a combination of what many of them know.

Move down to the listing of the New Letters for the lesson. Here is when you first introduce letter names. Ask:

"What connection is there between the *names* of these letters and the *sounds* that they make? In Hebrew, the first sound of a letter's name is usually the sound that the letter makes. On this and other Introduction Pages, the English sound that the Hebrew letter makes is written in the same color as the Hebrew letter."

As you move down the page and look at the New Vowel, remind the students of the mnemonic that you used when you frontally introduced the sound.

Next, read the story aloud, having students follow along with you. Spend no more than five minutes on the story, unless your schedule allows you an abundance of time with your class. The aim here is to deepen the students' understanding of this new word they can decode, not to teach a Judaica unit on שַׁבָּת.

f. Sound of ת

The ת symbol is not introduced until Lesson 8, when it first appears in vocabulary words (תַּחַת and אַתָּה). In the first edition of *Time to Read Hebrew*, the ת was introduced in Lesson 1 along with the ת, since both make the same sound. We learned that beginning readers confused the ת with the ב, rather than associating the ת sound with the ת sound. Therefore, the decision was made to delay the introduction of the ת, in accordance with the principles suggested by the reading research. (See the section on Research on Hebrew Reading on pages 17-20 in this Teacher Guide.) After Lesson 1, and until Lesson 8, you will find the letter ת used in instances where the ת is actually required. Students will not be exposed, however, to any vocabulary words with the incorrect symbol.

4. Using the Reading Page

The Reading Page (page 3) has been carefully designed to provide practice first with one syllable words, then progressing to longer and more complicated words.

Notice the relationship between lines 3 and 4. The difference between the words is that no vowel appears underneath the second letter in line 4. For example, בַּב on line 3 is directly above בַּב on line 4. On line 4, students have to blend a consonant, a vowel, and a consonant.

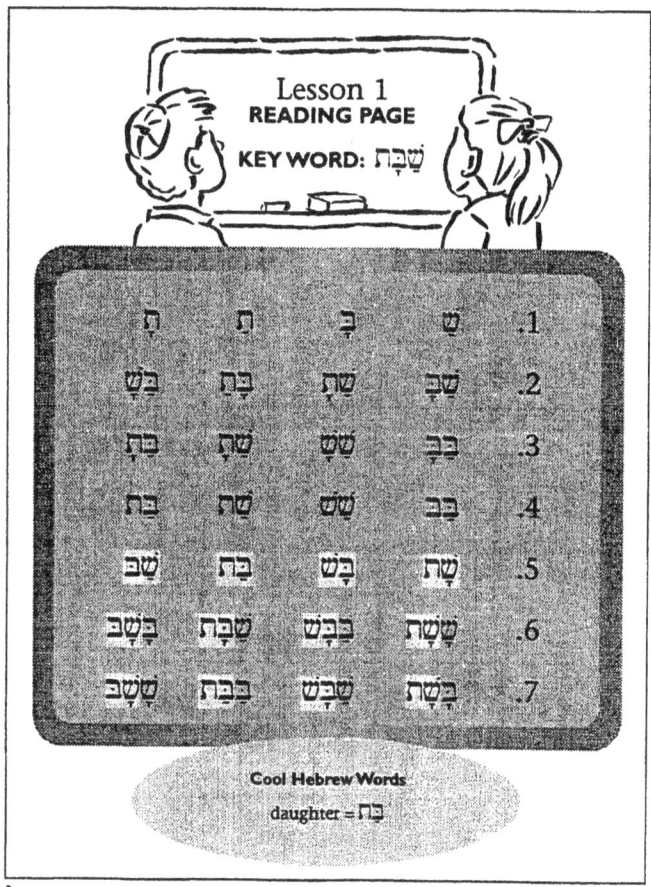

For many beginning readers, this will be the most difficult aspect of learning how to decode Hebrew, which is why it was recommended that you drill pairs like this with the flannel board. If a student demonstrates a problem with this now, you must progress very slowly with him or her, providing extra practice before going on to longer and more difficult words. Page 6 of the Workbook has more samples of these words, as does the זְמַן לִקְרֹא *Activity Book*.

Notice also the relationship between lines 5, 6, and 7. If the students read down the columns rather than across the lines, line 5 will help them to read lines 6 and 7. The last syllable is highlighted in each combination to help students with proper blending. Note on the bottom of the page the word בַּת (daughter). This is a word that you might want to share briefly with students now. It will not be introduced or reinforced later, except as part of the term בַּת-מִצְוָה. In future lessons, you will notice that interesting words like this are always placed on the bottom of the Reading Page. They are called Cool Hebrew Words or Cool Hebrew

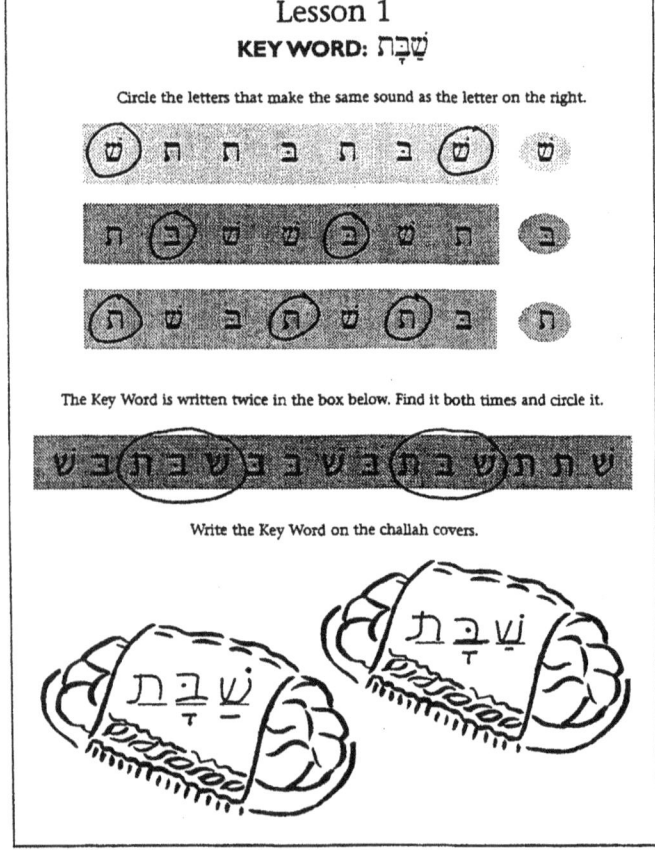

Phrases because they are worth knowing, but are not part of the sequential language component of the program. To review techniques for using the Reading Page, see the Introduction, page 15 in this Teacher Guide.

5. **Using the Worksheets**

Before using any worksheet in the classroom, be sure to go over it yourself, so that you know how to do it. Always have students first read from the Reading Page and then go on to the worksheets. This frees you to work with individual students who have difficulty with their reading while others are doing the worksheets.

Before students begin, explain how to do each individual worksheet.

Page 4: Make sure students are not writing the שׁ like a "W." Make sure students include the dot in the בּ, and that it doesn't look like a כ or a נ. Bring to class a *challah* cover or tray with the phrase לִכְבוֹד שַׁבָּת וְיוֹם טוֹב written on it. This will show students that they can read the word שַׁבָּת when it appears outside of the Workbook, and can also find it inside a phrase.

Page 5: Some students may circle the Key Word when the letters are in left to right order (backwards). Make sure to correct those students.

Page 6: At the top of the page, the picture of a word beginning with ת, such as *Torah*, was not included, because the word would begin with the ת, which has not yet been introduced. If you think their reading is fine, you can choose to have students read the pairs aloud to a partner, and listen only to those students about whom you are concerned.

6. **Prepare for Prayer**

The first Prepare for Prayer Page is in Lesson 5. There are not yet enough letters to make more than a few "prayer" words.

7. **Evaluation**

Ideally, each student should be evaluated individually before continuing to Lesson 2. As this is very time-consuming, you may have to modify your expectations. Students who shine in the frontal lesson do not need to be evaluated after every lesson. But, particularly at the beginning of the year, frequent evaluations are a way of monitoring each student's progress. Each student should be evaluated at least once before beginning Lesson 4. Begin the process while students are completing the worksheets. Let the students read out of their own Workbook while you mark a photocopied sheet. This way you can keep a record of each child's progress, even if students take their books home, or lose them.

If students are distracted by having to see the evaluations for upcoming lessons, you can photocopy the evaluations, cut them in individual strips, and laminate each onto card stock. Use the Class Evaluation Form on page 163 of this Teacher Guide to record student performance.

As the student reads the list of ten words, check off (√) each correctly read word. If a word is read incorrectly, write down phonetically what was actually said. It is not enough just to mark the words wrong. You and the student need to know what specific mistakes were made. The easiest way to do this is to write down the student's mispronunciation of the word in Hebrew script. The example on the following page shows how to do this.

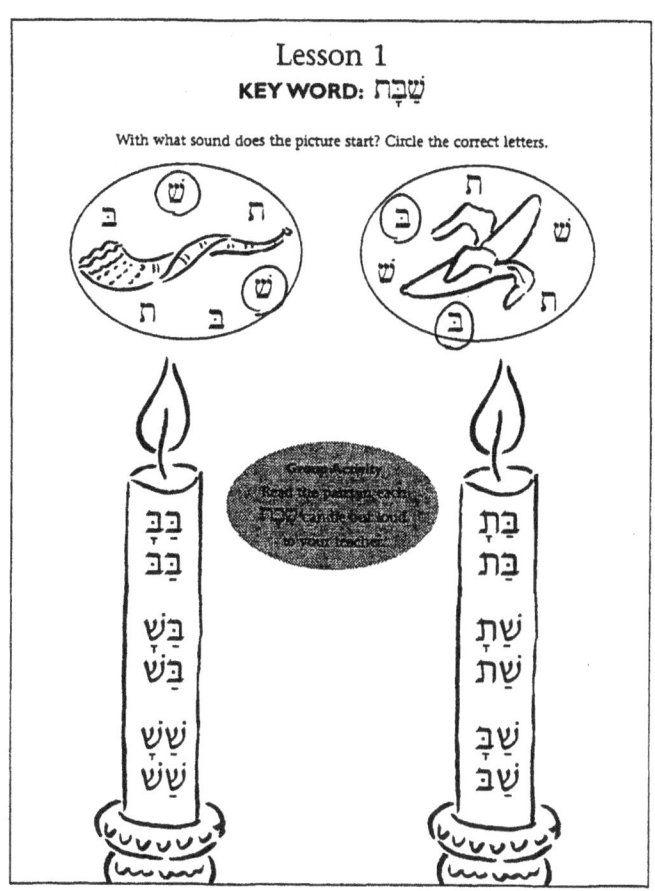

Problem Identification

Jonathan is having difficulty in two areas. He is confusing the ת with the ב and he is having difficulty blending consonant-vowel-consonant combinations. Since neither of these problems is consistent, it seems that he has learned some of the skills, but that he needs some extra attention. For this first lesson, Jonathan has made too many errors. Keep an eye on Jonathan.

Suggestions for Remediation

1. Letter confusion — Jonathan is probably confusing the letters ת and ב because they look similar when rotated. He may have a problem with visual memory. He is also not attending to a significant marking (the dot inside the ב). Therefore, isolate the letters and work on learning first one, and then the other. Have Jonathan sound out letter combinations with ת and שׁ, avoiding the ב. When you are confident that Jonathan knows the ת, bring in the ב. Remind him to look closely at every marking.

2. Blending error — Have Jonathan read lines 3 and 4 of the Reading Page in the following order.

בַּךְ בַּב שָׁשְׁ שָׁשֻׁ שָׁשׁ שַׁת שָׁתָ בַּתָ בַת

Explain the concept to him by contrasting it with English, using words like Bob and shot. Don't write down the English, as you don't want to make an association between the English vowel o and the Hebrew ָ or ַ.

Suggested Additional Activities

1. *Memory/Concentration* (see page 144 in this Teacher Guide). Use cognate picture cards and Hebrew letters.

2. Begin *Illustrated Letter Cards* (see page 150 in this Teacher Guide).

3. Begin *Illustrated Dictionary* (see page 150 in this Teacher Guide).

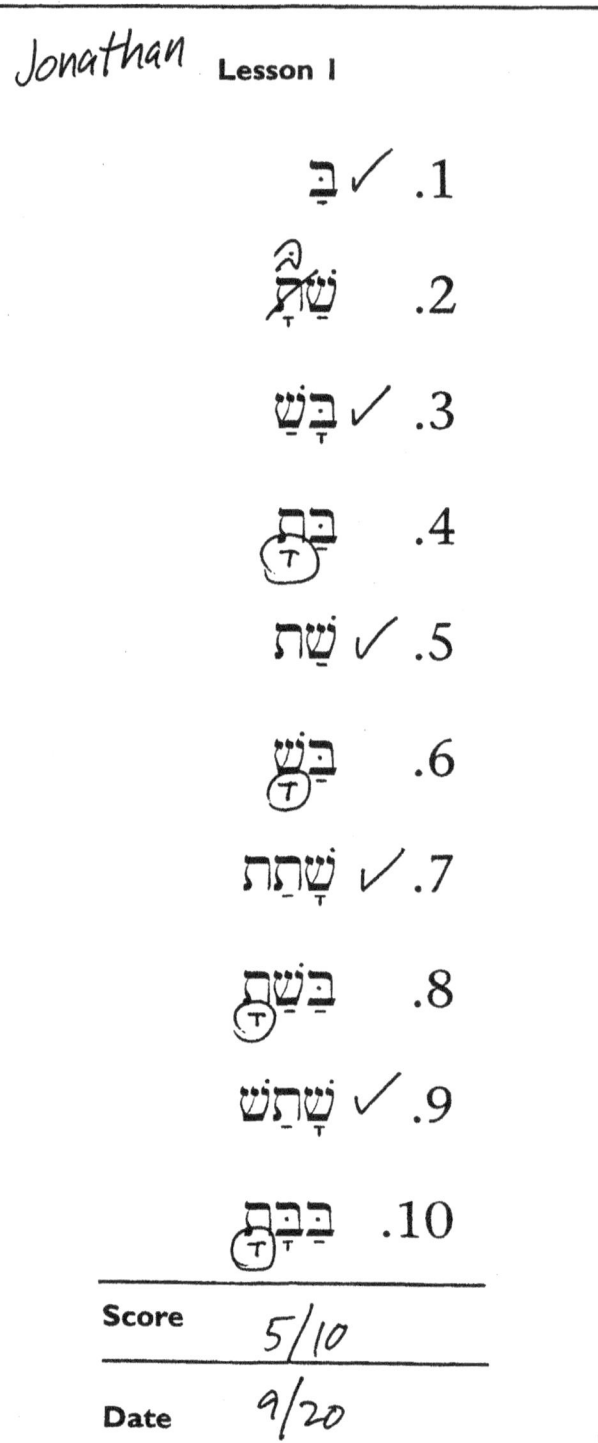

LESSON 2

Key Word: (fish) דָג
New Letters: ד ג

Oral Language Lesson (optional)

Other than the Key Word, no vocabulary is taught in Lesson 2. It is recommended that you begin at this time to introduce orally the vocabulary words that appear in subsequent lessons. In this way, students will know the words from hearing them before they see them.

The Key Word of the previous lesson שַׁבָּת may be reviewed at this time or during the review step (see below).

The Seven Lesson Steps

1. **Review**
Review the consonants and vowels taught in Lesson 1. Review the Key Word.

2. **Evoking the Key Word**
Ask students:
"What kinds of foods do people eat on Shabbat?"
Someone will probably mention fish or gefilte fish. Then, open the Workbook to page 7, the Introduction Page for this lesson. Tell the students that this lesson's Key Word is דָג. Ask them to point to one of the pictures of a דָג. Call on volunteers to point to a picture and say the Hebrew word. Don't expect the students to know the word דָג, this is one of the few Key Words that they won't know. They invariably learn it quickly when you tell them:
"In Hebrew, דָג isn't a dog, it's a fish!"

3. **Introducing New Letters and Vowels**
Close the Workbooks to introduce the new letters.
Again, you want the students to break the word into the component sounds. So first ask:
"What is the first sound you hear in דָג?"

Make sure that they can isolate the **d** sound.
"Have we learned the letter for this sound already?" (no)
Put a ד on the felt board and say:
"Notice that this letter has two lines and that the top line sticks out on the right." Draw a stick letter ד on the chalkboard.
Additionally, you can say:
"This letter makes a **d** sound as in the word "door." The Hebrew word for "door" is *delet* and it begins with ד. The ד even looks like a door — it has a hinge that sticks out." (DO NOT show or introduce the ר, so that students will not confuse the two later.)
Practice with the ד on the felt board in combination with the שׁ, בּ, ת, and the two vowels ָ and ְ.

Suggested sequence: דְשׁ דָבּ דָת שַׁדְ בַּדְ

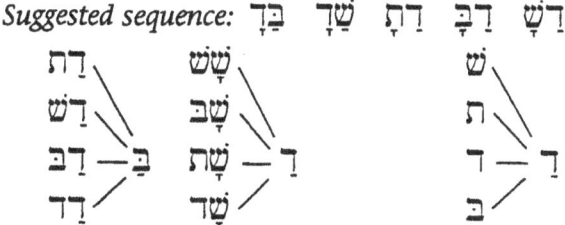

Note that the syllables are divided after the first letter/vowel combination, just as they would be in real Hebrew words.

Be careful that students are not confusing the sounds of the ד and the ת. If they are having difficulty with this, then don't show the ת initially. Just introduce the **d** sound and then, after they have learned it, bring back the ת.

Put דָ on the felt board again and ask:
"What does this say?"
""How do you say fish in Hebrew?"
"So what sound is missing?"
Put the ג next to the דָ and ask:
"What do you think this says? This says דָג. So what sound does this letter ג make?"
Now, take away the דָ and put on the board ג.
"What do you think this says?"

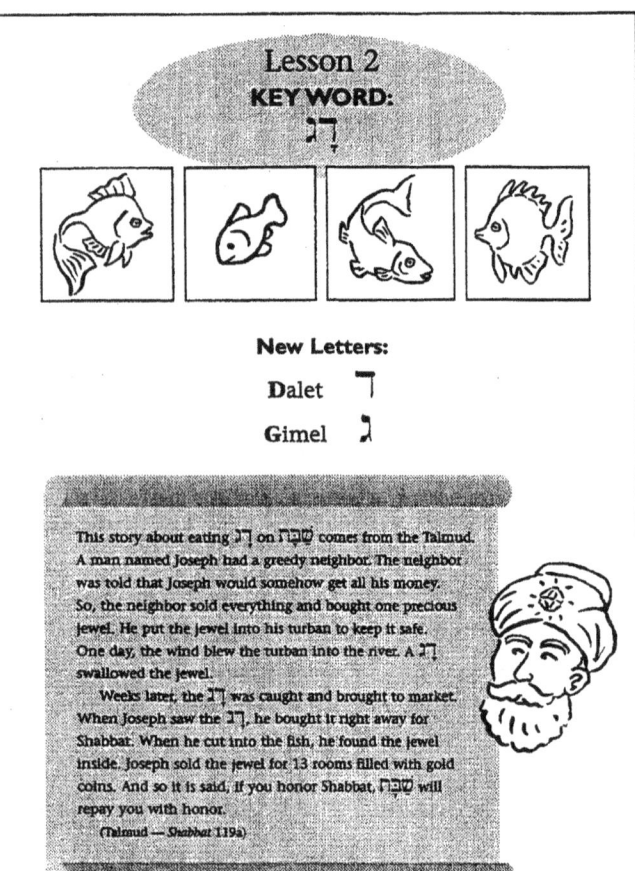

Refer back to page 7, the Introduction Page for Lesson 2. Call on several students to read the Key Word at the top of the page, to identify again in Hebrew the four pictures, and to say the names of the letters. Remind them that the first sound in the name of the letter tells them what sound the letter makes. Read the story aloud to the class. The story reinforces the Key Word, and explicitly connects it to the concept of שַׁבָּת. When the word דָּג appears in the story, students may try to read it from left to right, since it appears in the middle of English sentences. For this reason, the teacher should be the one to read the story. After the first few lessons, when directionality is less of an issue, there shouldn't be a problem with students reading these introductory stories.

If you have an abundance of time, you may want to read a longer version of the story found in the picture book *Joseph Who Loved the Sabbath* by Marilyn Hirsh (New York: Viking, 1986).

Practice now with the letters students have learned, except the ד. It is best when first introducing the ג not to practice with the ד also, as some children will confuse any two letters that are introduced at the same time.

Suggested sequence for the felt board:

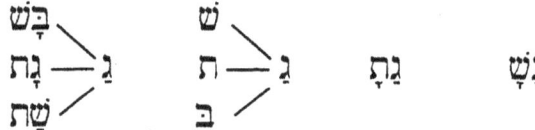

Notice how you are always progressing from easier words to harder words, starting with words that don't require blending, moving to words that do require blending, then changing the order of the letters, and finally moving on to longer words.

DO NOT show or introduce the נ (*Nun*).

4. Using the Reading Pages

Lesson 2 is relatively simple, as only two new letters are introduced. Here is your opportunity to make sure that students understand the concepts of blending and of reading from right to left, and that they have mastered the five consonants and the most common vowel sound in Hebrew. After this lesson, more vowels will be introduced. Do not progress yet to the next lesson with students who have not mastered the vowel sound ◌ and ◌. In general, students tend to confuse vowels even more than consonants.

On the first Reading Page of this lesson (page 8), there is a relationship between lines 2 and 3, 4 and 5, and 6 and 7. This is structured so as to help students realize the difference between words that end with a vowel sound and words that end with a consonant sound. Have students read the lines going down vertically, as well as across horizontally. Combinations on the next Reading Page (page 9) are more complex. Notice the relationship between lines 2–3–4 and 5–6–7. For example:

נָת

דָּגָת

שָׁגָת

Again, you can have students read down the page as well as across. The last syllable is highlighted in each combination to help students with proper blending.

6. Using the Worksheets

Page 10: Make sure students write the ד with an extended line, so that it does not look like a ר (*Resh*). Students complete the exercise on the bottom of the page.

Page 11: Students complete the worksheet. Make sure you have enough thin markers, colored pencils, or crayons in the five required colors. Directions and answers are self-explanatory.

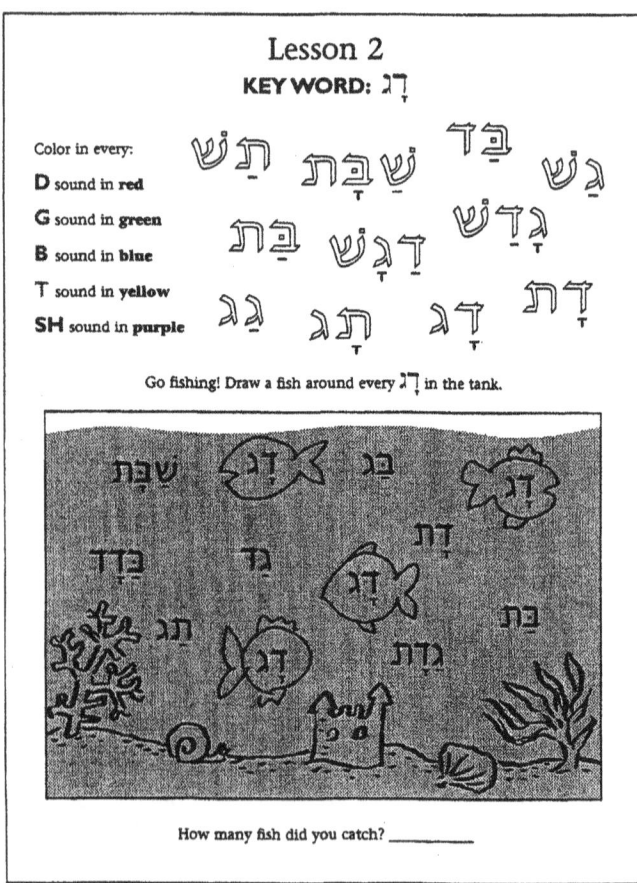

38

Page 12: All of the words on the top of this page are cognates, i.e., English or foreign words adopted into the Hebrew language with only small variations in pronunciation.

7. Evaluation

Evaluate individually any student who had difficulties in Lesson 1, and as many other students as you have time for. Remember that you will want to evaluate each student by the end of Lesson 4, and ideally you should evaluate as many students as feasible before continuing. The evaluation process is explained on page 16 in this Teacher Guide.

Suggested Additional Activities

1. *Connect-4* (see page 142 in this Teacher Guide).

2. *Around the World* (see page 146 in this Teacher Guide). Use words from the Reading Pages.

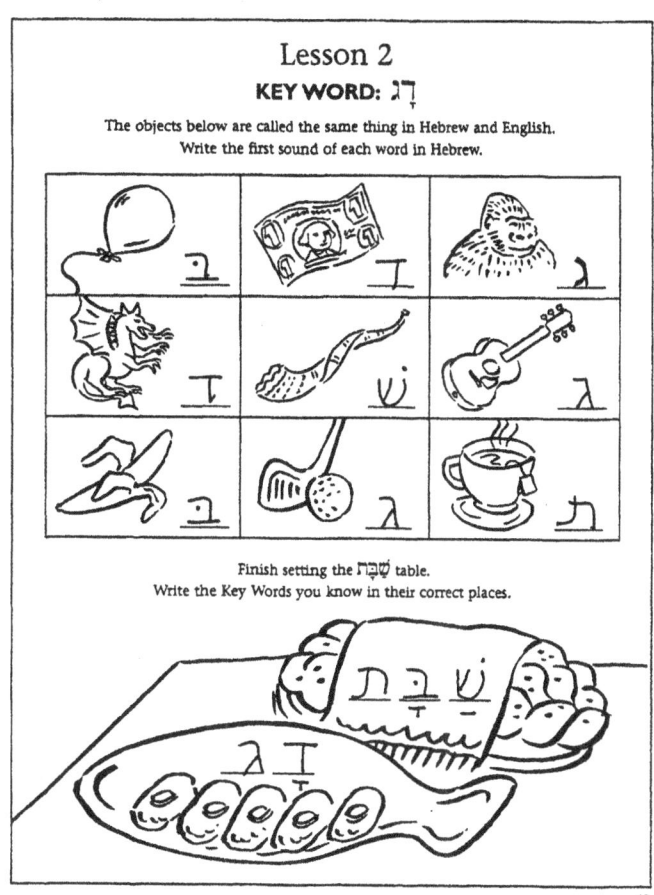

LESSON 3

Key Word: (mother) אִמָא (father) אַבָּא
New Letters: א מ
New Vowel: ָ

Oral Language Lesson (optional)

Other than the Key Words, no vocabulary is taught in Lesson 3. Continue to introduce the vocabulary of future lessons so that students can become familiar with it before seeing it in written form.

The Seven Lesson Steps

1. Review
Review the five letters learned thus far. Make sure students know the vowel sounds ָ and ְ before you teach the new vowel. Review the two Key Words.

2. Evoking the Key Word
Open the Workbook to page 13, the Introduction Page for this lesson.
Point to one of the pictures of a father and ask:
"Who is this?"
Point to one of the pictures of a mother and ask:
"Who is this?"
"Do you know the words for father and mother in Hebrew?"
If students do not know, point to the picture of the father and say:
"This is אַבָּא."
Try to establish a direct association between the picture and the word. Follow this principle throughout this program. It is easier to retain a word if it can be associated with an object that can be touched or a picture that can be seen, rather than with a written English word.

Optional Activity: Teach the song "*Shabbat Shalom,*" from זְמַן לְשִׁיר or the song "*Ema Aba*" from *Especially Wonderful Days* (A.R.E. Publishing, Inc.).

3. Introducing New Letters and Vowels
Say to students:
"You already know letters and vowels for all the sounds you need to write אַבָּא, but if we write it with just those letters and vowels, the word is going to look strange. Let's try it."
Spell it using just a ָ without a letter above it (בָּ ָ). Say:
"That doesn't look right. Something is missing. In Hebrew you can't have a vowel without a letter. So, we have to put a letter on top of the vowel, like this: אַבָּ. What sound do you think the א has?"
"Great! You are correct. It has no sound. It is silent. Here is another surprise. The Key Word is really spelled אַבָּא. The letter א at the end of the word is also silent."

Now, with the felt board, practice reading combinations of the א and the other letters that the students know. You can use the Reading Pages as your guide, but be careful not to use the מ or the ָ yet.

Suggested sequence:

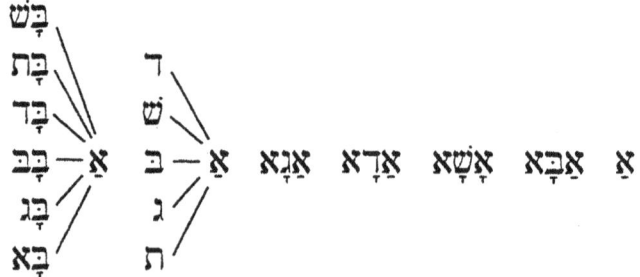

After you are sure that the silent letter is mastered, continue on to teach the word אִמָא. Say:
"Now we know how to say and read אַבָּא. How are we going to write 'mother'? How do we say 'mother' in Hebrew? (אִמָא) What is the first sound you hear?" (ee)

Proceed carefully here. You are about to introduce a second vowel sound. A few children may confuse this with the vowel sound previously learned, even though the two sounds are very different from each other. Ask:

"How will we spell **ee** in Hebrew? Do we know how to spell **ee**?"

You want students to deduce that אִמָּא will also start with the silent letter, and that underneath that letter will be a vowel different from the ones they have already learned.

Remove the ▨, replace it with a ▨ (*Chirik*) and say:

"This א now says **ee**."

Remove the א, replace with a שׁ and say:

"And what do you think שׁ says?"

Continue doing this with all the letters previously taught. Then say:

"What sound are we missing to get אִמָּא? Have we learned the **m** sound?"

Place a מ on the felt board and say:

"What do I have to put under this letter to make **mah**?" (מָ)

"Do you think something might be missing from the word אִמָּ?"

"Fantastic! Yes, we're going to put another silent א at the end of the word. Now we have the word אִמָּא!"

Suggested sequence for the felt board:

Open the Workbooks to page 13. Choose students to read the Key Words, identify again the four pictures, say the names of the new letters, and the sound of the new vowel. Remind students that the *Alef* is a silent letter — it does not make the **ah** sound as in the beginning of the word "*Alef*." This is one of the few cases in which the letter name is not a useful tool to remember the letter sound. Note that the vowel name is not given as it will not help students remember the vowel sound.

Read the story on page 13 aloud to the students. The story reinforces the Key Words, and deepens the concepts. You might suggest that they read it at home to their parents! The letters on the two tablets are versions of Hebrew script from the First Temple period. Students are not expected to be able to read them, but you can explain to those who ask that this is an old form of Hebrew writing.

If time permits, you can expand on the concept of honoring parents, asking students to give examples of ways they could honor their parents. If time is short, however, this entire part of the lesson can be done in about five minutes.

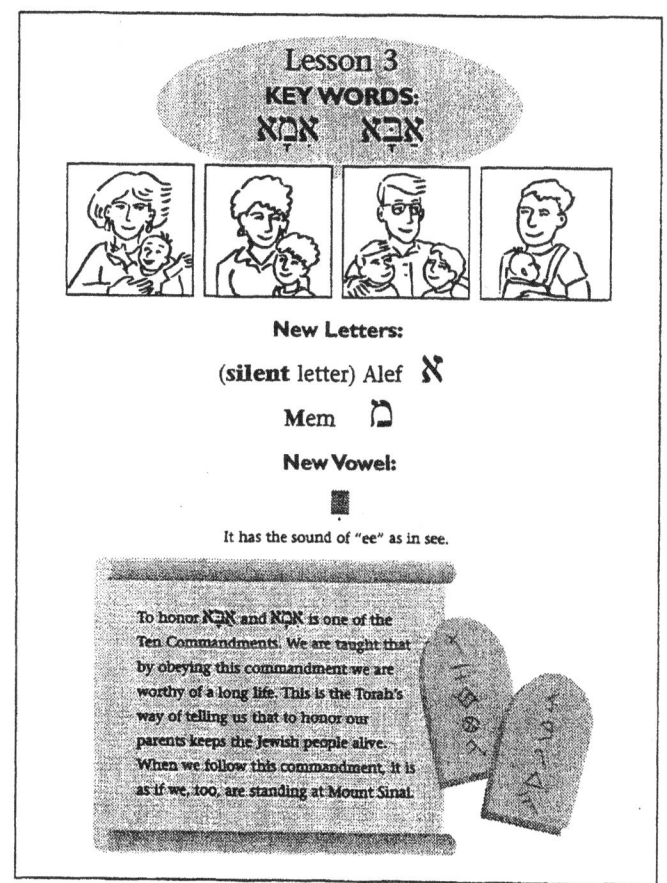

4. Using the Reading Pages

There are two Reading Pages for this lesson (pages 14 and 15). Since each includes both new letters and the new vowel, you will not be able to use these pages until you have introduced all the new concepts for this lesson.

On the first Reading Page, lines 1 through 4 feature simple combinations with the א in different places in the combinations. Lines 5 and 6 contain one syllable words in which only the vowel differs. Line 7 adds a syllable to the beginning of the words from line 6. Students can read lines 5-7 down as well as across. This kind of progression provides direct practice in blending and also increases attention to the vowels.

On the second Reading Page, lines 1, 2, 3, and 4, and lines 5, 6, and 7 are organized according to the same principles, and may also be read going down.

5. Using the Worksheets

Page 16: Make sure students are not writing the א as an "X." Students practice writing the מ and complete the matching exercise at the bottom of the page.

Page 17: The Vowel Hints are given here, in Lesson 3, because with the introduction of a second vowel sound, students may begin to confuse the two sounds. Until now, with only one vowel sound taught, there could be no confusion. Students who are auditory learners will find these hints useful, and when they make mistakes in sounding out the two vowel sounds, you can remind them of the hints. For students who are making many vowel errors on the Reading Pages, you may want to stop their reading, refer to the Vowel Hints on this page, and then return to the Reading Pages.

The coloring exercise at the bottom of the page results in the letters ת and א being colored in, with a dash between them. This dash is not supposed to represent the Hebrew vowel *Patach*; it is just a dash.

Lesson 3
KEY WORDS: אַבָּא אִמָּא

Practice writing the letter Aleph.

Practice writing the letter Mem.

Practice writing the letter Aleph with all of the vowels you have learned.

Match each picture to the correct sound.

Lesson 3
KEY WORDS: אַבָּא אִמָּא

Vowel Hints
Sometimes the doctor tells you to open your mouth and say "Ah." Then the doctor puts a stick in your mouth. This stick is called a "tongue depressor," and it looks like this:

When you see a Hebrew vowel that is shaped like a stick, (or a stick with a handle), remember to say, "Ah."

The "ee" vowel is one dot under a letter. It looks like a little bead.

Draw a tongue depressor around all the words that have the "ah" sound in them.
Draw a bead around all the words that have the "ee" sound in them.

 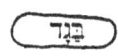   

Aleph א is the first letter of the Hebrew alphabet.
Tav ת is the last letter of the Hebrew alphabet.
Color in the spaces that contain the first or last letter of the Hebrew alphabet.

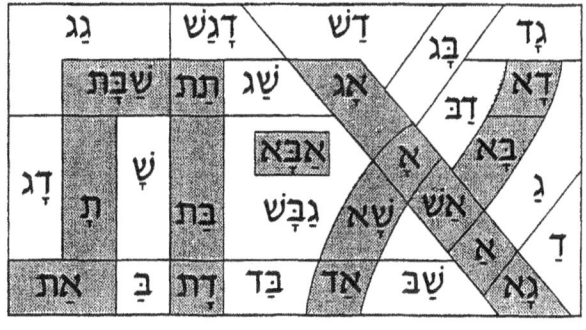

Page 18: Complete the pictures and the words. For the top part of the page, students are asked to be a little creative. The students must complete both the picture and the words based on the clues.

Page 19: Students complete the worksheet. Directions and answers are self-explanatory. Note the thematic connection to the lesson's Key Words.

6. Using the Prepare for Prayer Pages

These pages begin in Lesson 5, when students know enough letters to sound out a number of words that appear in the prayer book.

7. Evaluation

Evaluate each student individually. As students have now learned more than one vowel sound, they may make more mistakes in reading vowels. Mark a separate photocopy for each student so that you can pinpoint and keep track of the errors that he/she is making.

Suggested Additional Activities

1. *Open-ended Board Game* (see page 143 in this Teacher Guide). Use words from the Reading Pages. Either read directly, or put the words on cards. You will need a "judge."

2. *Break the Chain* (see page 142 in this Teacher Guide).

LESSON 4

Key Word: (Haggadah) הַגָּדָה (matzah) מַצָּה
New Letters: צ ה
Special Points: The two sounds of ה
New Vocabulary: (the) הַ ___

Oral Language Lesson (optional)

This lesson is the first time that an optional vocabulary word is introduced. These words will always be presented under the heading, "New Vocabulary." As opposed to the "Cool Hebrew Words" that appear on the bottom of most Reading Pages, these are words that will be used in subsequent language exercises. If your students will be completing the optional language component of the Workbook, they will need to learn each of the New Vocabulary words as they are introduced.

The New Vocabulary word for this lesson is הַ ___. Explain that it is a short word that is always attached to the next word, and that it means "the." In most cases, it is spelled with either a ַ or a ָ underneath it. Practice orally. Say:

"If הַ ___ means "the," what do you think הַשַּׁבָּת means? What about הַדָּג?" הַ ___ is one of the few words that must be introduced by translating it into English; any attempt at direct instruction would just be confusing for students.

The Seven Lesson Steps

1. Review

2. **Evoking the Key Word**
Both of the Key Words for this lesson have to do with Passover. While almost everyone will remember that they ate מַצָּה on the holiday, students may not know the word הַגָּדָה. Ask:
"Did your family read from a book at the Seder?"
"Do you know what that book is called?"
If you suspect that some of your students may not have attended a family Seder, or that their family's Seder was a holiday meal without any reading, you will need to phrase your question with sensitivity. Perhaps remind them of the school's model Seder last year, or assure everyone that they will participate in a model Seder this year in Hebrew School.

Bring in several samples of Haggadot that have the word הַגָּדָה written on the cover to show students. Once you have introduced the Key Word הַגָּדָה, students will be proud that they can read the word on the covers.

Teach the Sephardic/Israeli pronunciaton of the word הַגָּדָה — the second syllable is pronounced **gah** and the accent is on the last syllable.

Open the Workbooks to page 20, the Introduction Page for this lesson. Have students look at the pictures. Call their attention to the direction in which the two Haggadot open. They may not realize that Hebrew books (like their Workbook) open "backwards." Ask if anyone has an idea why the matzot are round and square. You might get some unusual answers! Have students point to each of the four pictures and say the Key Words.

3. **Introducing New Letters and Vowels**
Begin with הַגָּדָה. Here you will be teaching the silent ה and the voiced ה. Except for the voiced ה, the students can actually spell this word. If they try using the א at the beginning of the word הַגָּדָה, pronounce the word again, emphasizing the voiced **h** sound.

Put a ה on the board with a ַ underneath it and say:
"This is **ha**. What sound does the new letter make?"

It is very hard to pronounce the **h** sound

45

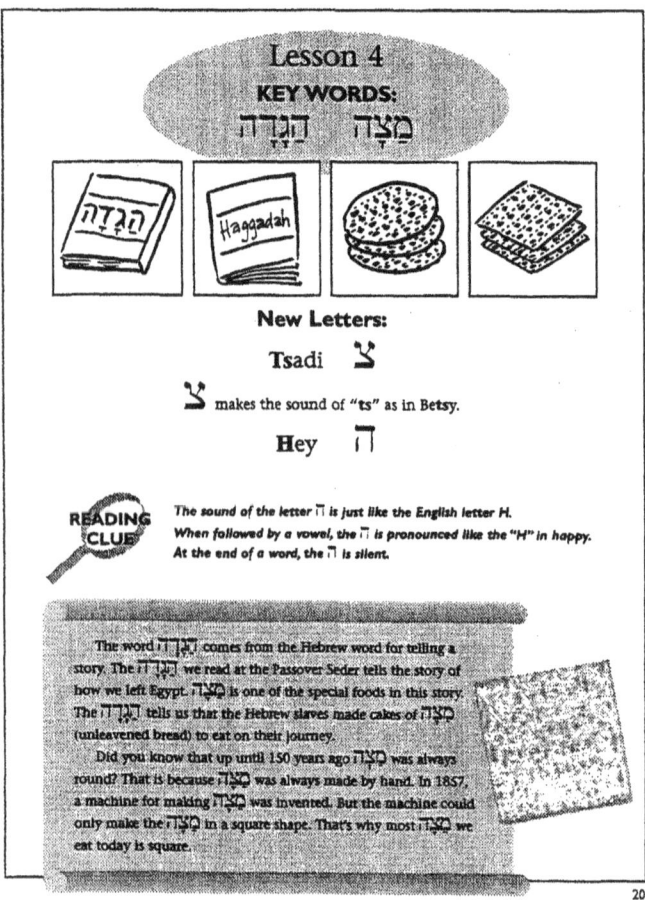

without a vowel, so don't spend much time trying to do that. Ask a student to come up to the felt board to spell the word *Haggadah*. They will probably spell it without the ה at the end: הַגָד, and will likely switch the ◌ֶ and ◌ַ vowels. Say:

"Right. That is read *Haggadah*. However, this word is spelled differently in Hebrew."

Place a ה at the end of the word to make הַגָדָה, correct the vowels, and say:

"This is the correct spelling of the word *Haggadah*."

Remove the ה from the end of the word and say:

"This also reads *Haggadah*. So, what is the sound of this letter?"

If students reply (incorrectly) "h," say:

"Listen carefully. Both words say *Haggadah*. You can't hear any difference at the end of the word."

Encourage the students until they come up with the rule that a ה at the end of a word is silent when there is no vowel under it. You can also compare the letter ה to the English letter "h" — the "h" is silent at the end of a word and

voiced when in other positions (e.g., oh, yeah, Sarah, Leah, helicopter, hippo).

With the felt board, have students practice reading different combinations using both the silent and the voiced ה. By now you understand the principle of the sequences used with the felt letters and the felt board. From this lesson on, follow the same principles that were demonstrated in Lessons 1 through 3 and make up your own sequences. You may choose words from the first Reading Page, progressing from easy words at the top of the page to more complex words at the bottom of the page.

At this point, you can either read page 21, the first Reading Page of this lesson, or introduce the Key Word מַצָה. If your students need their concepts broken up into small sections, it is best to read the first Reading Page before saddling them with another new letter. Also bear in mind that students may prefer to have a break between the reading of the two Reading Pages.

Introduce מַצָה by saying:

"What is the first sound in מַצָה?"

Students already know the **m** sound, so they will be able to spell מַ. If you are placing the letters on the board, use the correct vowel. Ask:

"What is the sound after **mah**?"

The **ts** is a very difficult sound for English speaking students because it does not exist as a separate letter in English. Two English letters give you the sound: "ts" in "cats" or "zz" in "pizza." Get students to pronounce the sound. If they know the word צִיצִית, or will be learning it during the year, you can practice saying it. Otherwise, use examples from known words such as pizza, *matzah*, Mitsubishi, Betsy, and itsy-bitsy. Try to avoid examples with the "ts" at the end of the word, since you are not teaching the final צ, and not having them read any Hebrew words with the צ in the final position. Don't belabor the point. After additional practice, most students learn to pronounce צ, and correcting them over and over at this point may just embarrass them.

After you have introduced the צ, the students can spell the word מַצָה in Hebrew. They will probably spell it initially without the ה. Say:

"Yes, that is pronounced מַצָה, but that isn't the way you spell it. Does anyone have an idea how you might spell it?"

Someone will probably come up with מַצָה, because they already had the silent final ה in הַגָדָה. Or, they might come up with מָצָא, which is also an excellent suggestion, albeit a different word. You can give a hint — that the word ends with this lesson's silent letter.

Have students practice reading various combinations of letters and vowels on the felt board. Then, read the story on the page 20 Introduction Page. Resist the temptation to make this an in-depth Passover unit — this should be a 5 to 10 minute presentation of the Key Words.

4. Using the Reading Pages

The first Reading Page (page 21) reinforces only the ה, so you can separate your lesson into two parts. Use the first Reading Page after הַגָדָה is introduced. If students have difficulty with lines 3 and 4, have them read down the columns for lines 2 through 4. Alert the children to the fact that in line 7 all the words begin with הַ. Review the meaning of the word הַ and see how many of the words on line 7 the students can understand.

Use the second Reading Page (page 22) after you have taught both מ and צ. Line 3 can help students read line 4. Line 6 can help students read line 7.

5. Using the Worksheets

Page 23: Students practice writing the new letters and complete the exercise at the bottom of the page. "Tsetse fly" will be unfamiliar to most students, but is included as it is an English word with the צ sound. Encourage students who are having trouble pronouncing the צ sound to say these English words aloud to themselves as they complete the page.

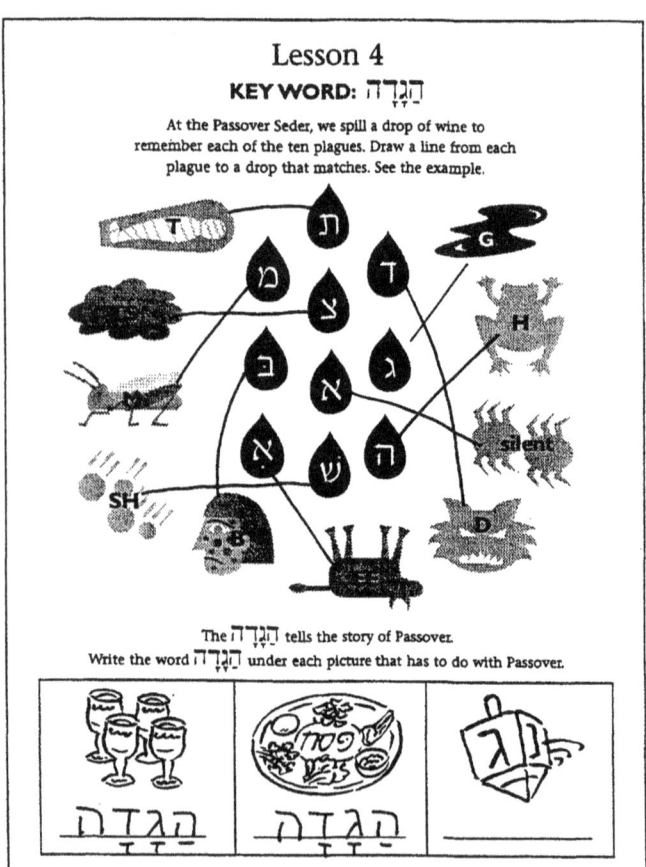

Page 24: The exercise on the top of the page simply requires students to match the Hebrew letter with its English sound. The pictures of the ten plagues and the drops of wine are used to connect the exercise thematically with the Key Words. The pictures have no connection to the sounds on them, nor are students expected to know the plagues in Hebrew. The exercise at the bottom of the page is conceptual. Briefly discuss the symbols of Passover so students will be prepared to complete this worksheet.

Page 25: The exercise in the הַגָּדָה graphic at the top of the page teaches the ה_ as a vocabulary word. Make sure you have introduced the ה_ before students reach this exercise.

Before students complete the crossword puzzle at the bottom of the page, point out to them that some clues begin with the word "the." Tell them to be sure to include the Hebrew word for "the" in their answers to these clues.

6. Using the Prepare for Prayer Pages

The Prepare for Prayer Pages begin in Lesson 5, when students know enough letters to make a number of words that appear in the prayer book.

7. Evaluation and Remediation

Evaluate individually any student who you have not yet evaluated. Even a student you are sure is doing well deserves the individualized attention, and occasionally you may be surprised to find that a bright, cooperative student actually has a reading problem. Be sure also to evaluate any student who did poorly on previous evaluations. Now may be the time to speak to your Director of Education about these students and to devise a plan to address their difficulties.

Make a note of students who are not correctly pronouncing the צ. Some students may still pronounce it as ס, ז, or ת. It is crucial that all students understand that the צ says **ts**. You can verify a legitimate speech difficulty by asking the student to read several English words that contain this sound.

Make sure students are pronouncing the voiced ה and not reading it as an א.

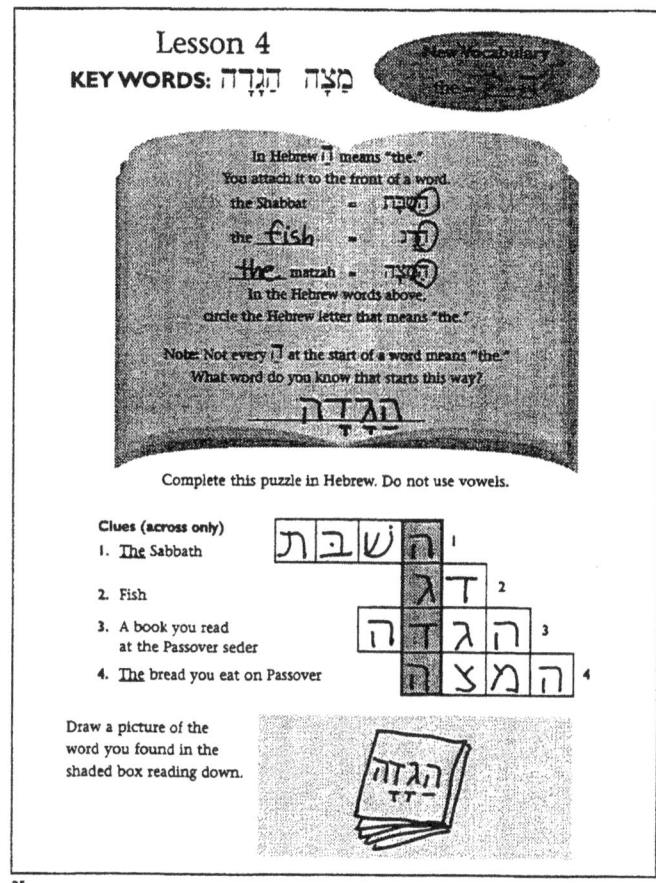

Suggested Additional Activities

1. Bring in samples of *Haggadot*. Look through them and find the words מַצָּה and הַגָּדָה. You will also find the words אַבָּא (in "*Chad Gadya*"), and הַשַׁבָּת (in "*Dayenu*"). Students will be proud that they can already read these words!

2. Play *Human Tic-tac-toe* or *Chalkboard Tic-tac-toe* as a class (see page 146 and page 145 in this Teacher Guide).

3. In a learning center, students can make or play with *Two Piece Puzzles*, matching letter sounds and/or matching vocabulary (see page 147 in this Teacher Guide).

LESSON 5

Key Word: (hand) יָד (I) אֲנִי
New Letters: נ ׳
Special Points: ◌ָ = ◌ָ   ◌ִי = ◌ִ   נ ≠ ג
New Vocabulary: (in the house) בַּבַּיִת   (in the) בַּ___   (house) בַּיִת   (who) מִי

Oral Language Lesson (optional)

Introduce the new word מִי through the use of a puppet. Tell the students:

"My puppet [give it a name] wants to meet our class. He wants to know who you are."

Have the puppet look through your roll book and say:

"מִי יוֹסֵף?"

The student will reply by raising a hand. Later in the lesson, after you have introduced the Key Word אֲנִי, the student can reply,

"אֲנִי יוֹסֵף."

Continue this with other children's names.

You can also use pictures. Display pictures of an אִמָּא, an אַבָּא, and people the children know. Again, have the puppet ask questions, e.g.:

"מִי אַבָּא?"

Pick a student to come to the front of the class and point to the correct answer.

There are many ways to teach the concepts of בַּיִת and בַּבַּיִת. Bring to class pictures of a house and of people, or an actual doll house. After you teach the vocabulary, students can "illustrate" sentences with these props. e.g.,

אִמָּא בַּבַּיִת   אַבָּא בַּבַּיִת   דָג בַּבַּיִת

One excellent activity is very simple and requires little preparation. Draw a large outline of a house on the chalkboard (large enough so that a full head would fit in the frame). Stand in front of the chalkboard, as if you are *in* the house and ask:

"מִי בַּבַּיִת?"

Have students come to the chalkboard one at a time as you repeat the question. Then, the class as a whole (or volunteers) can answer the question.

The Seven Lesson Steps

1. Review

2. **Evoking the Key Word**

The Key Word יָד means both "hand" and a "Torah pointer." Show the pictures on page 26 or, better yet, show a real Torah pointer. Ask if students know what the pointer is called. If they don't know, ask:

"What does this look like?"

They will say that it looks like a hand. Say:

"Raise your hand. In Hebrew the Torah pointer is called a יָד, and so is your hand."

Explain that when reading the Torah one does not touch the parchment with one's own יָד.

Now evoke the Key Word אֲנִי. Students are not likely to know this word. However, it is easy to teach. They know your name already, so just say:

"אֲנִי _____"
(your name)

If you have a puppet, demonstrate by having the puppet say:

"אֲנִי _____"
(puppet's name)

With these two examples, students should understand what the word means. Go around the room and have children introduce themselves by saying:

"אֲנִי _____"
(child's name)

After the children introduce themselves, ask them to tell you what אֲנִי means. They may think it means "my name is" or "I am." Refer back to the Introduction Page (page 26). Have students point to all four pictures and identify them in Hebrew.

Notice that both Key Words are connected with the idea of "myself." This also ties in with the Key Words from Lesson 3, אִמָא and אַבָּא. You can expand on this to make an oral Hebrew unit on "Me and My Family."

3. Introducing New Letters and Vowels

In order to spell יָד, students are only missing the first sound, so ask:

"What is the first sound in יָד?"

Put the י on the felt board and alert students to how small the letter is. In fact, you may want to write it on the chalkboard next to the ד so they can see how small and elevated it is.

With the felt board, practice reading words with the letter י, along with all the other letters that have been taught. At this point only use the י in positions where it is voiced, i.e., makes the consonant y sound.

Continue and teach the second Key Word אֲנִי. Ask:

"What is the first sound you hear in the word אֲנִי?"

When trying to spell it, students will probably use either אָ or אַ. Leave it at this point and do not correct the vowel. Go on to teach the נ. Say:

"What is the next sound you hear in אֲנִי?"

Put a נ next to the א. Students can tell you which vowel to put under the נ.

Before continuing, practice reading words on the felt board with the נ. Initially, when you form words with the נ, DO NOT use the ג. Only when you are sure that everyone in your class knows the נ, should you bring back the ג. Do so first without the נ, and then use both letters together. Notice, too, that both the נ and the י are very small letters. Initially, you do not want to drill with the י until you are sure that the students know the נ.

Do not put the נ in a final position. If students suggest this, try to avoid the issue, as the Final ן will be taught in the next lesson.

Now teach the ֲ (Chataph-Patach). Explain that there is another vowel with an **ah** sound and show the vowel ֲ. If you have a set of letters that has only ַ, add two dots with a dark marker. Ask:

"Since ַ and ֲ both make an **ah** sound, what sound are the two dots actually making?"

Elicit from the students the concept that the two dots are silent, as this will help them when the silent ה is taught in Lesson 9.

Write the word אֲנִ (with the א, but without a י). Say:

"This is pronounced **anee**, but that is not the way the Key Word is spelled. It is spelled like this: אֲנִי."

Have students discover the rule that the י does not change the pronunciation. They might think that this is only true when the י occurs at the end of a word, as was the case with the silent ה. Therefore, show other examples where the silent י is not at the end of the word, such as in the word אִישׁ.

Open the Workbooks to page 26, the Introduction Page. Read the entire page with students, reviewing the Key Words, as well as the new letters and vowels, and reading the story. After they have deduced the Reading Clue on their own, and practiced reading words that follow it, they are now introduced to a formal statement of the rule. Make sure everyone understands it. Ask

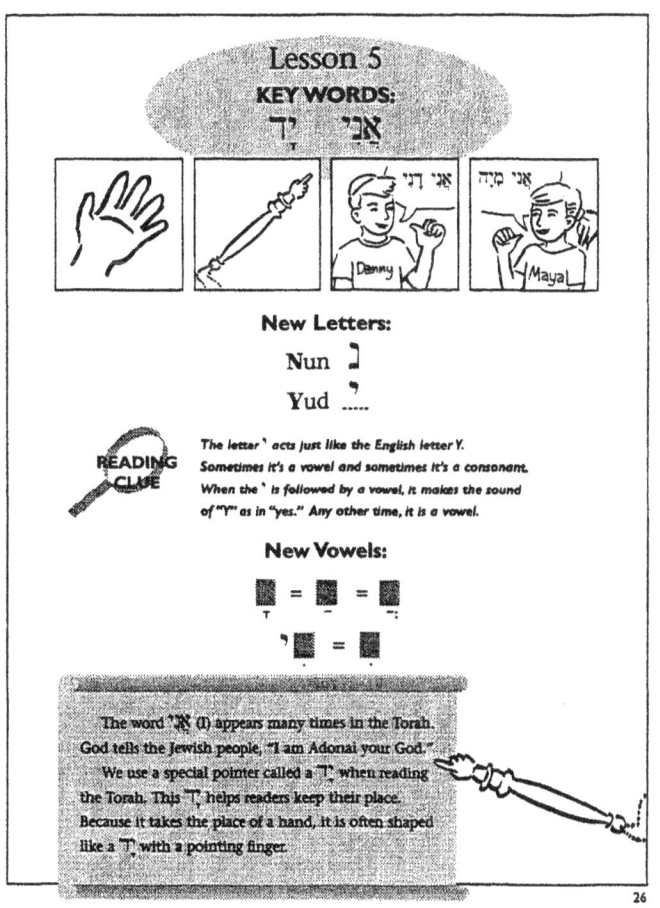

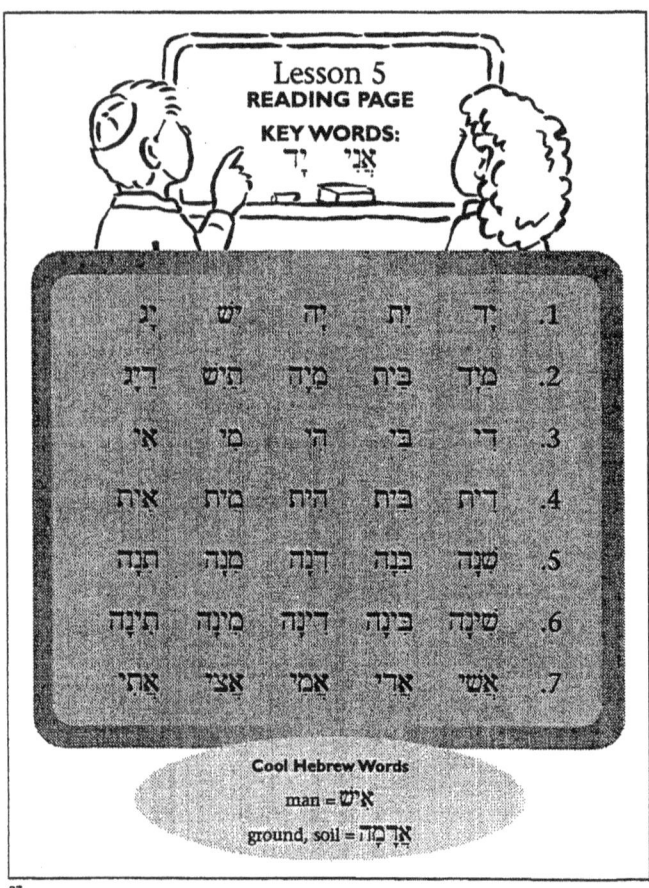

them to give you examples from the Introduction Page of words in which the י is a consonant and in which it is a vowel. They will need to understand this in order to complete page 31.

4. Using the Reading Pages

All the new letters and vowels appear on both pages. On the first Reading Page (page 27), the first two lines enable the students to practice the י when it is voiced (a consonant sound). Notice the relationship between lines 3 and 4, and 5 and 6. While the vowel ְ appears only under certain letters, including the א, there is no need to explain the grammatical reason for this.

The second Reading Page (page 28) is a review of the concepts taught in Lesson 5 using more difficult words. Line 1 consists of Hebrew names. In line 2 the י appears in a middle position with a ְ under it. This is to alert students to the fact that the י is a voiced consonant when there's a vowel under it, even if the vowel is ְ. Refer students back to the Reading Clue on the Introduction Page (page 26) if this gives them difficulty. Lines 6 and 7 each contain words from one "root." Line 6 words all have to do with presenting or presentations. You can say to students that line 7 words all have to do with telling, and ask them why they think the Key Word הַגָּדָה belongs in this word family. Many of the Reading Pages that follow will also have lines with words from the same root.

5. Using the Worksheets

Page 29: Make sure students write the י correctly, small and above the line, so that it does not look like a ר or a ו. Have a *dreidel* on hand to show which letters to write. Or, play *dreidel* as a motivating way to learn the נ and to review the other letters. This is especially relevant if Chanukah is approaching, but children will enjoy playing *dreidel* any time of year. For those who have completed the worksheets, set up a learning center for playing *dreidel* with instructions in English and tokens with which to play.

Page 30: Students write the Key Word יָד next to the three pictures of hands and the Torah pointer. Children may have a variety of different answers to the "cross out the word" exercise. For example, some may cross out אֲנִי in question 2, thinking that דָג is eaten on שַׁבָּת. Others might cross out שַׁבָּת, saying that אֲנִי and דָג are both alive. Any answer that students can support is acceptable here. The main purpose of the exercise is to have students read the words and understand what they are reading.

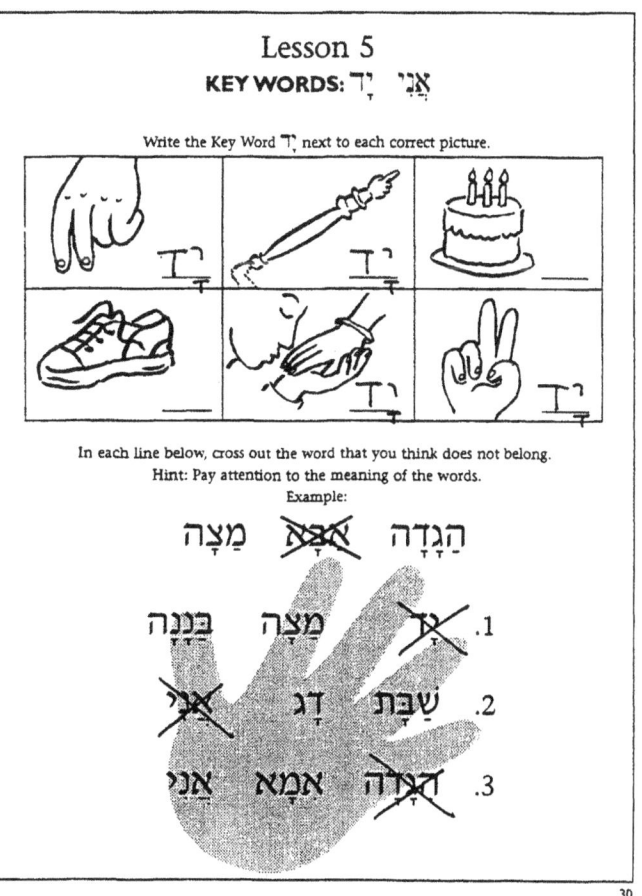

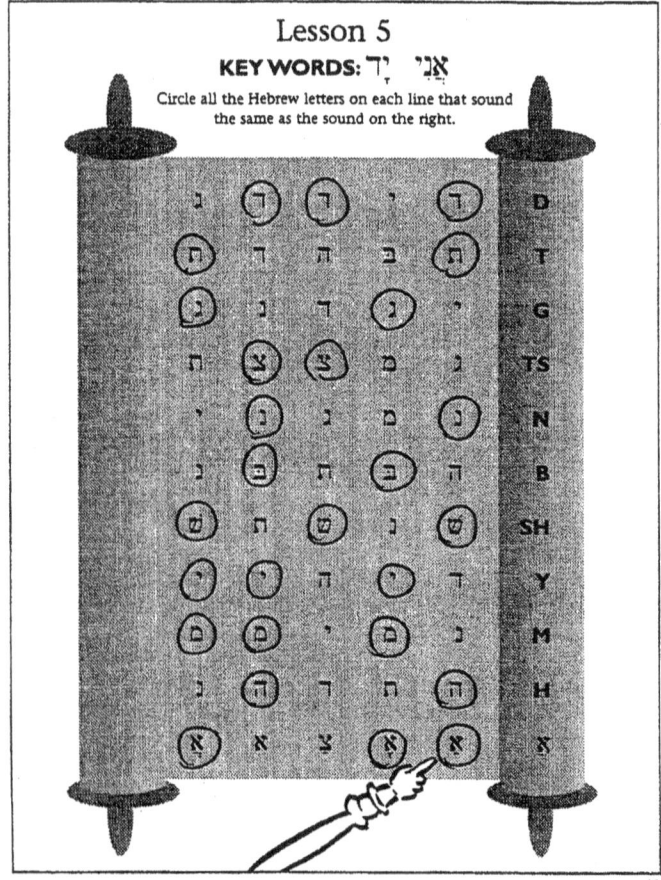

Page 31: Students must read the words to determine if the ׳ makes a vowel or consonant (voiced) sound. Refer back to the Reading Clue on the Introduction Page (page 26). Don't worry if students manage to complete the exercise correctly by applying the vowel rule and not actually reading the words. This is a much harder task and demonstrates that they have mastered the concept.

Page 32: The English is placed on the right side of each line to encourage students to scan the lines from right to left, the Hebrew direction.

Page 33: This page is for students who are doing the language component of the program. Before completing this page, students should already know the vocabulary from the oral lesson. Make sure students read and understand the Hebrew questions, as the question word מִי is the new concept. They may tend to ignore the three questions that refer to the bottom exercise, thinking that they can just fill in the speech bubbles.

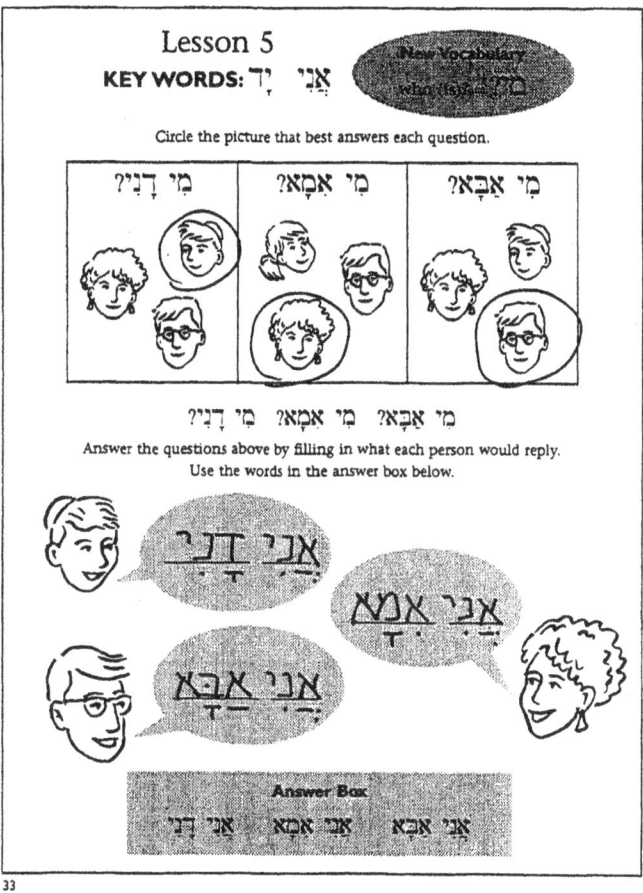

Page 34: This page is also for students who are doing the language component of the program. Students are to complete the pictures using the captions below each to tell them what to draw inside each house.

6. Using the Prepare for Prayer Pages

Page 35: This is the first Prepare for Prayer Page. Congratulate students on having reached this milestone in their reading instruction. Especially for students who are finding Hebrew a challenge, knowing that their body of knowledge is growing may help with motivation. For the first time, students know enough letters and vowels to read a whole page of words that come from the prayer book. Read the introductory paragraph aloud to them, or convey its ideas, and have students read it later to themselves. Make sure everyone knows what a בִּימָה is. While the partners read the words to each other, circulate through the room to make sure students are reading correctly, or to resolve any disagreements. If your class gets out of hand doing this kind of activity, or if you are concerned that many mistakes are being made, you can complete the page as a class activity. Conversely, if you think your students have had plenty of decoding practice with the new concepts, and time is short, the page can be skipped, as no new concepts are introduced.

7. Evaluation and Remediation

If students are confusing the ג with the נ, review each letter separately and then have them read words that contain both letters. Give them a hint to remember each letter: the ג is going on its little leg, while the נ has nothing special about it, or looks like the side, top, and bottom of a נֵר. They will not be able to read the word נֵר yet, so you will have to give the hint orally. But they may already know the word from candle blessings or the pre-primer *Kadimah!* If not, you can teach the word orally, if you think it will help a student remember the נ letter. Later in the Workbook, נֵר will be a vocabulary word.

Make sure that the י is being correctly pronounced, as this is a difficult concept. Often, with more reading practice, students suddenly grasp the concept.

Suggested Additional Activites

1. *Speed Reading* (see page 142 in this Teacher Guide).

2. *File Folder Houses* (see page 147 in this Teacher Guide). Write the English letters B, Y, D, and N on the envelopes and sort Hebrew word cards that have one of those sounds. If you are doing the language component of the program, label each "house" בַּיִת.

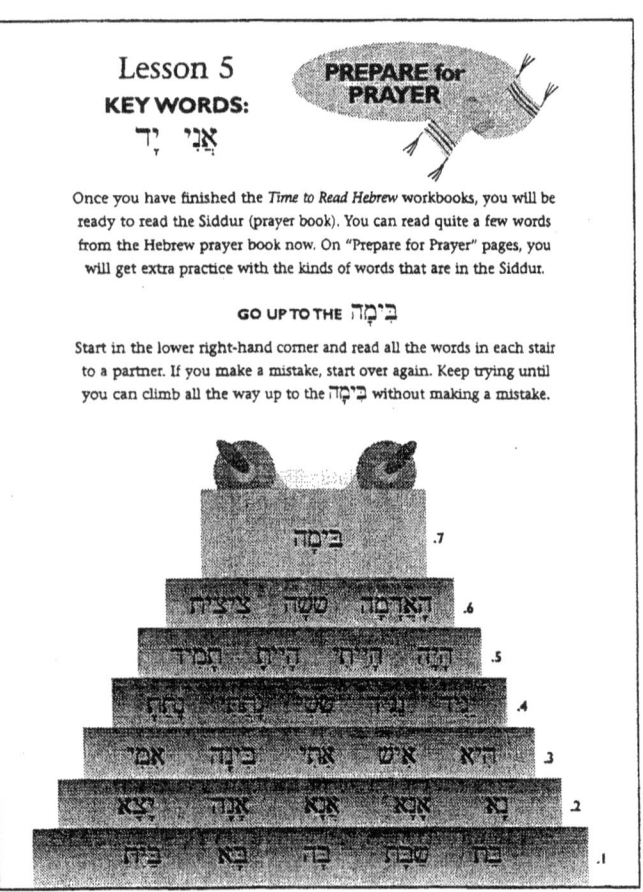

LESSON 6

Key Words: (wine) יַיִן (Kiddush) קָדוֹשׁ
New Letters: ק ן
New Vowel: וּ וֹ
Special Points: ן = נ
New Vocabulary: (what) מַה

Oral Language Lesson (optional)

The new vocabulary for this lesson is מַה. Review the vocabulary learned in the previous lesson. Review the question מִי בַּבַּיִת?. Ask students:

"If I want to ask you what you have in your house, I cannot use the word מִי, because it refers only to people. I have to use a different word. I have to use the word 'what.' Does anybody have any idea how to say 'what' in Hebrew?"

"I'm sure many of you actually know the word. It is the first word of the Four Questions that you ask at Passover." You may want to hum or sing the beginning of the Four Questions to see if this jogs anyone's memory.

If no one knows the word, tell students what the word is. Then show them the correct spelling.

Now play a game with the question מַה בַּבַּיִת?. Draw a house on a large piece of card stock. Cut a door flap that can open and close (the opening should be at least 4" x 8"). Place the house on the chalkboard ledge. Prepare picture cards using pictures of Hebrew objects that students know, such as דָג and הַגָדָה. Also use cognate pictures (see page 167 in this Teacher Guide), such as "guitar." Do not use people or words that are unfamiliar in Hebrew. Show the children the picture cards and review the Hebrew word for each object. Then ask "מַה בַּבַּיִת?" after hiding a card in the house. The student who answers correctly, with a full sentence, gets to place the next card in the house and ask the question.

Now drill the contrast between the two questions, מַה בַּבַּיִת? and מִי בַּבַּיִת?. Place two magazine pictures on the chalkboard, one showing a person in the house, the second showing an object in the house. The students do not need to know how to name these people or objects in Hebrew, as you will be drilling only the questions, not the responses. Say:

"I am going to ask a question about one of these pictures. See if you can figure out which picture I'm asking about."

Then ask either מַה בַּבַּיִת? or מִי בַּבַּיִת?. After you have done this a few times, have a student volunteer choose the picture and ask the question. Have a variety of pictures to enliven the game, the more humorous the better. Instead of a cardboard house, you can draw a house on the chalkboard, as in Lesson 5.

The Seven Lesson Steps

1. **Review**

Review the previously learned vowels, as there is a new vowel in this lesson. Ask:

"What is the difference between this vowel and the other vowels that you have learned so far?"

"By now we have learned four vowels. Three of them make the same sound. What is that sound?" (ah) Ask:

"Who would like to write/place the three ah sounds on the chalk/felt board?"

"What is the other sound that we have learned?" (ee)

Review the ב and the כ, as they are look-alike letters and tend to get confused. A review of the נ is also useful because in this lesson the Final *Nun* is taught.

2. Evoking the Key Words

The Key Words in Lesson 6 are both tied into Shabbat, as is the Key Word in Lesson 8, חַלָּה. Ask students:

"What was the first Key Word that you learned?"

"In this lesson you are going to learn two more words that have to do with Shabbat. Let's see if you can guess these words. I'll give you a hint — both words have something to do with welcoming Shabbat around the dinner table."

Students will probably mention many things, including the *challah*. If they do, say that this is also a Key Word, but not in this lesson. If they mention the drinking of the wine, ask:

"Do you just drink the wine, or is there a blessing? What is the blessing called?" Open up the Workbooks to page 36, the Introduction Page, and identify the Hebrew for each picture. The students will probably not be familiar with the picture on the left, the wine press. Tell them it is a device used to squeeze the juice out of grapes in order to make wine.

Talk about the קִדּוּשׁ blessing. Explain that the word קִדּוּשׁ comes from the Hebrew root meaning "to be special," and that with this blessing we are calling attention to how special Shabbat is.

In this particular lesson, you will want to evoke both Key Words at the same time. In the second part of the lesson, break the words down into their component sounds.

When you teach the Key Word יַיִן, tell the students that it sounds very much like its English equivalent (wine).

3. Introducing the New Letters and Vowels

Ask students:

"What is the first sound you hear in קִדּוּשׁ?"

They have not yet learned this sound, so once they say **k**, put the ק on the felt board. Tell students that this letter is different from letters they have learned earlier because it extends below the line. They will not be able to see this if the letter is a card on a felt board or appears in isolation. ק is, incidentally, the only non-final letter that extends below the line.

Practice with this letter before teaching the new vowel. When practicing with the ק initially, DO NOT use the ה, as they look alike. Then bring in the ה and practice some combinations without the ק. Only then bring the two together. Illustrate on the chalkboard the visual differences between the two letters.

After students know the ק quite well, continue spelling the word קִדּוּשׁ until you need the new vowel sound. Ask:

"What sound comes after the ד?"

"Today we are going to learn this vowel sound."

On the felt board, form the word קִדּוּשׁ with the correct spelling. Point to the וּ (*Shuruk*) and ask:

"What sound do you think this makes?"

"Is this a consonant or a vowel?"

"In what way is the new vowel different from other vowels we have learned?"

Keep the word קִדּוּשׁ on the board, spelled correctly. Prompt students to notice that this vowel is on the letter line. (DO NOT show or introduce the וֹ, so that students will not confuse the two.) Practice forming and reading words with the new vowel. If students are capable of learning the second Key Word (יַיִן), proceed to introduce it. If not, you can use the first Reading Page to practice the new consonant and vowel.

Before you spell יַיִן, tell students that they know all the letter sounds and that they might think that it is spelled like this: יַיִנ. Say:

"This sounds correct, but there is a mistake here that you have no way of knowing about. The letter נ is one of five letters in Hebrew that has a final form. You may remember that we read about this on the first page of the Workbook, before you knew any letters. You can't put this נ at the end of a word. Instead, you have to use a Final *Nun*, which looks like this: ן. Whenever we have the **n** sound at the end of a word, we have to use this form of the letter." Ask:

"In what ways are the נ and the ן similar?"

See if the students can suggest that the ן looks like נ with its tail stretched out. This kind of comparison will be very important later on when they learn ף, ך, and ץ.

Open the Workbooks to the Introduction

Page, page 36. Read the entire page, asking students once again to identify each picture, read the Key Words, and the names and sounds of the letters. The new vowel combination on this page presents a challenge. There is no exact English equivalent for the sound made by וִי. The closest approximation is the vowel combination in "gooey," but the correct Israeli pronunciation of וִי actually has the י sounded slightly as a consonant. Students may also wonder about the rationale for the pronunciation, asking, "Why does it make that sound? Why not just 'oo'?" Rather than getting into complicated explanations, assure them that it's just one of those unique things in Hebrew reading. While there is no Key Word with this sound, it will be drilled on page 38, which is why it is introduced here.

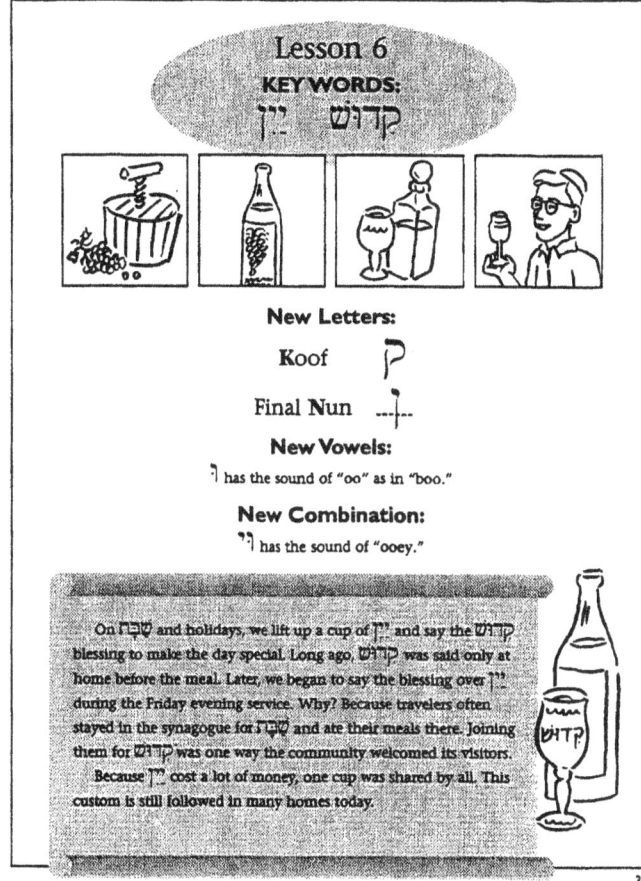

4. Using the Reading Pages

On the first Reading Page (page 37), only the ק and the ו are introduced. Therefore, you can teach this lesson in two parts.

The second Reading Page (page 38) consists primarily of practice in the ן. This page is best read in columns, especially lines 1 through 4. In line 6 you are practicing the וי combination. Line 7 has words from the same Hebrew root, ד.י.נ. Words from this root have to do with judging.

5. Using the Worksheets

Page 39: Students practice writing the new letters and complete the exercise at the bottom of the page. Make sure they make both letters extend below the line.

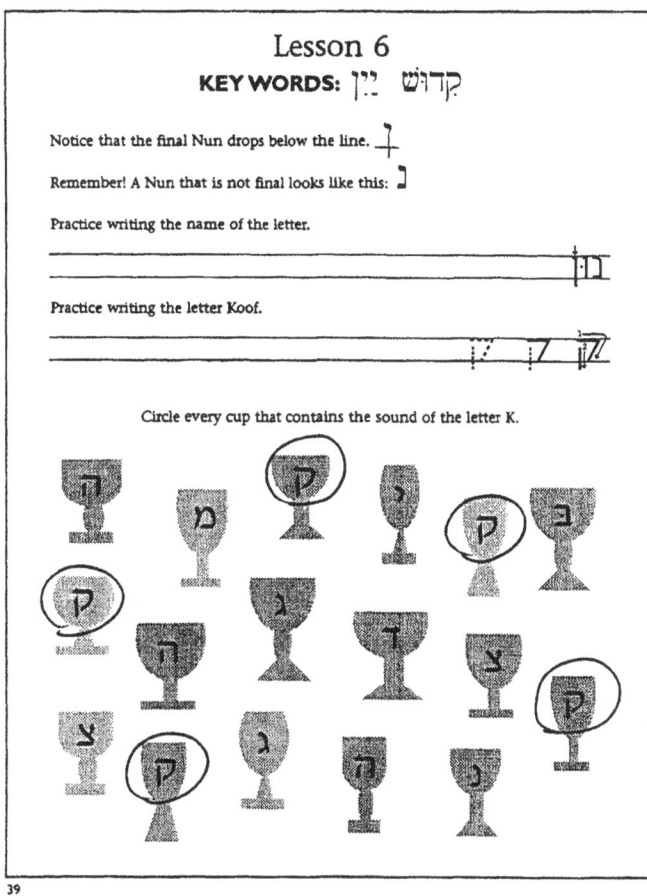

Page 40: Explain to students that they have to choose between a נ and a ו in the exercise at the top of the page. The exercise at the bottom of the page is for students who are having trouble blending with the new vowel sound. Some beginning Hebrew readers will initially try to put a vowel sound before the ו, sounding a combination such as נו as "**nah-oo**." Most students can sound out the combinations with a friend. If you sense some students are having trouble, have these students read to you or your aide.

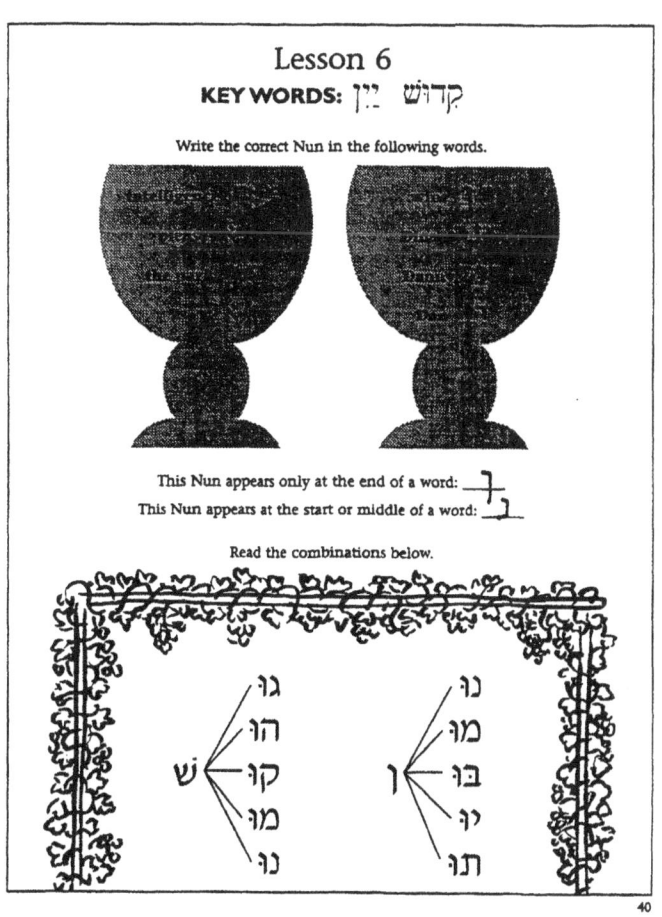

61

Page 41: Have students use a pencil to color the picture silver or grey.

Page 42: This page is for students who are doing the language component of the program. It deals with the distinction between מָה and מִי. Provide students with sufficient oral practice with this kind of exercise before they complete this page.

6. Prepare for Prayer

Page 43: The game on this page is similar to *Connect-4*, described in more detail on page 142 of this Teacher Guide. If students mark the boxes with pencil, they will be able to play the game only once. You can lay a plastic sheet on the page and use erasable markers so that they will be able to reuse the sheet. This game is a student favorite, as it involves strategy as well as reading.

7. Evaluation and Remediation

Problem Identification

Jonathan, our imaginary student, has been doing quite well so far, although he had some trouble learning the וּ vowel. In this lesson some new problems appear, much like the blending problems in Lesson 1. Here Jonathan is breaking up a word into syllables in the wrong place (#8), and on occasion adding the **ah** sound before the vowel וּ.

Suggestions for Remediation

To work on the blending problem, have Jonathan read two letter words that have an וּ (e.g., בּוּ, שׁוּ, תוּ), and then add a final consonant to these words (בּוּת, שׁוּת, תוּת). Here is a word game that students enjoy very much. Start telling a (short) story and write some of the words in Hebrew letters.

On my foot I wear a שׁוּ. When it rains I wear a בּוּת.

A cow says מוּ, to scare someone you say בּוּ.
What do you דוּ when יוּ are in a good מוּד?

Suggested Additional Activities

1. *Baseball* (see page 146 in this Teacher Guide). The questions you ask are words to read in Hebrew.

2. *What's Missing?* (see page 149 in this Teacher Guide). Use this game to review vocabulary and the question word מָה.

3. *Hot Potato* (see page 143 in this Teacher Guide). Use this game to practice phonetic reading.

Jonathan Lesson 6

1. קָנוּ
2. הַגָּן ✓
3. אָנוּ ✓
4. יָמָה ✓
5. בְּקָשָׁה ✓
6. אַיִן ✓
7. צִיוּד ✓
8. בְּטָנוּן
9. דָּקִיק ✓
10. דָּגָן ✓

Score 8/10

Date 10/25

LESSON 7

Key Word: (Purim) פּוּרִים
New Letters: ם ר פּ
New Vocabulary: (chalk) גִיר (water) מַיִם (Rabbi) רַבִּי
Special Points: ר ≠ ד   ם = מ

Oral Language Lesson (optional)

Spend a few minutes teaching the word מַיִם. Students may know it from the song *"U'sh'avtem Mayim."* You can teach students to read מַיִם only after you have taught the Final *Mem*. The other vocabulary word (גִיר) will probably not be familiar to students. Show students what the word means by pointing to a piece of chalk. Ask students to try to spell the word after you have introduced the ר. The cognate רַבִּי is also taught in this lesson, but should be obvious to students.

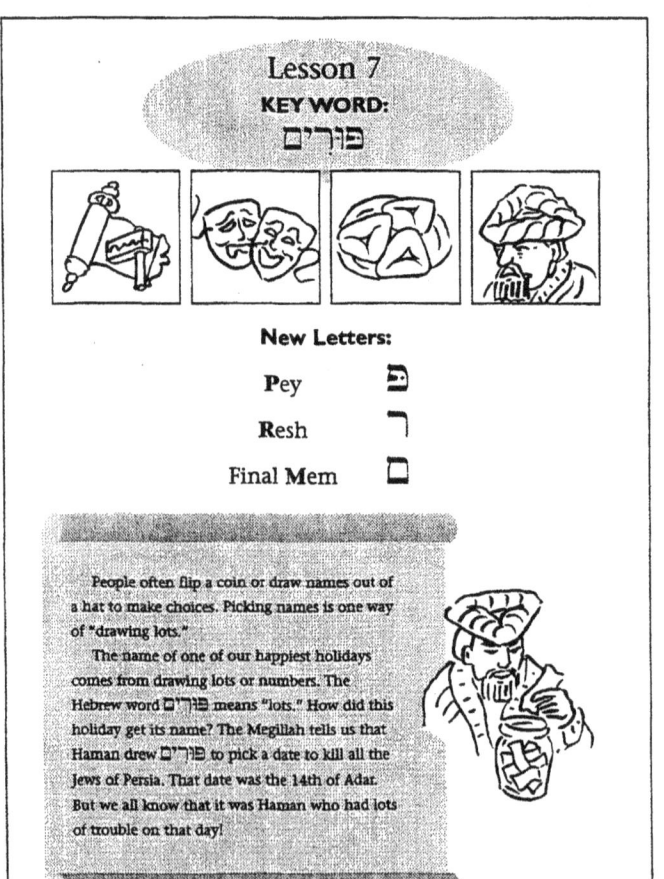

The Seven Lesson Steps

1. Review
Review the concept of final letters. Review נ and ן. Review מ in preparation for teaching ם.

2. Evoking the Key Word
Say:
"Today we are going to read the name of a particular Jewish holiday. What Jewish holidays do you know?" Then have students open the Workbooks to page 44. Ask if they know what holiday is being pictured. Make sure they understand what each of the pictures depicts: evil Haman, *hamantaschen*, masks (because we dress up in costumes), and the *Megillah* with a noisemaker. Students will need this information to complete the Worksheets. Note that the pictures are discussed in right to left order, reinforcing the Hebrew direction.

3. Introducing the New Letters and Vowels
Say:
"What is the first sound in the word Purim?"
After you have taught the פּ, practice various combinations. DO NOT mention or show the פ at this time.

Teach the ר. Make sure when first introducing it that you DO NOT show the ד. Then after you have practiced the פּ and the ר, take away the ר and practice only the פּ and the ד. Bring back the ר only when you are sure that the distinction has been made.

This lesson can be divided into two parts. In the first part, teach only the פּ and the ר, and in the second part, teach the ם. Students will think that they know how to spell Purim after they have learned the פּ and the ר, but they don't yet know about the ם. Now read from the first

Reading Page. Notice that at the top of the Reading Page (and on the Worksheets), the ם appears. Students might realize on their own that this makes the **m** sound at the end of a word, as they learned the concept of the final letter in the previous lesson.

If you do break the lesson into two parts, after you have completed the first Reading Page, teach the ם. Help students come to the realization that they now know two final letters.

4. Using the Reading Pages

Notice that there is no ד on the first Reading page (page 45). This is so students don't confuse the ד with the ר.

The second Reading Page (page 46) provides an opportunity to practice reading the ם and the ן, as well as to review the two other new letters. The ד appears in four words on line 2. On line 7, a ד and a ר appear in all the words. Notice that although these words look as if they are from the same root, they are not.

5. Using the Worksheets

Page 47: Students practice writing the new letters and complete the exercise at the bottom of the page. Students have to choose between the מ and the ם. Some of the words will be taught later in this lesson's worksheets.

Page 48: Students will need to know the vocabulary word רַבִּי to complete the exercise at the bottom of the page. As the word is a cognate, all students should learn it. The exercise at the bottom of the page could also be done in a learning center as a card sort. Photocopy the exercise and paste each word on an index card. Have students sort the cards in two piles — words that contain a ר, and words that don't. You can use words from the Reading Pages for this as well. Make the exercise self-checking by marking the cards on the back with two different markings.

Page 49: Students review letter sound correspondences. The noisemaker illustrations reinforce the Key Word.

Page 50: This is an exercise based on cognates, words that are similar in English and Hebrew. Make sure students can identify each picture before completing the page on their own. The Ninja may be unfamiliar to some.

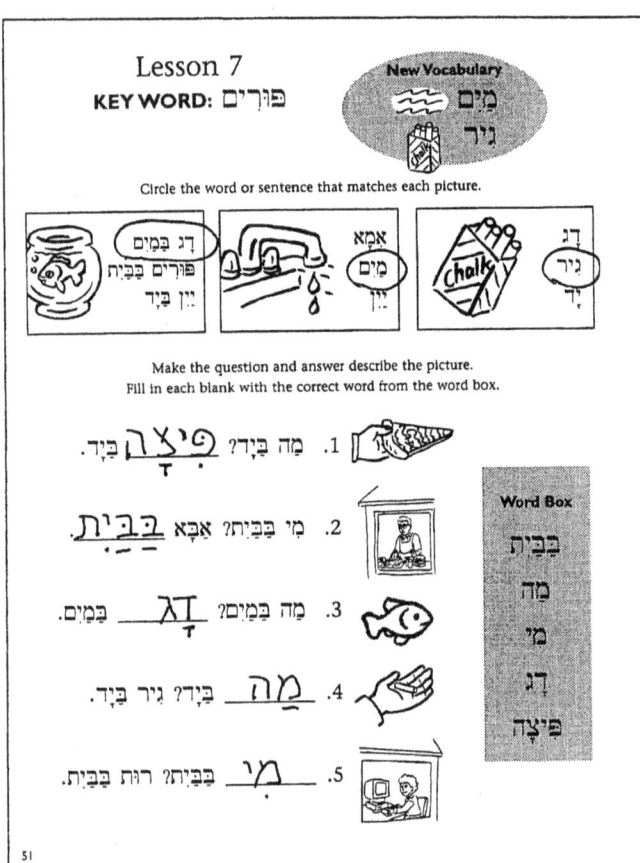

Page 51: This page is for students completing the language component of the program. Show pictures or act out situations similar to those pictured. Ask similar questions, leaving a word out of your answer. Then, leave out the question word, as is done on the page. Make sure students understand that the pictures on the page correspond to the questions and answers, and that they do not need to match the pictures to anything.

Page 52: Students read this conversation as a small play. This is their first meaningful text in Hebrew. All students should complete this page, even if they are not completing the language component of the program, as the vocabulary words used are either Key Words or cognates. Have students read the play in groups of three, encouraging lots of expression. Any group that wishes can then perform for the class.

6. Prepare for Prayer

Page 53: This page offers more practice with words containing the new letters. If your time is limited and/or your students are reading well, you do not need to read this page, as no new material is presented, other than the Cool Hebrew Words section at the bottom of the page. Lines 4 to 7, when read in columns going down, contain words from the same root. The concept of roots will be introduced on the Lesson 9 Prepare for Prayer Page, but you may want to call students' attention to it here. Ask:

"Looking down the column, do you notice anything similar about all the words?"

Students will probably say that the words look alike or sound alike. You don't need to go into a detailed grammar explanation; it is enough to say that all the words in the column have similar meanings.

7. Evaluation and Remediation

Pay attention to confusions between the ד and ר. If students are confusing these two, review each letter separately and then have them read words that contain both letters.

Suggested Additional Activities

1. *Connect-4* (see page 142 in this Teacher Guide).

2. *Computer Index Cards* (see page 148 in this Teacher Guide). Write a Hebrew vocabulary word and give three English translations. Use this in a learning center with individual students working independently.

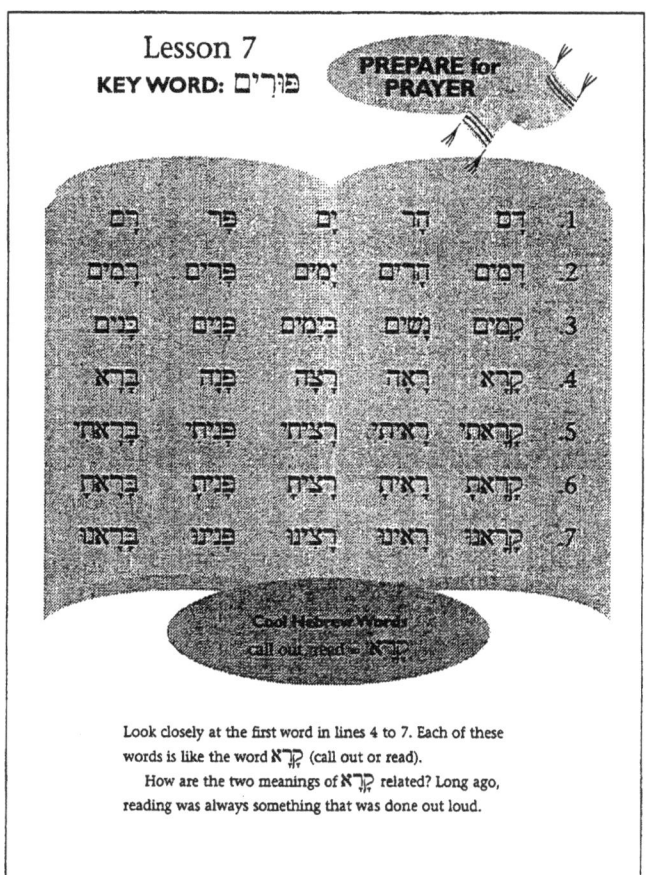

LESSON 8

Key Word: (challah) חַלָה
New Letters: ת ל ח
New Vocabulary: (cat) חָתוּל   (under) תַחַת   (you, masc. sing.) אַתָה
Special Points: ח ≠ ק   ה ≠ ח

Oral Language Lesson (optional)

Before introducing the word אַתָה, review the word אֲנִי. Go around the room and have each student say אֲנִי and his or her name. Then point to several boys and say to each, "אַתָה" plus his name. Get the class to respond as a group. Point to a boy and the whole class as a chorus says:
"אַתָה _____"
   (name)

See if students will notice that no girls have been called up.

The students will probably not know the second vocabulary word, תַחַת. Give each student pictures of objects students can name in Hebrew (e.g., בַּיִת, דָג, חַלָה, מַצָה, etc.). Then recite short sentences using the word תַחַת. As you speak, demonstrate your sentences by placing the picture of one object under that of another. Have students follow your example. Sample sentences:

"מַצָה תַחַת הַגְדָד."
"בַּיִת תַחַת יָד."

After the students start to understand the concept, give instructions without your demonstration. Break the class into smaller groups, giving each group a different instruction. Teach the new vocabulary word חָתוּל with this technique, using either a picture or a stuffed cat. Review the use of בְּ__, using phrases such as "חַלָה בְּיָד." (See page 148 in this Teacher Guide for a more complete description of the Listen and Do! technique.)

The Seven Lesson Steps:

1. Review
   Review the similar looking letters ד and ר. Review the Key Words related to Shabbat.

2. Evoking the Key Word
   Tell students that the Key Word for this lesson is also related to Shabbat. As a hint, tell them it's something we eat, particularly on Shabbat. Bring in a challah and share with the class. Open the Workbook to page 54 and look at the picture of challah.

3. Introducing the New Letters
   The first sound in חַלָה is often difficult for an English speaking child to pronounce. Practice pronouncing this word correctly, as well as other words that start with this sound (e.g., חַי, חֲנֻכָּה).

   The second letter (ל) is not difficult to pronounce. Ask students if there is something unique about the size/shape of this letter. See if they notice that it is the only letter learned so far that extends above the line, as opposed to the ן and ק, that extend below the line. The ל also looks quite different in various styles of type. Compare, for example, the felt letter ל with the ל as it appears in the Workbook on page 54.

   Before you continue to the Reading Page, you must teach the תּ (with the Dagesh). In this program, both the ת and the תּ make the same sound: t. This symbol was not introduced in Lesson 1 simultaneously with the ת, because of the potential for confusion with the ב. It is being introduced in this lesson because this is the first time where students will be shown either a Key Word or vocabulary word that is spelled with a תּ, in this case both תַּחַת and אַתָּה. There are other Hebrew letters that are written with a *Dagesh* that doesn't change the sound of the letter. These symbols are used for grammatical reasons. *Dageshim* that do not change the pronunciation of the letter are not taught in this Workbook (but will be introduced in the זְמָן לִתְפִילָה program). The ת is taught because in some communities it does make a different sound. In addition, the parents or grandparents of many students in your class may have learned Hebrew with an Ashkenazic pronunciation. By identifying both ת and תּ as **t** in the Workbook, the current use of Sephardic pronunciation is made explicit. The approach here is perhaps inconsistent, but was chosen for pedagogic reasons. The goal is to give students the maximum amount of information with the minimum of confusion.

You can tell students that the תּ is generally used at the beginning of the word, and other times as well. This reading program, and most Jewish communities today, pronounce the ת and תּ the way it is said in the State of Israel, where the ת is pronounced exactly like the תּ. In the Ashkenazic (Eastern European) prounounciation, the ת is said as **s**, and the תּ as **t**. This is why people may pronounce words like שַׁבָּת as "*Shabbos*" or בְּרִית as "*Bris.*"

As you read the Key Word story on page 54 with students, you may find some objection to the idea that the חַלָּה could have its "feelings" hurt. Make sure that students understand that the point of the story is that we must be very careful of each other's feelings, not that we really believe that the bread is going to be insulted!

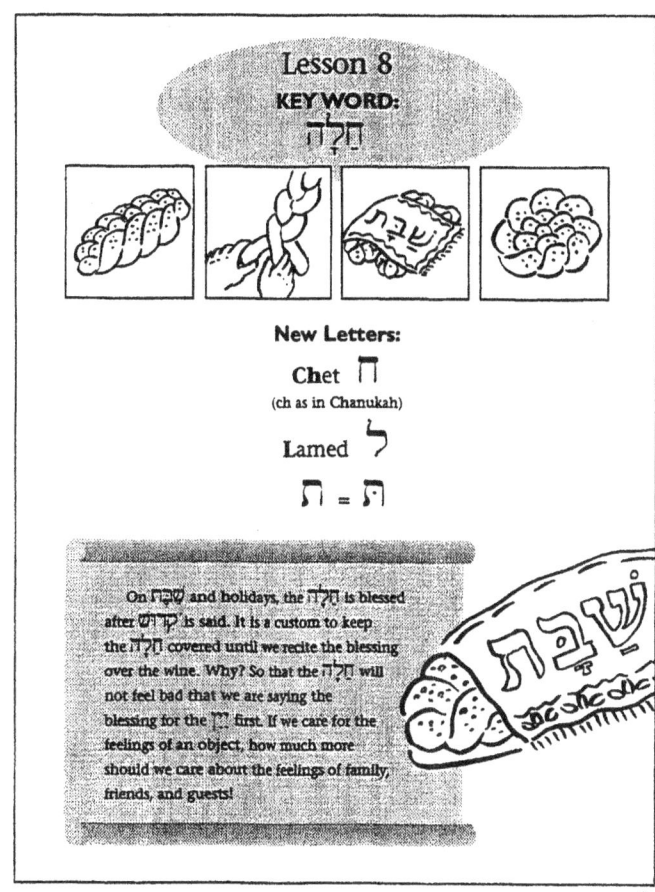

4. Using the Reading Page

The Reading Page (page 55) provides for practice in reading the ח when it appears in different places in words. In line 6 all the words have a ֲ (Chataph-Patach). Ask students if they notice something special about line 6. Tell them that the ח, like the א, will sometimes take this vowel.

The word חוּפָה appears at the bottom of this page and on page 60, "A Wedding," that depicts the wedding of two cats. Although the preferred spelling for this word is חֻפָּה, students have not yet learned the ֻ, and the spelling used here is acceptable.

5. Using the Worksheets

Page 56: Students practice writing the letters *Chet* and *Lamed*, and then complete the exercise on the bottom of the page.

Page 57: Students decide which items relate to each of three Jewish holidays. Make sure that everyone is familiar with the items.

Pages 58-59: These pages are for students who are doing the language component of the program. They should be done only after an oral introduction of the words. Page 58 reviews and practices אַתָּה. Page 59 reviews and practices תַּחַת.

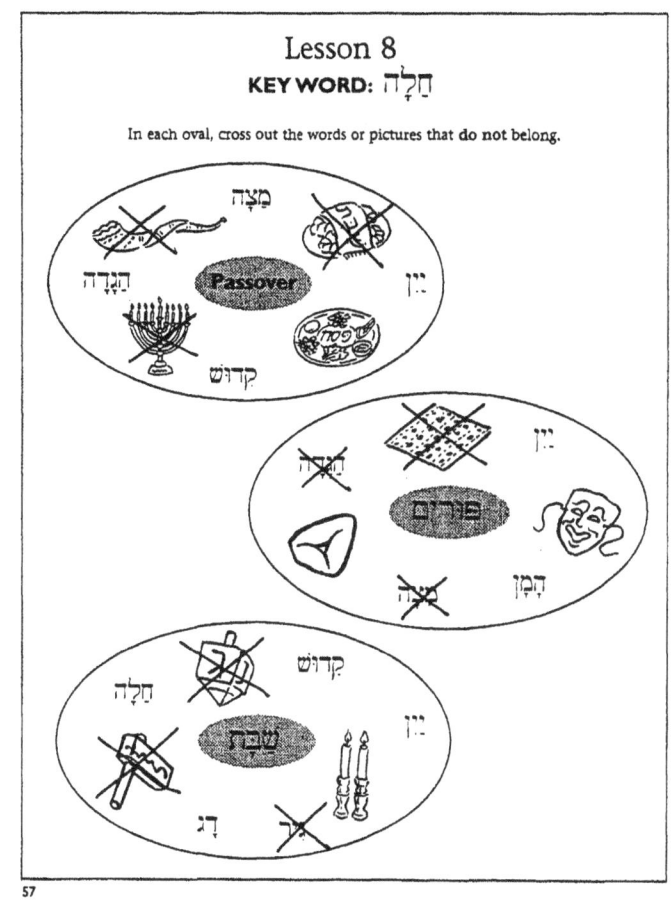

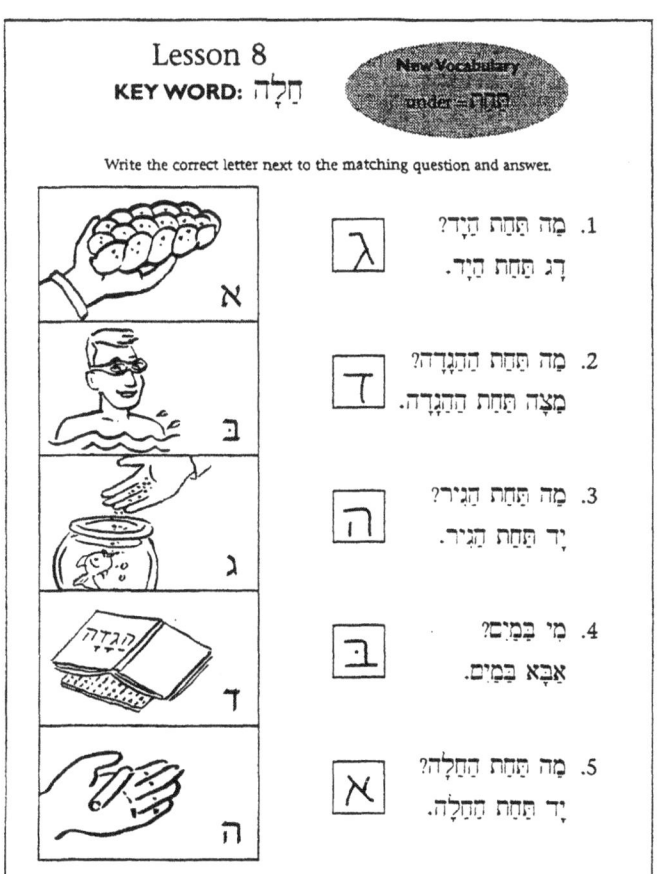

Page 60: This page is purposely humorous, with little text. Note that the new vocabulary here is not reinforced later, except for the word חָתוּל. Therefore, use the page for additional decoding practice. Students doing the language component of the program will need to learn the vocabulary. As an extra activity, students might do their own illustrations of this story (see *Little Books* on page 150 in this Teacher Guide).

6. Prepare for Prayer

Page 61: This page offers highly structured reading practice with the types of words that appear in the *Siddur*. Classes that are limited in time and reading well may skip the page, as no new concepts are introduced.

As adults, we may have difficulty with the idea presented that God "always gives you a second chance." We think of Nazis or terrorists, and hope that God punishes them. If a child brings up this idea, you may want to say that God gives *you* (the child) a second chance, not necessarily really evil people. This concept of a forgiving God is an important one for children to internalize; children should not worry that an all-powerful entity is judging them and potentially punishing them.

7. Evaluation and Remediation

Students who have trouble *pronouncing* the ח may still go on to Lesson 9, provided that they have no difficulty in recognizing that letter.

Suggested Additional Activities

1. *Floor Board Game* (see page 146 in this Teacher Guide). Students must correctly read Hebrew words to advance their team. Write words from the first Reading Page on large cards so that all the students can see them.

2. *Bingo* (see page 144 in this Teacher Guide). Illustrate the vocabulary and Key Word from Lessons 1-8.

LESSON 9

Key Words: (mitzvah) מִצְוָה (Havdalah) הַבְדָּלָה
New Letters: ב ו
New Vowels: silent ְ
New Vocabulary: (family) מִשְׁפָּחָה (you, fem. sing.) אַתְּ
(Bat-Mitzvah) בַּת-מִצְוָה (Bar-Mitzvah) בַּר-מִצְוָה
Special Points: ו ≠ ן   ו ≠ ר   ב ≠ בּ   בּ = ו

Lesson 9 is a critical lesson. It presents one of the more troublesome areas for the novice reader, the medial or silent *Shva*, as well as two symbols for the V sound. Make sure to allot enough time to teach the lesson thoroughly, probably two class sessions.

Oral Language Lesson (optional)

Review the pronouns אֲנִי and אַתָּה. Teach אַתְּ in the same way that you taught אַתָּה, but with girls called up, of course (see page 70 in this Teacher Guide). Have students understand that both of these Hebrew words mean "you."

Teach מִשְׁפָּחָה by showing a picture of a family in a house. Say as you point to each person in the picture:

"אַבָּא בַּבַּיִת."

"אִמָּא בַּבַּיִת."

"דָּוִד בַּבַּיִת."

"מִרְיָם בַּבַּיִת."

Then point to all the people in the picture and say:

"מִשְׁפָּחָה בַּבַּיִת."

Ask students what they think מִשְׁפָּחָה means. Display several pictures showing a variety of situations that can be described in Hebrew. Include pictures of the new word in this selection. Say a sentence and ask students which picture matches the sentence you have said. This is a good preparation for the worksheet on מִשְׁפָּחָה on page 70.

The Seven Lesson Steps:

1. Review

2. Evoking the Key Words

Explain that a commandment in Hebrew is called a מִצְוָה, and that a Bar or Bat Mitzvah is one who keeps the commandments. Ask students for suggestions of what they think a מִצְוָה is. (See *Teaching Mitzvot: Concepts, Values, and Activities* by Barbara Binder Kadden and Bruce Kadden and *Mitzvot Copy Pak*™ by Zena Sulkes and Al Sulkes, both published by A.R.E. Publishing, Inc.) The meaning of the pictures on page 62 will not be immediately apparent to students. The first is a puzzle map of the world. This signifies the mystical concept of our world being "broken," and our task to "fix" or "complete" the world by the performance of מִצְוֹת. On a child's level, this means we all need to work together to make the world a better place. Rituals, social action, and treating each other kindly and fairly are all מִצְוֹת. The second picture shows a Torah with the number 613 written across it, representing the traditional number of מִצְוֹת in the Torah. Children may be surprised to learn that there are more than ten commandments, but on reflection will be able to list many commandments that are not part of the ten. Ritual examples would be: anything having to do with celebrating the biblical holidays, observing the laws of *kashrut*, and affixing a *mezuzah*. Additional ethical commandments include: giving צְדָקָה, visiting the sick, not speaking badly of others, and protecting the environment.

The first הַבְדָלָה picture depicts a night with three stars out. This is the time that הַבְדָלָה is said on Saturday night by traditional Jews. The last picture is of a הַבְדָלָה set. Briefly describe the ceremony; the story at the bottom of the page will reinforce the information you provide.

3. Introducing New Letters and Vowels

This lesson can be divided into two parts. First, teach the new vowel, then the new consonant sound.

From this lesson on, you do not need to ask students to break the Key Word(s) into all of their component sounds. Instead, have them identify the new sounds. In this lesson you ask students to isolate the sound of v (represented by both ב and ו), which they have not yet learned.

First, teach the new vowel. Before introducing the silent *Shva* (◼), have students read two syllable words that normally should have a *Shva*, but put a space between the syllables, and omit the *Shva*, as is done on Reading Page 63, lines 1 to 6, the first column. Then, put the two syllables together. Students will most probably read these words correctly. Then, go back and add the vowel *Shva*. Emphasize that the pronunciation doesn't change. Can students guess the sound of ◼? The concept of the silent *Shva* should be easy to understand if it is introduced this way. For reading purposes, treat any single *Shva* in the middle of the word as a silent *Shva*. While there are exceptions to this rule, they have been avoided in this Workbook, other than קָדְשָׁנוּ in Lesson 18. DO NOT mention at this time the voiced *Shva* or practice any letter/vowel combinations in which the *Shva* is voiced (i.e., when a *Shva* occurs at the beginning of a word or when two occur in a row). After you introduce the *Shva*, have students read page 63, the first Reading Page. They will not be able to complete any of the worksheets, as each contains the new letters as well.

Introduce the two new letters at the same time, so that students will associate the two very different shapes with the same sound. Ask students to try to spell the Key Word מִצְוָה. What sound are they missing? Introduce the ו. DO NOT show words with the vowel וֹ at this point. Next, show the students how to spell הַבְדָלָה. Explain that we use another letter that makes the v sound. Introduce the ב. Ask students if this letter looks familiar. They will say that it looks like the בּ without the dot. However, DO NOT reintroduce the בּ at this point. Practice words with the ב. Once this is solidly learned, bring back the בּ. Students may ask why there needs to be two symbols for the same sound; make the comparison to English where there are two symbols for the k sound (c and k) and the s sound (s and c).

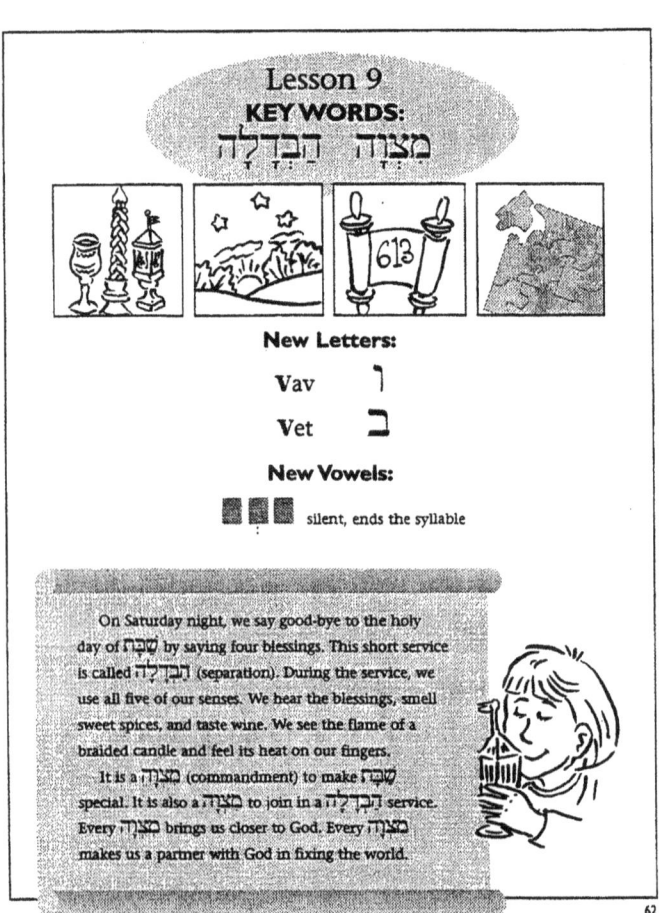

4. Using the Reading Pages

The first Reading Page (page 63) is very carefully constructed to provide direct practice in words that contain the *Shva*. In lines 1 to 6, the same word is written three different ways. Lines 7 to 9 each have four verbs from the same root. Some recommendations for using the Reading Page follow:

a. Starting with the first line, teacher reads the first part of each word, class responds with the second part. For example: teacher reads יְל (first part), class responds דָה (second part). Continue in like manner with all the words in lines 1 to 6, then reverse roles and have students read the first part.

b. After you have read lines 1 to 6 in this fashion, read the first syllable and have the students read the second syllable. Then read the two syllables together.

c. Divide the class in half. One group reads the first part of the words, the second group the second part.

d. One student volunteers to read the first part, and the class responds with the second part.

e. Divide the class into two groups. One group reads the first part, the other group reads the second part.

f. Go around the room in order asking each student in turn to read the second part after you read the first part. Then, at random, call on individuals who are having difficulty to read the second part.

g. When you have completed these steps with lines 1 to 6, have students read lines 7 to 9.

Notice how this exercise was structured. You began with the easiest form of responding (a group response to the teacher's invitation to participate), then you moved to a group inviting and another group responding. You then went on to smaller groups, and then to teacher calling on individuals, first in order and finally at random. In addition, you began by breaking the word into syllables, and ended with reading the entire word. By the end of this exercise, all students should be able to read two and three syllable words that contain a silent *Shva*.

77

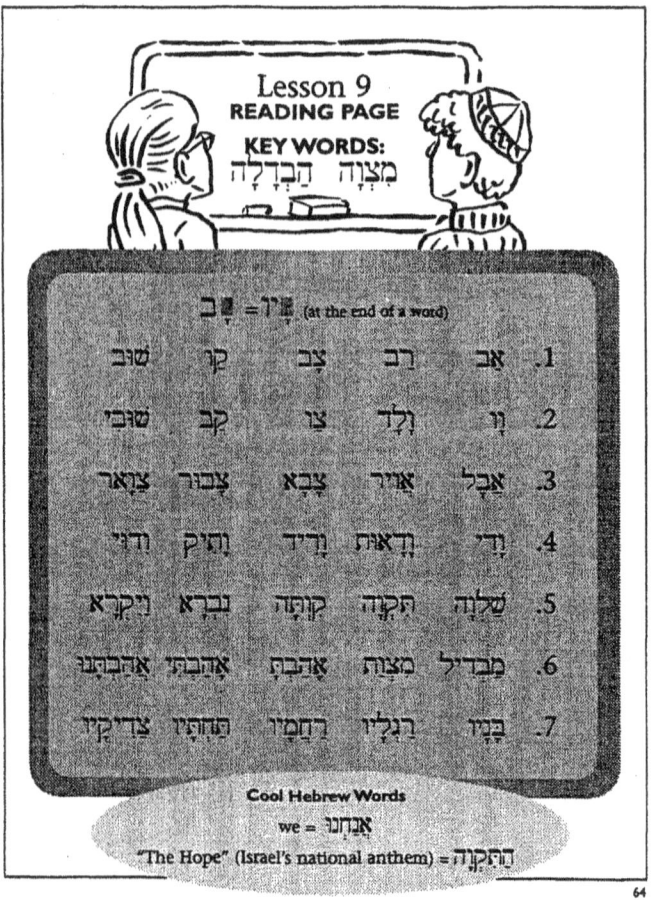

On the second Reading Page (page 64), the words are more difficult. ב and ו are drilled on this page, and the *Shva* reviewed. The vowel combination וְי is presented here. Since the י does not change the pronunciation, students can be told to ignore it and read the combination the same as וְ.

5. Using the Worksheets

Page 65: Students practice writing the two new letters together to reinforce the concept that they make the same sound.

Page 66: This activity provides practice in writing the Key Words and in identifying their meaning.

Page 67: This is an enjoyable activity that is geared toward teaching discrimination of letters that look alike — the ן, ב, ו, ר, and י. Tell students to read each word to themselves before they color it, and have them color in lightly so that they can read the words back to you when you go over the page. They will need to use colored pencils or crayons rather than markers so that you will be able to read the words.

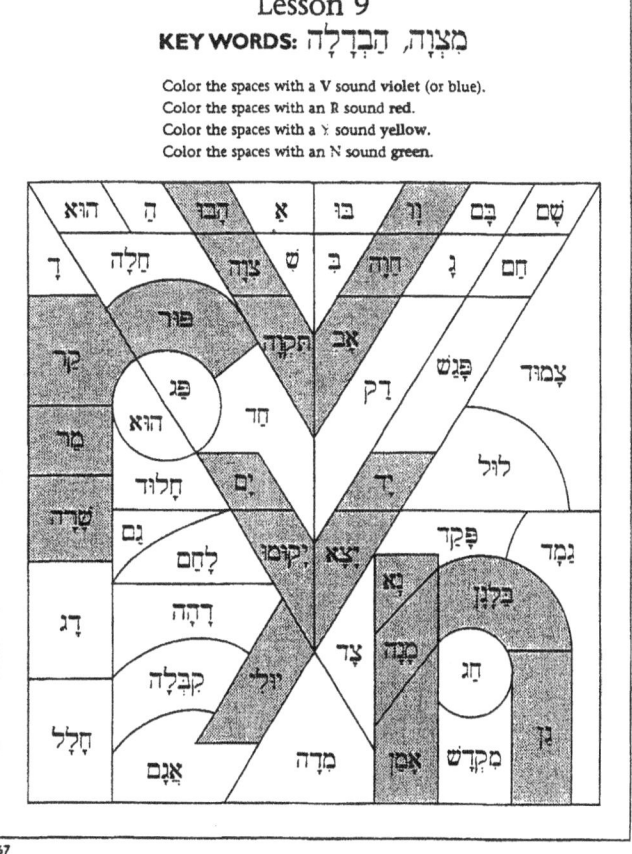

Page 68: The words used in the exercise on this page are cognates or words that the students should know in Hebrew. They may not recognize the names אַבְרָהָם and יִצְחָק, or the clue for יִצְחָק. They should be able to figure it out by process of elimination, but be sure to explain the clue to them (Sarah laughed when the angel told her she was going to have a baby. The name יִצְחָק comes from the root of the Hebrew word for laugh, צ.ח.ק).

Page 69: This page is for students who are doing the language component of the program. Students fill in the blanks with the correct pronoun or name.

Page 70: This page is for students who are doing the language component of the program. Have students describe the pictures orally to you before completing the page independently. Or, describe a picture and have them tell you which letter it is. Remind them that not every numbered sentence will be matched to a picture. When you go over the page, you can have volunteers illustrate the three leftover sentences.

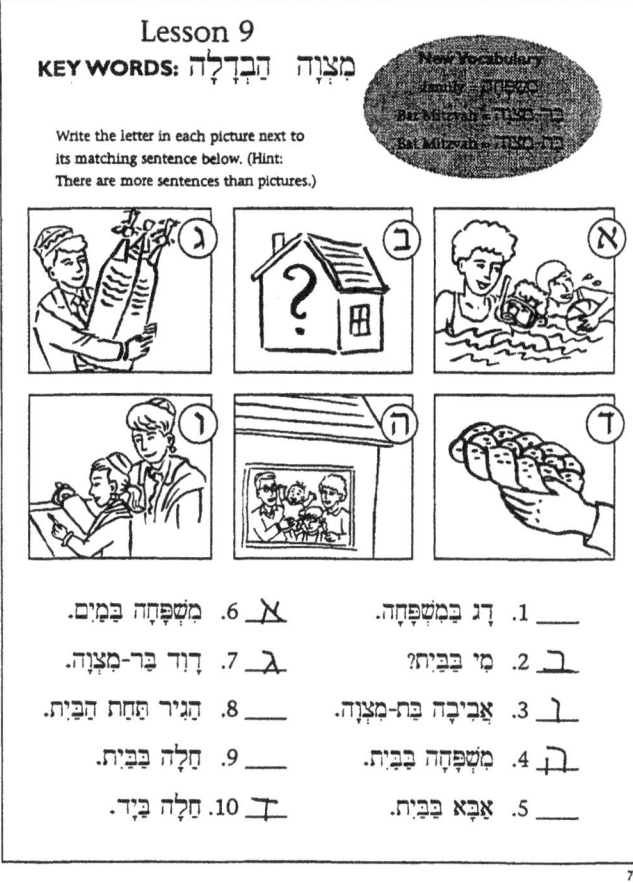

6. Prepare for Prayer

Page 71: This page must be done by all students. The concept of Hebrew roots is formally presented here for the first time. Note that actually translating each member of the word family is neither required nor suggested, as some of the word forms are obscure. The words were chosen because they contain the two new letters, בּ and ו, and because all three root letters show up in them. Thus, the obscure words הִקְוָה and מִקְוָה are used rather than the more common קָוִיתִי, which contains only two of the three root letters.

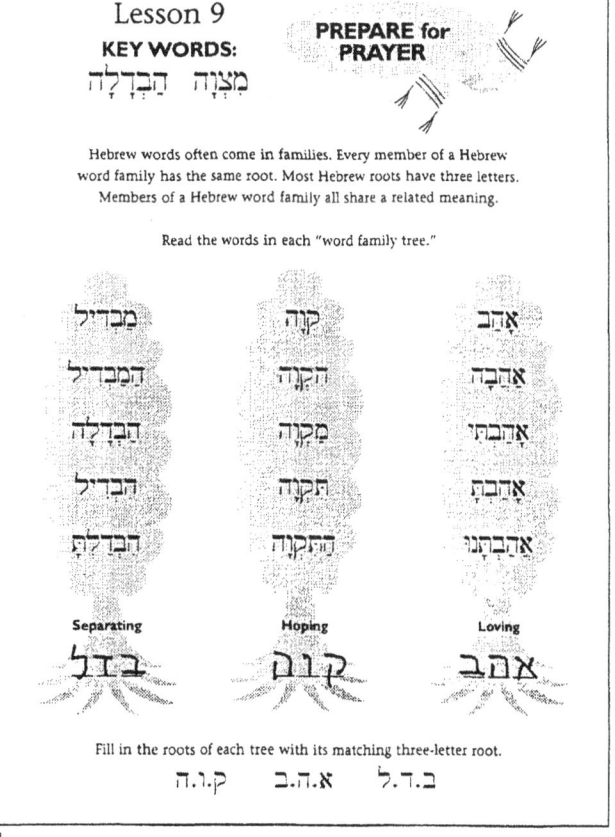

7. **Evaluate and Remediate**

Evaluate each student individually. This is a lesson in which students commonly make errors. See the sample evaluation in the right-hand column of this page. Remember, reading the silent *Shva* as ◌ is a mistake.

Problem Identification

Jonathan is having a problem with blending, as might be expected. He was definitely not ready for the evaluation. His teacher should have realized that he did not understand the concept of the *Shva*. He also read ו as נ. Since he did this only once, it is probably not a major problem.

Suggestions for Remediation

Highlight with a special pen (preferably yellow) the first syllable of words in lines 1 to 6 and the second syllable of words in lines 7 to 9. Following a procedure similar to the one outlined in the "Using the Reading Pages" section on page 77 above, read the first syllable and have Jonathan read the second syllable. Then have him read the entire word. Alternately, he reads first and you finish. Once he has mastered this stage, use the actual Reading Page. If Jonathan has difficulty with this, form words with foam or felt letters.

Note that Jonathan's score of 4/10 is meaningless. He knows much more than 40%, but he missed the basic concept of this particular lesson and should not progress to Lesson 10 before the problem is remediated. Did you notice that he got 4 plus? That is because some of his pronunciations were unclear.

(Note: Jonathan's evaluation should have been stopped when he made the *Shva* error for the third time.)

Suggested Additional Activities

1. *Shva Cubes* (see page 143 in this Teacher Guide).

2. *Chalkboard Races* (see page 145 in this Teacher Guide). Say a vocabulary word in Hebrew and have the two students race to write or illustrate the translation on the board.

3. *File Folder Puzzle* (see page 147 in this Teacher Guide). Use the two syllable words and their English translations from the exercise on the top of page 66. Since you are matching puzzle pieces, the two matching syllables must be opposite each other, not in a mixed up order as on page 68. Thus, you will need to copy the words over. Example:

an "ice" house	לוּ	אַג
lunch outdoors	נִיק	פִּק
a spring month	רִיל	אַפ

LESSON 10

Key Word: (Hebrew) עִבְרִית (class, classroom) כִּתָּה
New Letters: ע כ
New Vocabulary: (next to) עַל־יַד (on) עַל (in the classroom) בַּכִּתָּה
Special Points: ע ≠ צ כ ≠ ב ע = א כ = ק

Oral Language Lesson (optional)

Teach the new word בַּכִּתָּה. To reinforce, fill a grab bag with common objects found in the home or in the classroom (a toothbrush, a chalkboard eraser, a washcloth, an alarm clock, a textbook, etc.). Divide the class into teams. A volunteer from one team reaches into the bag and feels for an object. Without looking, he must say בַּכִּתָּה or בַּבַּיִת. The object is then pulled out, and if the student is correct, his or her team scores five points. The students do not need to know the Hebrew names of the objects used, as they will not be saying those words.

Review the two position words בַּ___ and תַּחַת. Teach עַל and עַל־יַד in the same way תַּחַת was taught in Lesson 8 (see page 70 in this Teacher Guide). Then, call two student volunteers to the front of the room. Give them both the same instruction to carry out. The winner is the one who correctly completes the task the quickest. After they have practiced, have students give instructions to each other.

The Seven Lesson Steps:

1. **Review**
   Review the א and ק, as their sound-alikes will be taught in this lesson.

2. **Evoke the New Key Word(s)**
   To evoke the first Key Word ask:
   "What language are you studying?" (עִבְרִית)
   To introduce the word כִּתָּה, ask:
   "Where are you studying it?" (בַּכִּתָּה)
   If students do not know these words, have them look at the pictures on page 72, the Introduction Page. Tell students that the Hebrew script on the left is a sample of Torah script. Can they recognize any of the letters? What's missing? Tell them that the Torah is written without vowels. כִּתָּה is used in Hebrew to refer both to a physical classroom and to a class or grade of students, just like the English word "class."

3. **Introduce New Letters and Vowels**
   Introduce the ע. Practice forming words with it, making sure not to use the צ at this time. After they have learned the ע, have a student spell the Key Word using the new letter (עִבְרִית).

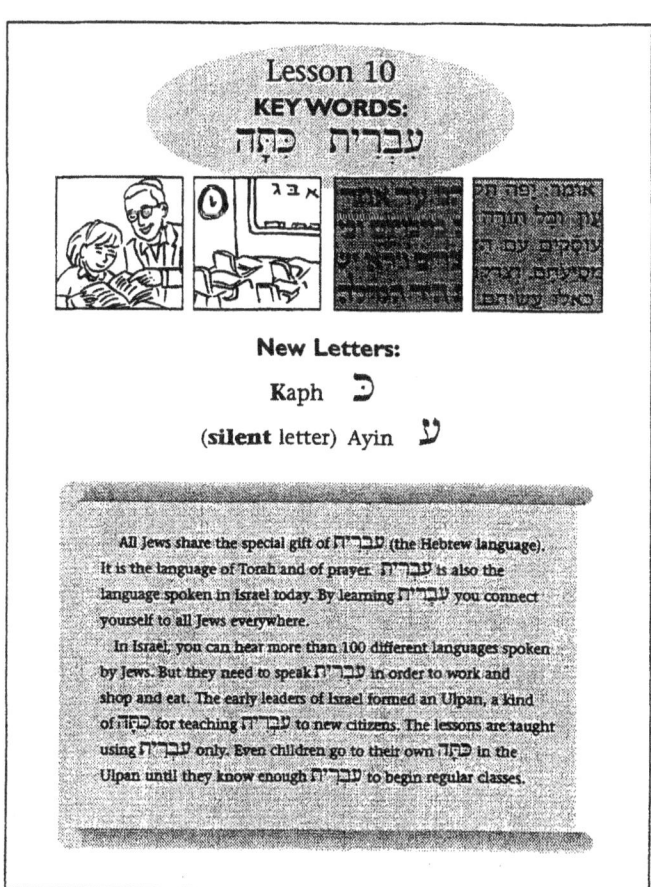

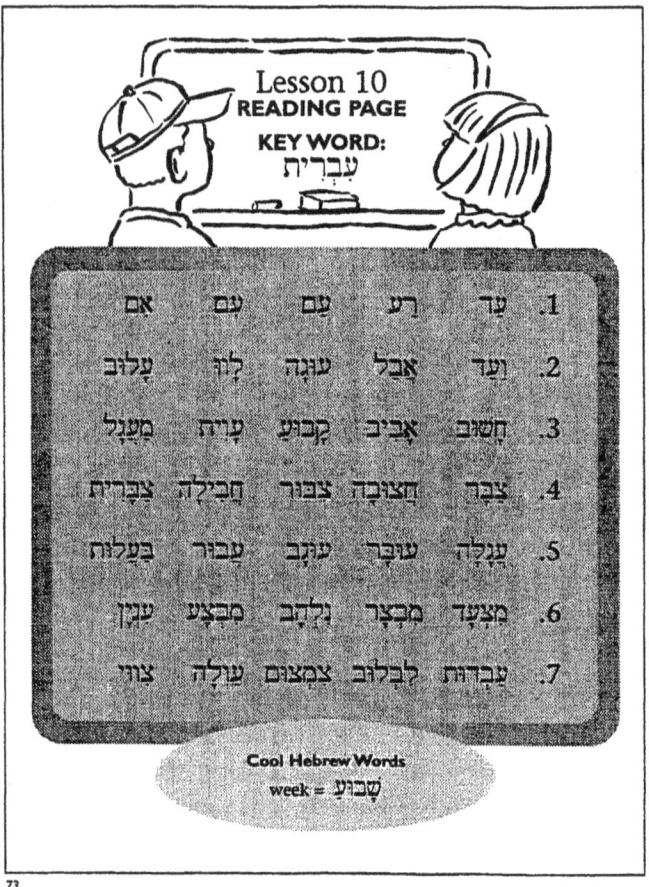

The emphasis in this lesson is on the alternative letters for the sounds: ע = א and כ = ק.

Open the Workbooks to page 72, the Introduction Page. Read the Key Words and new letters. Make sure students understand that the ע is a silent letter, not a vowel that makes the ay sound. Read the story on the Introduction Page with the students. Now may be an appropriate time to discuss how the students feel about learning Hebrew, as they near completion of Volume One. Emphasize the kinds of positive ideas presented in the story, while praising them on how far they have come.

4. Using the Reading Pages

The first Reading Page (page 73) drills the new letter ע. The second Reading Page (page 74) provides practice in reading the new letters ע and כ, and their sound-alikes, א and ק. On line 3 there are several words with a ◌ֲ under the ע. Line 6 words are all past tense verbs, first person singular. Line 7 contains nouns that follow a similar pattern.

5. Using the Worksheets

Page 75: Students practice writing the new letters and the two letters that have the same sounds. Since the "sound alike" pairs of ק = כּ and א = ע were not taught at the same time, students need now to make the association that both members of the pair sound alike. This is very important if the students are going to remember both members of a pair, and not just the first one they were taught.

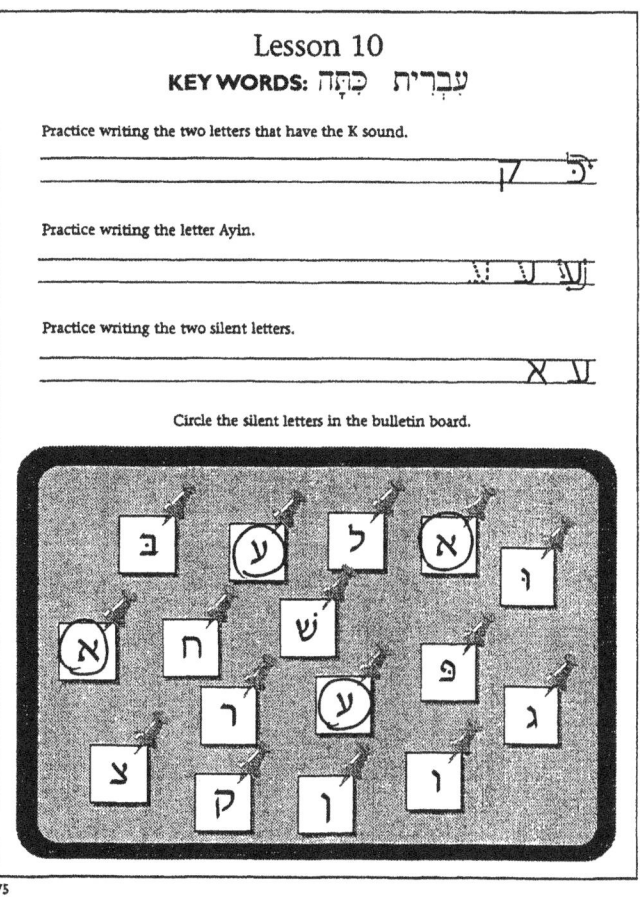

Page 76: This worksheet utilizes all the sound-alikes that have been taught so far. The words in this activity are homophones whose sounds match. Every word used is a real Hebrew word, though some are very obscure. Since students are not reading for meaning here, it is unimportant what the words mean. However, they should not be exposed to combinations that cannot or do not occur in Hebrew.

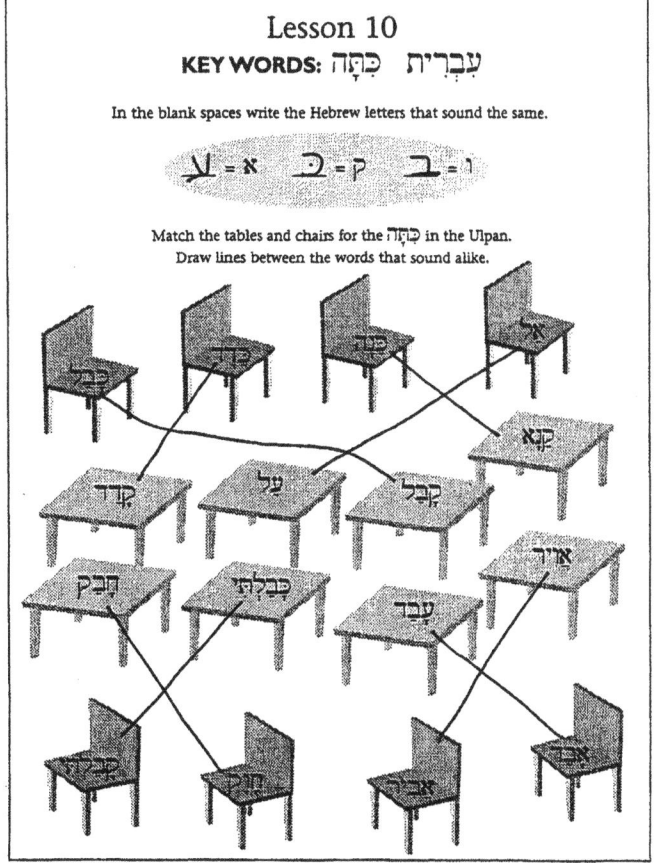

Page 77: This page is for students who are doing the language component of the program. The vocabulary should be taught orally before students are asked to do these pages. For the top activity, act out similar situations using a stuffed animal. For the bottom exercise, show a variety of pictures and have students chorally respond either "בַּבַּיִת" or "בַּכִּתָּה."

Pages 78 and 79: These pages are for students who are doing the language component of the program. The answers to the questions on page 78 are on the bottom of the page. The pictures on page 79 illustrate the answers for page 78.

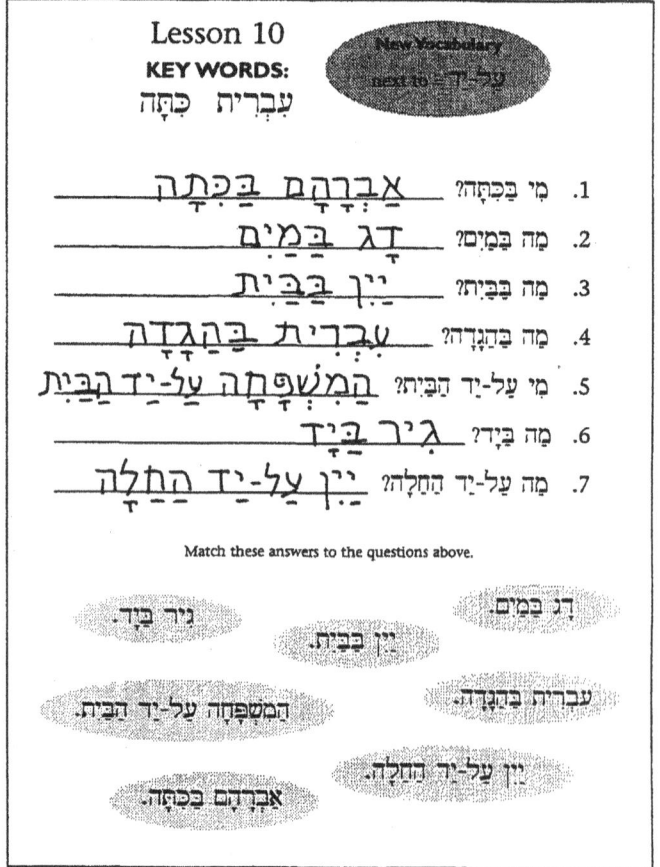

6. Prepare for Prayer

Page 80: This page should be completed by all students, as the concept of roots is reviewed. Refer students back to Lesson 9, page 71, and remind them that Hebrew words come in word families that share similar meanings and three-letter roots.

7. Evaluate and Remediate

If students are not ready to begin Lesson 11 (Volume Two), do a general review of the Reading Pages, using any of the reading games suggested in the "Games and Other Activities" section, beginning on page 141 of this Teacher Guide.

Language Review

Page 81: This page is for students who are doing the language component of the program. It contains a review of most of the vocabulary taught so far. If desired, use this page as a vocabulary quiz. The only words missing from it are בַּת-מִצְוָה, בַּר-מִצְוָה, and עַל-יָד. Some students don't enjoy word searches; it is fine for them just to translate the words.

Suggested Additional Activities

1. *Jeopardy* (see page 145 in this Teacher Guide). This is a nice activity for a *Siyum* (finishing the Workbook) party. This game provides for a thorough and enjoyable review. Possible categories: בַּבַּיִת, בַּכִּתָּה, *Shva* words, silent symbols, and sound-alikes.

2. *Go Fish* (see page 144 in this Teacher Guide). This is a good choice for students who are advanced, especially if you want the whole class to begin using Volume Two at the same time.

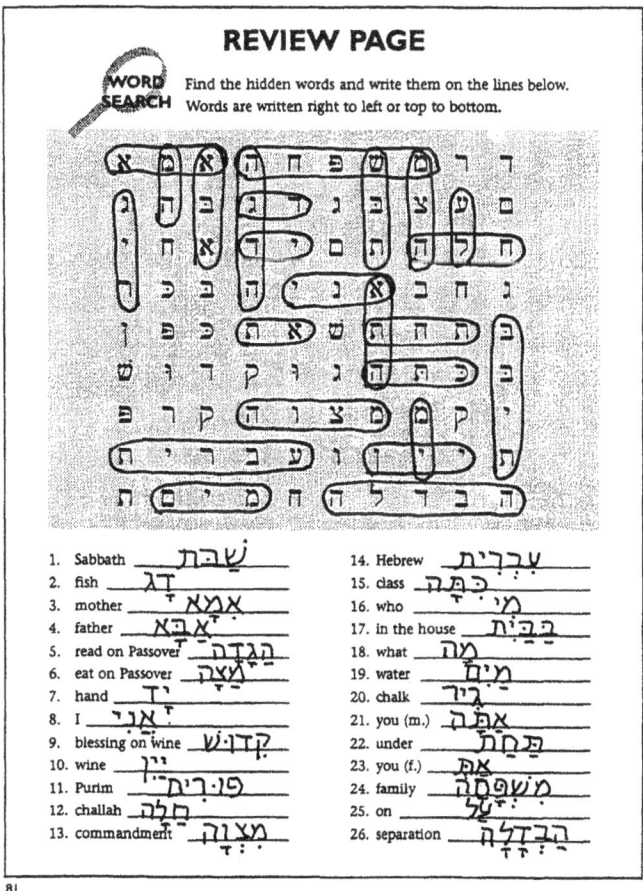

LESSON 11

Key Words: (Israel) יִשְׂרָאֵל   (Passover) פֶּסַח
New Letters: ס שׂ
New Vowels: ▨ ▨ ▨
New Vocabulary: (boy) יֶלֶד   (girl) יַלְדָּה   (flag) דֶּגֶל
(notebook) מַחְבֶּרֶת   (Magen David, shield of David) מָגֵן דָּוִד
Special Points: ס = שׂ   שׂ ≠ שׁ   ס ≠ ם

With this lesson, we begin Volume Two of זְמַן לִקְרֹא. First, read together the letter to the students; later, allow students to complete the exercise. If your school starts Volume Two after summer vacation, you will need to do an extensive review before proceeding with Lesson 11. You can use the first half of זְמַן לִתְפִלָּה Book 1 for your review.

Oral Language Lesson (optional)

The new vocabulary in this lesson continues to focus on classroom objects. Additional vocabulary that relates to the classroom can be found in Lessons 12 through 16. Teach these words using the classroom as a context and using the actual objects. Since students already know the words בַּ___, עַל, עַל-יַד, and תַּחַת, you can play a variety of games in which students first merely respond to oral commands (e.g., יָד עַל מַחְבֶּרֶת) and then say what was done. (See *Listen and Do!* on page 148 in this Teacher Guide.)

As mentioned in the Introduction, it is best to introduce vocabulary orally before it is introduced in the Workbook. Therefore, some combinations are listed here that include the vocabulary in later lessons:

גִּיר עַל סֵפֶר   עִפָּרוֹן עַל מוֹרָה
דֶּגֶל עַל-יַד כִּסֵּא   עִפָּרוֹן בַּמַחְבֶּרֶת
מַחְבֶּרֶת תַּחַת לוּחַ   יַלְדָּה עַל-יַד חַלָּה

Although students might not know how to read these words, they can still learn their meanings. Try some humorous and unexpected combinations. For additional games, see *What's Missing?* and *What's in That Bag?* on page 149 of this Teacher Guide.

The Seven Lesson Steps:

This lesson teaches two symbols for the s sound, each of which can be confused with a different symbol, and three vowel symbols that make either one or two sounds, depending on your congregation. Count on spending an extra class session on this lesson.

1. **Review**
Review the new letters learned in Lesson 9 and 10. Avoid the שׂ. Review classroom related Key Words learned in Lesson 10 in preparation for the new Key Word יִשְׂרָאֵל.

2. **Evoke the New Key Word(s)**
This lesson has two Key Words, יִשְׂרָאֵל and פֶּסַח. The Key Word יִשְׂרָאֵל is likely to be in the students' vocabulary. Ask:

"What is the name of the Jewish State?" The pictures on page 2, the Introduction Page, show the symbol of the State of Israel and an Israeli postage stamp.

Everyone will know the holiday of Passover, but they may not know its Hebrew name. Show the pictures on page 2, the Introduction Page. Tell students that the holiday pictured is called פֶּסַח in Hebrew, and have them tell you what the holiday is in English by looking at the pictures. Remind them of the two other Key Words they have learned that relate to the holiday, הַגָּדָה and מַצָּה.

3. **Introduce New Letters and Vowels**

In this lesson you will introduce *Tserey* (◌ֵ), *Segol* (◌ֶ), and *Chataph-Segol* (◌ֱ). In Israel and in spoken Hebrew, they are pronounced identically, as a short **eh** (as in bed). In American worship, the ◌ֵ is usually pronounced as a long **ay** (as in day). This pronunciation is a vestige of one of the classical Hebrew pronunciations. (See the section "A Note about Pronunciation and Spelling" on page 10 of this Teacher Guide.) When Hebrew was primarily a written language, through almost 2,000 years of the Diaspora, changes in pronunciation were much more infrequent than is currently the case. As a living, spoken language in Israel, Hebrew is constantly evolving. Currently in Israel, the Ministry of Education has instructed language teachers to teach that any variation of ◌ֵ, ◌ֶ, or ◌ֱ makes an **eh** sound, even when followed by a י, ה, or א. The teachers report, however, that students are still "mispronouncing" words, in other words, using one of the older pronunciations. As a teacher of this reading program to children who live outside of Israel, it is crucial for you to realize there is no "right" or "wrong" way to pronounce the ◌ֵ — there is only what we refer to as "Bimah Standard," the way your congregation pronounces the vowel. Your Rabbi, Cantor, and Director of Education should all be in agreement, so that your students learn the pronunciation they will use when worshiping with your congregation. The ◌ֵ followed by a י as in בֵּין is always pronounced as a long **ay** (unless you are a language teacher in Israel!) and is taught in Lesson 15. The sound of ◌ֵ followed by א, ה, ◌ֶה, or ◌ֲע is also open to discussion, and is presented in Lesson 15.

If the new vowels make the same sound for your congregation, teach them at the same time, even though they don't appear in the same Key Word. Teach the new vowels before you teach the new letter. To avoid teaching four concepts at a time (◌ֵ, ◌ֶ, ס, and שׂ), use other words to teach the ◌ֵ and ◌ֶ initially, for example כֵּן (yes) and יֶלֶד (boy).

Now, introduce both letters that make the **s** sound. You want to introduce the שׂ and ס together so that students associate the two symbols that make the same sound. When introducing the שׂ you are teaching the second of a pair of look-alike consonants. As with all confusing pairs, introduce the שׁ first and make sure it is well learned before reintroducing the שׂ. When teaching the ס, make sure that at first you avoid the ם. Alert students to the fact that although the letter ס may look like a ם, certainly if it appears at the beginning or in the middle of the word, it cannot be a ם.

If your congregation pronounces the ◌ֵ and ◌ֶ differently, you will want to introduce them separately. In this case, first introduce the ◌ֶ and the ◌ֱ, both of which make the "eh" sound. Then, introduce both letters that make the **s** sound. You can use the Key Word פֶּסַח to introduce the ס, but you will need to wait until you have taught the ◌ֵ in order to teach the Key Word יִשְׂרָאֵל. So, choose another word to introduce the שׂ — perhaps שָׂרָה or שִׂמְחָה, both of which appear later in the lesson. You want to introduce the שׂ and ס together so that students associate the two symbols that make the same sound.

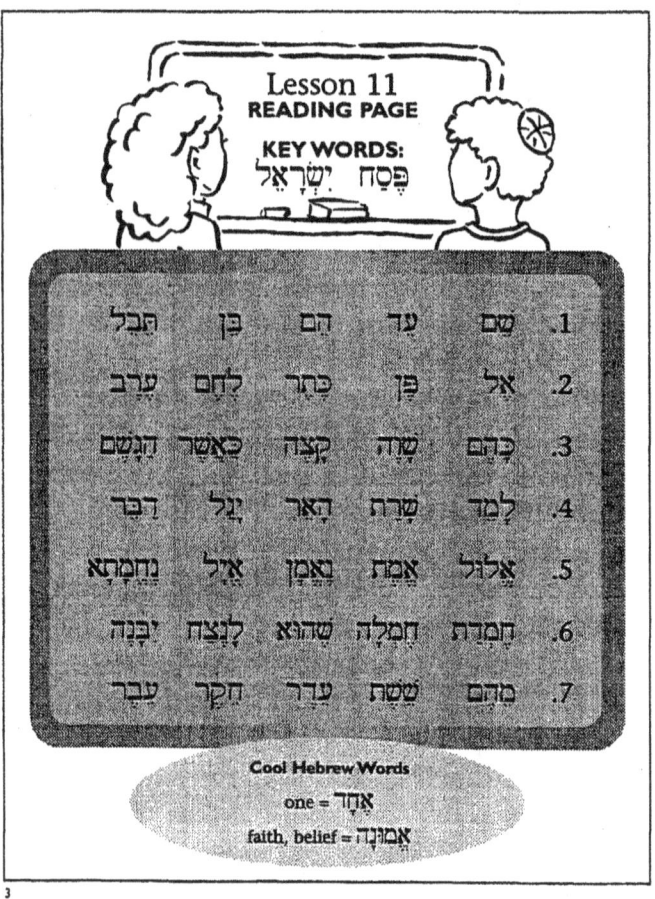

Initially, avoid the ▓, which some children confuse with the ▓ and ▓. To help remember the new vowel, give students the mnemonic from page 8 in the Workbook that the vowel looks like three or five "eggs" clustered together (or two eggs, if your school pronounces ▓ as "eh"). Students are also likely to confuse the new vowels with the ▓ and ▓ vowels since they look similar. Because of this, the two sounds are introduced very far apart in this program. Remind students of the mnemonic for the ▓ sound, also found on page 8.

When you read the Introduction Page (page 2) with students, have them fill in the way that ▓ is read in your synagogue community. Once you have taught the Key Word יִשְׂרָאֵל, ask students if they can read the Key Word on the postage stamp. They will be surprised to realize they can recognize it even without vowels. Explain that in Israel Hebrew is written without vowels (just like in the Torah).

4. Using the Reading Pages

Note that on the first Reading Page (page 3), the new vowels are introduced, but not the new letters. On the second Reading Page, the first three lines feature the ס and שׂ, but the שׁ with which the שׂ is most likely to be confused is avoided until line 5. The ם, which can be confused with the ס, is reintroduced on line 3, while line 4 contrasts the ם and the ס in the final position.

These Reading Pages were constructed so that you may break the lesson into two parts, first teaching only the new vowel sound. If your congregation pronounces the vowels as two separate sounds, do not divide your lesson this way (see explanation above).

5. **Using the Worksheets**

Page 5: Students complete the worksheet. Directions and answers are self-explanatory. Note that this kind of comparison between the שׁ and the שׂ is done only after students have been introduced to the new symbol and practiced reading words with it.

Page 6: This page provides practice in reading the Key Words. Students unscramble or fill in the blanks with words that are either previous Key Words, cognates (אָמֶרִיקָה), or Hebrew words that should be part of their Jewish background knowledge (כַּרְפַּס).

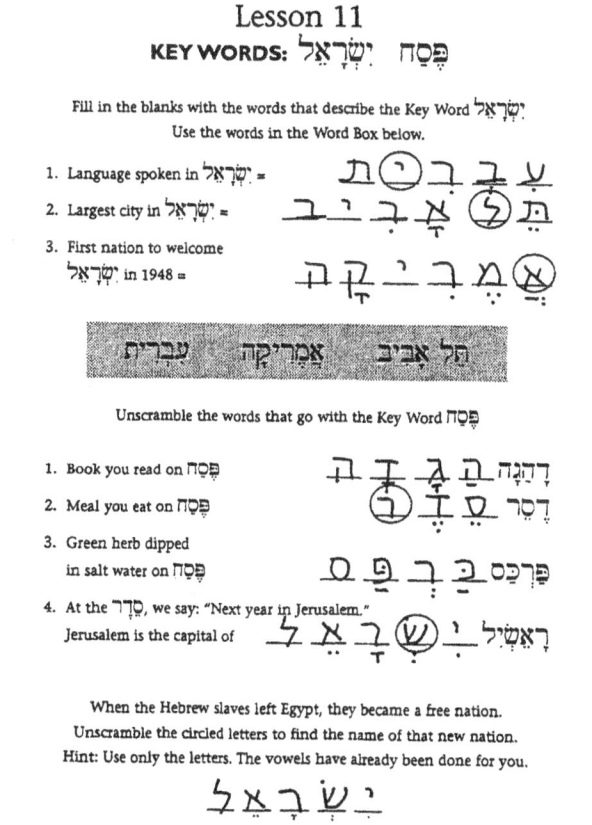

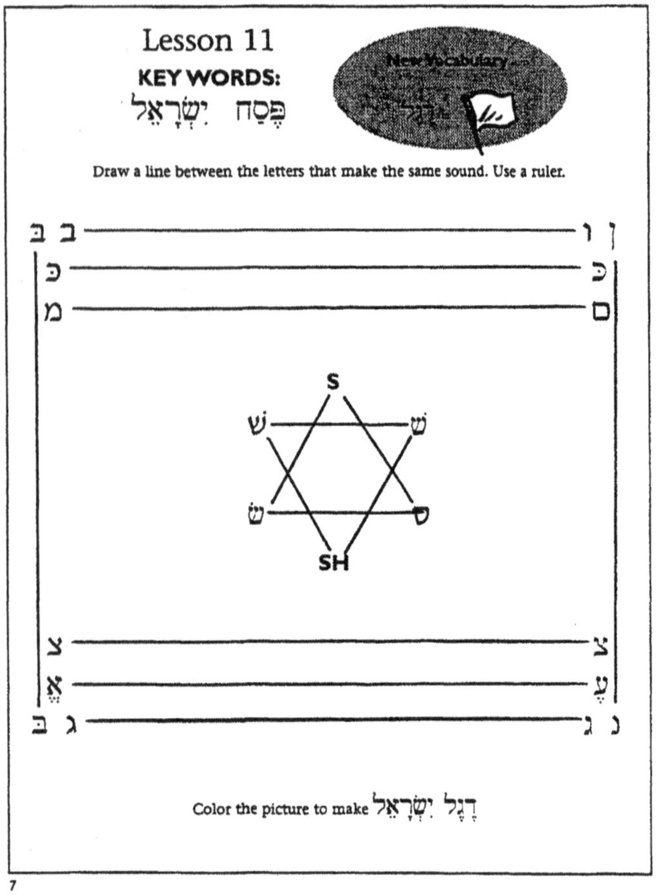

Lesson 11

KEY WORDS: פֶּסַח יִשְׂרָאֵל

New Vocabulary

Draw a line between the letters that make the same sound. Use a ruler.

S

SH

Color the picture to make דֶּגֶל יִשְׂרָאֵל

7

Page 7: When students connect the matching letters, an Israeli flag is formed.

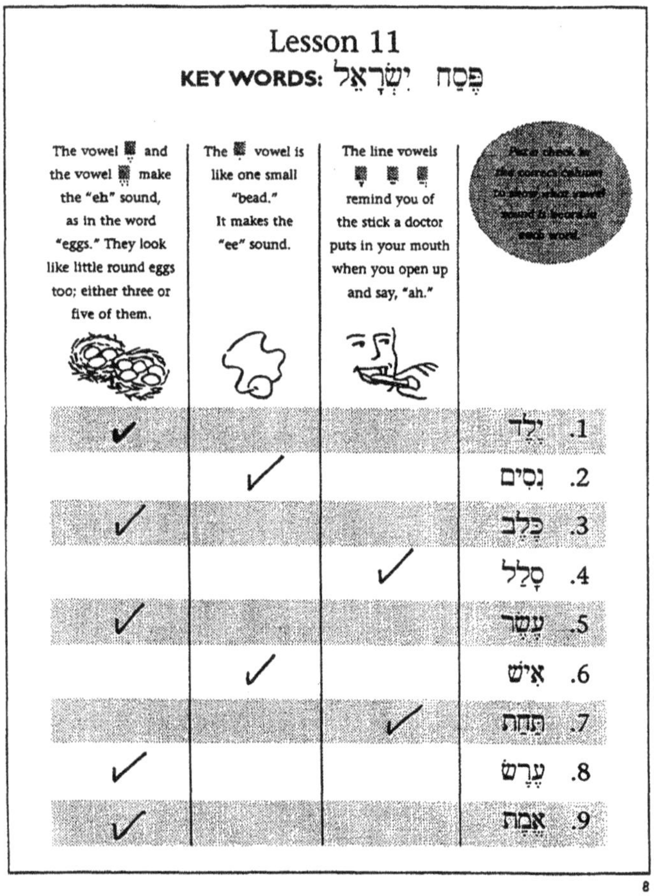

Lesson 11

KEY WORDS: פֶּסַח יִשְׂרָאֵל

The vowel and the vowel make the "eh" sound, as in the word "eggs." They look like little round eggs too; either three or five of them.	The vowel is like one small "bead." It makes the "ee" sound.	The line vowels remind you of the stick a doctor puts in your mouth when you open up and say, "ah."	
✓			1. יֶלֶד
	✓		2. נִסִּים
✓			3. כֶּלֶב
		✓	4. סַלָּל
✓			5. עֶשֶׂר
	✓		6. אִישׁ
		✓	7. תַּחַת
✓			8. עֶרֶשׂ
✓			9. אֶמֶת

8

Page 8: This page is excellent reinforcement for any student having trouble remembering the new vowel sounds. The was purposely not included because different schools pronounce it differently. You can turn this page into a learning center sorting game. Have three boxes or envelopes labeled with the vowel hints. Print on cards the words from this page and any other words you choose that have just one vowel sound. Students sort the cards. To make the activity self-checking, make three different marks on the backs of the cards.

Page 9: All students should complete this page. Read the Hebrew names at the bottom of the page with the entire class before students do this exercise. Discuss the biblical names. Some names are not clearly male or female for a non-native speaker of Hebrew. Discuss the principle of the הָ and ת as female endings, and have students identify the girls' names that do not follow this rule. Students completing the language component of this program may also note that אַתָּה does not follow this rule. Praise this discovery, and explain that it is an exception. Follow up with a discussion on the Hebrew names of students in the class. See if these follow the gender rules.

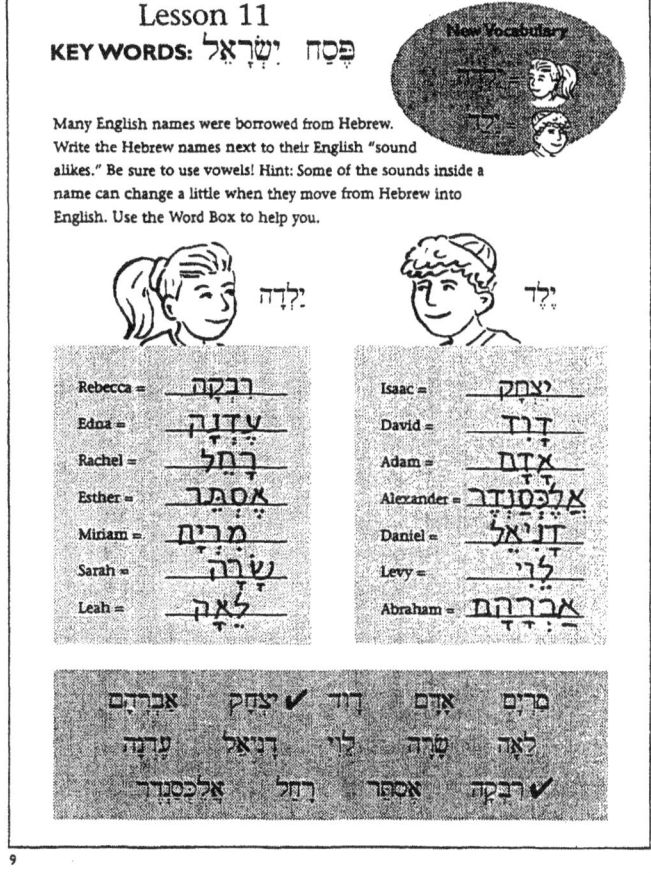

Page 10: This page is for students who are doing the language component of the program. Do this exercise together as a class if you suspect it will be difficult for individuals to complete.

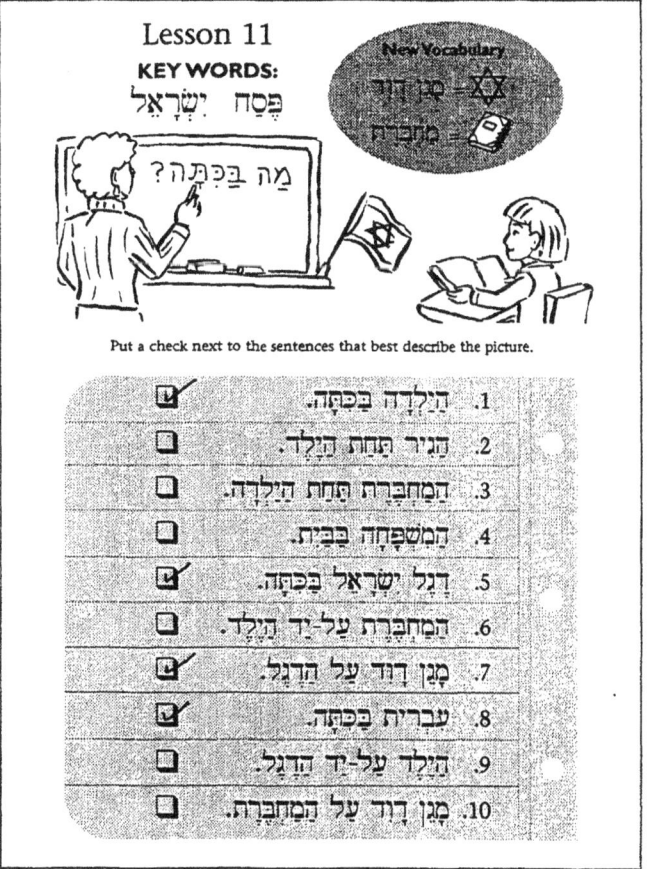

Page 11: This page is for students who are doing the language component of the program. Notice that the answers to the riddles may be found both in the box on the bottom of the page and in the illustrations.

6. Prepare for Prayer

Page 12: All students should complete this page, since it reviews the concept of Hebrew roots. Remind students (particularly if they are completing Volume Two after summer vacation) that many Hebrew words are members of word families that share the same three letter roots. One of the Key Words in Lesson 15 (חַג שָׂמֵחַ) comes from the root ש.מ.ח, so you may want to introduce it orally here.

7. **Evaluate and Remediate**

Pay attention to students' pronunciation of the new vowel sound. It is likely that despite your best efforts to keep the שׁ and שׂ separate, some students will still confuse the two. In this case, go back and review each letter separately, and then review them together. While there are mnemonics for this pair of confusing letters, none of them work very well with young students (most children don't realize that we shake hands with the **right** hand).

Suggested Additional Activities

1. If you are teaching vocabulary, have students begin filling in the dictionary at the end of the Workbook. They should continue to do this for every lesson.

2. Spend some additional time working on יֶלֶד and יַלְדָה, both orally and in writing. For example, if you are a יֶלֶד, do the following: יָד עַל גִיר, but if you are a יַלְדָה, do this: יָד עַל מַחְבֶּרֶת.

3. Play *Break the Chain* (see page 142 in this Teacher Guide).

4. Play *Chalkboard Tic-tac-toe* (see page 145 in this Teacher Guide).

LESSON 12

Key Word: (Alef) אָלֶף (book) סֵפֶר
New Letters: פ ף
New Vocabulary: (dog) כֶּלֶב
Special Points: ף = פ   פ ≠ פּ

Oral Language Lesson (optional)

In this lesson there is only one new vocabulary word, כֶּלֶב. Review the prepositions עַל, עַל־יָד, and תַּחַת while teaching it. Use magazine pictures or a stuffed toy dog rather than translating the word for dog.

The Seven Lesson Steps:

1. **Review**
Review the new vowel sounds taught in Lesson 11, as well as other previously learned vowels. Review the ס and the שׁ. This lesson is much less complex than the previous one; take the opportunity to make sure students have mastered the new concepts.

2. **Evoke the New Key Word(s)**
Students may have learned סֵפֶר as an oral vocabulary word in Lesson 11. Point to a book and ask what it is called in Hebrew.
To teach the second Key Word, point to the letter א and ask if anyone remembers what it is called. Once students know the name of the letter (Alef), see if anyone can guess the origin of the word "alphabet." The pictures on the Introduction Page (page 13) show a book and a Torah scroll, since we call the Torah scroll a סֵפֶר תּוֹרָה. The אָלֶף pictures show how the א developed its shape and illustrate the number value for the first six letters of the Hebrew alphabet.

3. **Introduce New Letters and Vowels**
Ask students to identify the sound of the new letters, פ and ף. When teaching the פ, avoid the פּ.
The text on the Introduction Page (page 13) may spark student interest in the topic of how the letters developed. Posters are available that show how all the Hebrew letters developed.

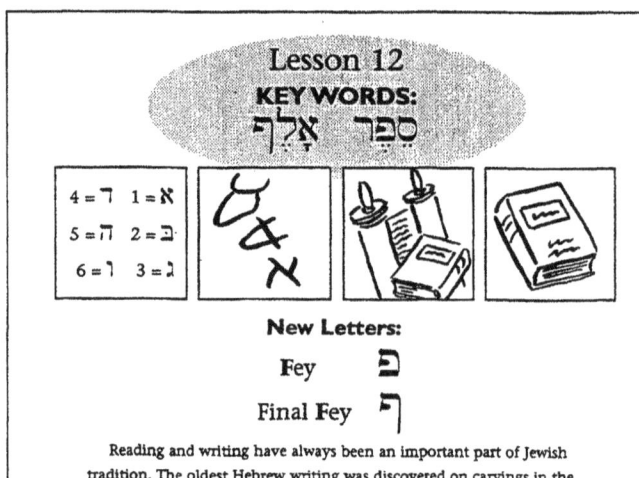

New Letters:

Fey   פ

Final Fey   ף

Reading and writing have always been an important part of Jewish tradition. The oldest Hebrew writing was discovered on carvings in the Sinai Desert. These carvings are more than 3,500 years old. At first, Hebrew was written in picture writing like the kind used in Egypt. Later, letters got their names from the words they pictured, and each letter stood for the first sound in its name. For example, the letter א was an ox head: ⌀. Its name comes from an ancient word for ox. If you look closely, you can still see the ox's head in the א.

Here are some other examples of Hebrew letters that come from picture writing.

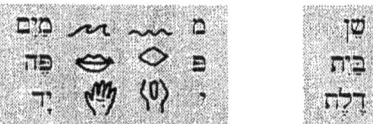

Every Hebrew letter also stood for a number. For this reason, the word סֵפֶר (book) is related to the word מִסְפָּר (number).

4. Using the Reading Page

This lesson has only one Reading Page because only one new sound is taught. In line 4 there are words in which the ס is intentionally placed at the end of the word. Make sure a ס at the end of a word is not read as a ם. Line 6 has words from the ס.פ.ר root, while line 7 has words from the א.ל.פ root.

5. Using the Worksheets

Page 15: Students practice writing the פ in both its forms. In the middle of the page, they have to decide which is the correct form. Make sure students use the regular, not final, forms of the מ and נ in the riddle at the bottom of the page.

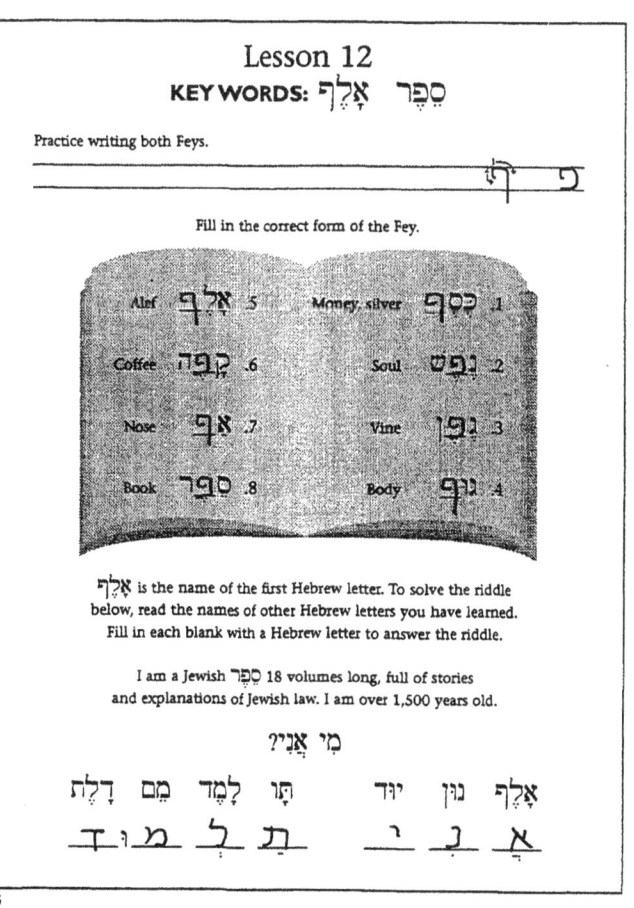

Page 16: This page offers a general review of the consonants taught so far. Thematically, it is connected to the Key Word סֵפֶר.

Page 17: All the words on the bottom of the page that rhyme have at least one common vowel and the same ending letter. This is a challenging exercise. First, practice orally with rhyming and non-rhyming English words and then with Hebrew words. Some English examples are:
1. bat, bit, can, cat
2. before, remote, adore, repose

Page 18: This page is for students who are doing the language component of the program.

6. Prepare for Prayer

Page 19: This game is similar to *Connect-4*, described in more detail on page 142 of this Teacher Guide. Students played the game before in Volume One, Lesson 6 of the Workbook, page 43. If students mark the boxes with pencil, they will be able to play the game only once. You can lay a plastic sheet on the page and use erasable markers so that they will be able to reuse the sheet. This game is a student favorite, as it involves strategy as well as reading.

7. Evaluate and Remediate

When you evaluate, be aware of the possible confusion between the פ and the פּ.

Suggested Additional Activities

1. *Play Connect-4* (see page 142 in this Teacher Guide).

2. Make *Little Books* using sentences like those on page 18 in the Workbook (see page 150 in this Teacher Guide).

LESSON 13

Key Words:	(good morning) בֹּקֶר טוֹב
	(hello, good-bye, peace) שָׁלוֹם
New Letter:	ט
New Vowels:	וֹ ָ
Special Points:	ט ≠ מ ט = ת וֹ = ׁ
New Vocabulary:	(teacher, fem. sing.) מוֹרָה (teacher, masc. sing.) מוֹרֶה
	(learn, fem. sing.) לוֹמֶדֶת (learn, masc. sing.) לוֹמֵד (Torah) תּוֹרָה
	(yes) כֵּן (no) לֹא

Oral Language Lesson (optional)

This lesson is particularly heavy on vocabulary, so you may need to allot more time to complete the language component of the lesson. As with all lessons, it is best to have students familiar with the new vocabulary even before the lesson is introduced. This lesson features seven new words, six of them related to the classroom, in addition to the Key Words.

For the first time you will be teaching a verb, and can therefore work on matching the pronouns (אַתָּה and אַתְּ) to the verb forms.

Here are some phrases you can now make using the new vocabulary:

מָה אַתְּ לוֹמֶדֶת?   אַתְּ מוֹרָה?
מָה אַתָּה לוֹמֵד?   אַתָּה מוֹרֶה?
אַתָּה לוֹמֵד בִּיוֹלוֹגְיָה?   מוֹרָה בְּכִתָּה?
מִי לוֹמֵד מוּסִיקָה?   מִי הַמוֹרָה?

For very advanced students, you can even construct some complex sentences or questions using the adjective טוֹב (for example, מִי יֶלֶד טוֹב?).

The Seven Lesson Steps:

1. Review

Review concepts learned in the most recent lessons. Avoid using the וֹ vowel as you will be teaching וֹ, since these two are often confused.

2. Evoke the New Key Word(s)

Look at Lessons 13 through 15 and you will see that most of the Key Words for these lessons are polite expressions and greetings. Students are likely to know the Key Words in Lesson 13 (and probably also the greetings in Lesson 15). Ask:

"What do you say in Hebrew when you meet someone? What word in Hebrew means peace, good-bye, and hello?" (שָׁלוֹם)

Discuss how one word can have all of these meanings. When you read the story on the Introduction Page (page 20), students will learn the actual meaning of the root שׁ.ל.מ. Next ask:

"And with what words do we greet each other in the morning?" (בֹּקֶר טוֹב)

When teaching "good morning," teach that "morning" = בֹּקֶר, and "good" = טוֹב. This information will be useful for Lesson 15. If you want to challenge skilled students, ask what they think יֶלֶד טוֹב (good boy) means, or how you would say good wine, good book, good father. Get students to notice that the adjective in Hebrew follows the noun.

If students start using feminine nouns, see if they can come up with טוֹבָה, the feminine adjective for "good." Knowing that ָה is the feminine form, they might be able to deduce טוֹבָה from טוֹב.

Have students identify the pictures on the Introduction Page. The completed puzzle of the world map illustrates the meaning of "completeness" expressed by the Key Word שָׁלוֹם. Remind

100

students of the picture used in Volume One to introduce the Key Word מִצְוָה (on page 62). There the identical picture had one piece out of place, illustrating the concept that each מִצְוָה helped to repair our world and bring it to wholeness. Show students the picture from Volume One, since their Workbooks have probably been sent home already.

3. **Introduce New Letters and Vowels**

Ask students to identify the vowel sound which they have not yet learned (וֹ and ׇ).

a. Vowels

וֹ has no precise English equivalent. It is most often taught as the long "o" in "over," which is the mnemonic used to reduce confusion with the וּ. This pronunciation is not exact. Since some students may not even hear the difference, model the correct pronunciation in such familiar words as Torah and שָׁלוֹם. (Do not persist in correcting students if they continue to pronounce it as a long "o"). If you can't pronounce the vowel correctly, you can invite a "guest speaker" to come to class and model the correct pronunciation (perhaps a native Hebrew speaker on staff).

Note: DO NOT reintroduce the וֹ initially until you are absolutely sure all students know the וֹ and ׇ. Present the וֹ first, because it is the more common form of the vowel.

b. Consonant

Notice that you are introducing a letter (ט) that often gets confused with the מ. Make sure that initially you only show the ט. Create the sound association with the ת and ה by showing all three letter forms at the same time. Only when all students have mastered the ט, reintroduce the מ.

Read the Introduction Page (page 20), together with students.

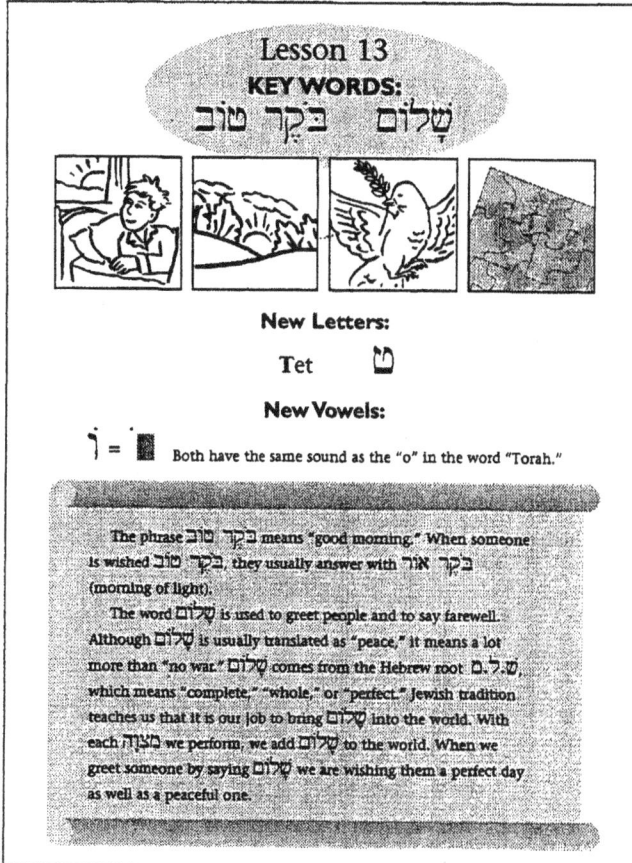

4. Using the Reading Pages

This lesson can be taught in two segments. In the first segment, teach and reinforce only the new vowel by using the first Reading Page (page 21). Notice that lines 3 and 4 are verbs in masculine and feminine forms. In advanced classes you may want to teach these verbs as vocabulary. Line 6 consists of more vocabulary related to the classroom.

When using the second Reading Page, you will be drilling the *Cholam-Chaser* ( ) and the new letter ס. The words on line 3 and 4 are the names of colors, which you may want to teach as vocabulary.

5. Using the Worksheets

Page 23: Before doing this page, teach students the Hebrew word בֹּקֶר (morning).

Page 24: Students practice writing the new letter ט along with the ת and תּ to reinforce the idea that all three make the same sound. The word pairs in the bottom exercise all are real words. This page requires the students to pay close attention to both look-alike and sound-alike letters. Students must circle the letter in the correct column to indicate if the words sound the same (are homophones) or sound different. The letter that is circled has no significance other than enabling them to answer the riddle at the bottom of the page.

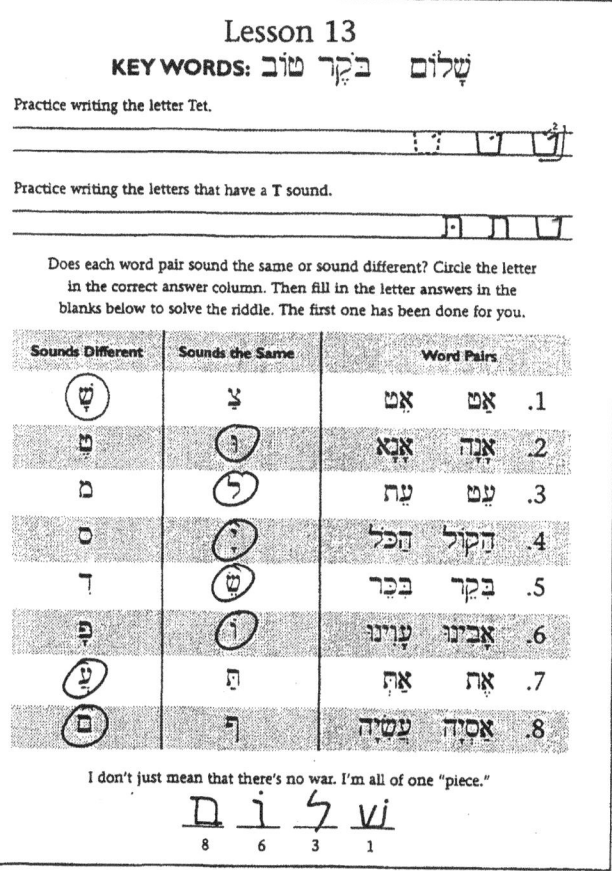

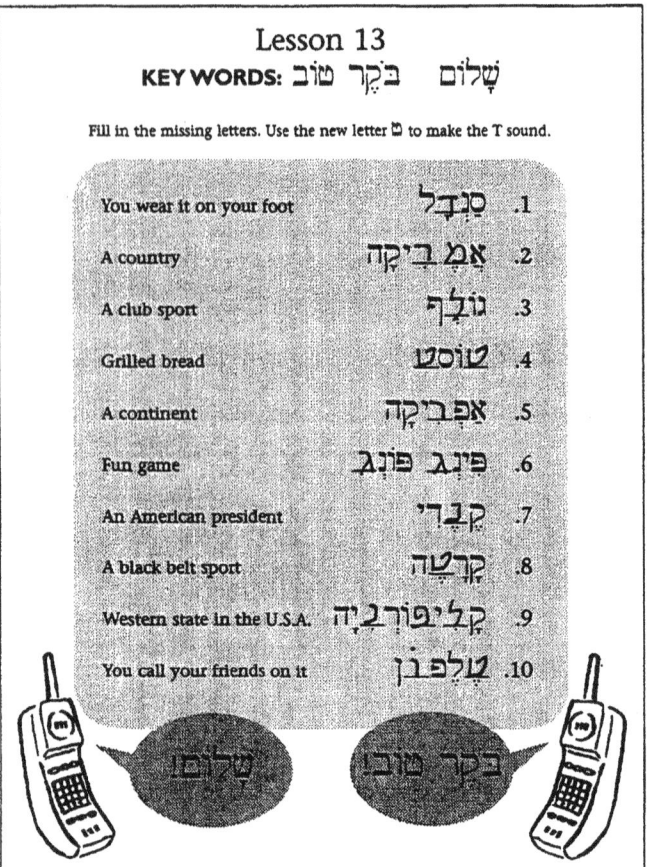

Page 25: Words on this page are all cognates. Some are pronounced slightly differently in Hebrew than in English.

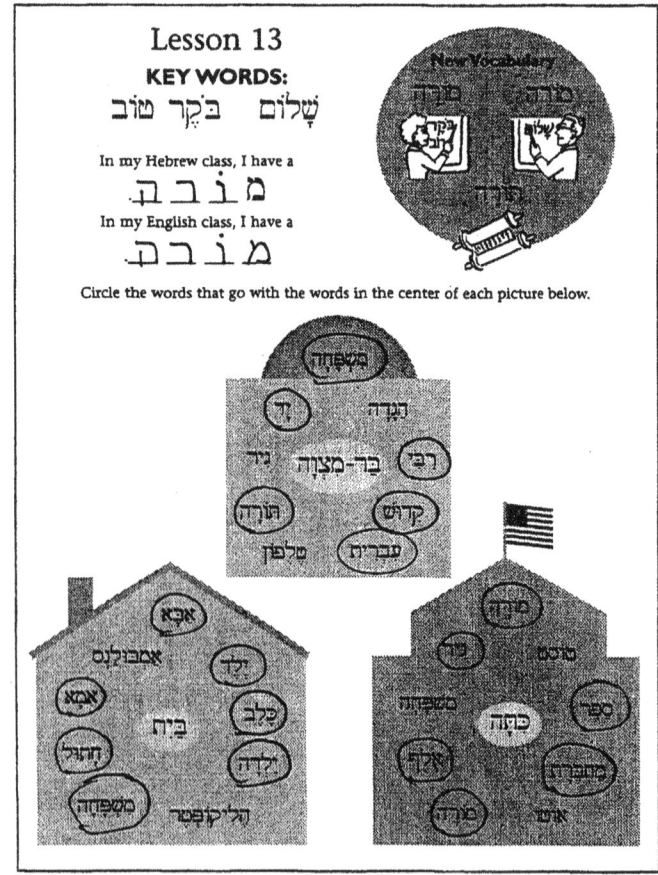

Page 26: This page is for students who are doing the language component of the program. Review the new vocabulary (מוֹרֶה/מוֹרָה) and the other words in the circles before students complete the worksheet. Go over at least two examples from the exercise at the bottom of the page.

Page 27: This page is for students who are doing the language component of the program. Teach the verb forms (לוֹמֵד/לוֹמֶדֶת) before students complete this worksheet, and do this exercise orally with the entire class before they complete the worksheet.

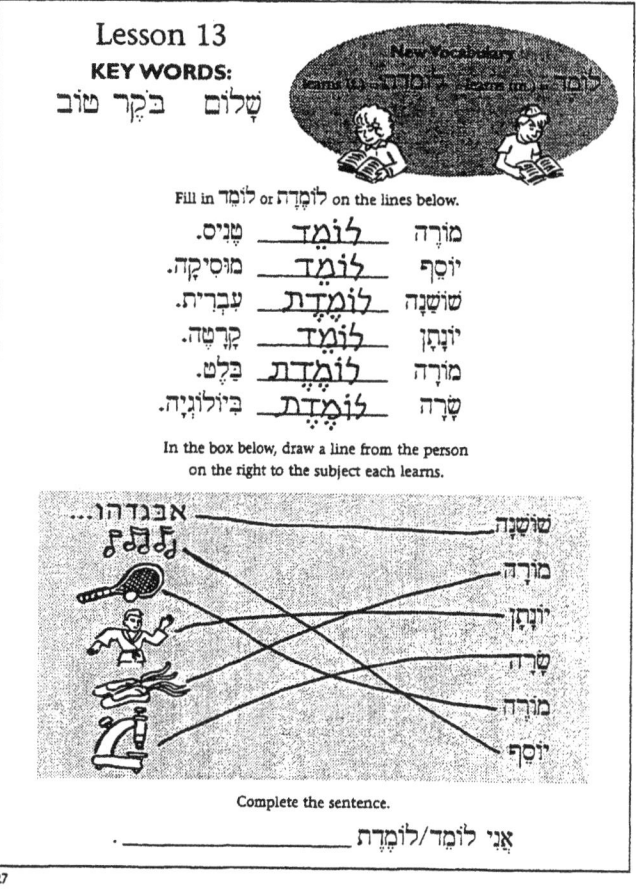

Page 28: This page is for students who are doing the language component of the program. Teach the Hebrew words for "yes" and "no" before assigning this worksheet.

Page 29: This page is for students who are doing the language component of the program. This worksheet provides the first real conversation in this volume. Read it as a group (assigning roles), and have students complete the sentences on their own. See *Dramatic Play* (page 148 in this Teacher Guide).

6. Prepare for Prayer

Page 30: This page continues the presentation of Hebrew roots and should be completed by all students.

7. Evaluate and Remediate

Pay close attention to students' pronunciation of the new vowel sound, making sure that they are not pronouncing it as an וֹ. Vowels are usually much more troublesome for novice readers than consonants. Do not let students who have not mastered the new vowel sound proceed yet to Lesson 14.

Suggested Additional Activities

1. *Climb the Ladder* (see page 143 in this Teacher Guide).

2. *Around the World* (see page 146 in this Teacher Guide). Good for reviewing all the new vocabulary found in this lesson.

3. *Computer Index Cards* (see page 148 in this Teacher Guide). Let students individually review the new vocabulary.

LESSON 14

Key Words: (excuse me) סְלִיחָה
(please) בְּבַקָשָׁה
New Vowel: initial voiced ְ
New Vocabulary: (and) וְ__ (with) עִם (charity, justice) צְדָקָה
(love, like – fem. sing.) אוֹהֶבֶת (love, like – masc. sing.) אוֹהֵב
Special Points: initial voiced ְ ≠ silent medial ְ

Oral Language Lesson (optional)

In this lesson you will be teaching the second verb taught in this program, אוֹהֵב (love or like, masculine singular) and אוֹהֶבֶת (love or like, feminine singular). Create a variety of sentences in Hebrew that use the new verb, and act out the word as you recite the sentences. Students should figure out the meaning of the word. Use this opportunity also to practice the pronouns אַתְּ, אַתָּה, and אֲנִי.

The distinction between עִם and וְ__ is illustrated in the humorous conversation on page 35. Teach וְ__ (and) first, since the focus of this lesson is the beginning *Shva*. Additionally, explain to the students that וְ__ is a prefix, just like הַ__ and בְּ__, that is attached to the word that follows.

When teaching עִם (with) demonstrate orally, as well as with objects, the distinctions between this word and עַל (on), תַּחַת (under) and עַל-יַד (next to). If students confuse these words, focus on any two of them at a time by having students manipulate actual objects.

The Seven Lesson Steps:

1. Review
Notice that this is a short lesson in which only one vowel is taught. It is, however, a vowel sound that can cause great difficulty. In this lesson segment, review and make sure students are proficient in what they have learned so far. This is especially necessary since the lessons ahead introduce new vowels and vowel combinations.

2. Evoke the New Key Word(s)
The Key Words in this lesson most likely will not be known to students. However, they are related to the greeting words in Lessons 13 and 15.

Act out situations or show appropriate pictures in which these two words would be used.

Ask students to identify the initial sound in the Key Words.

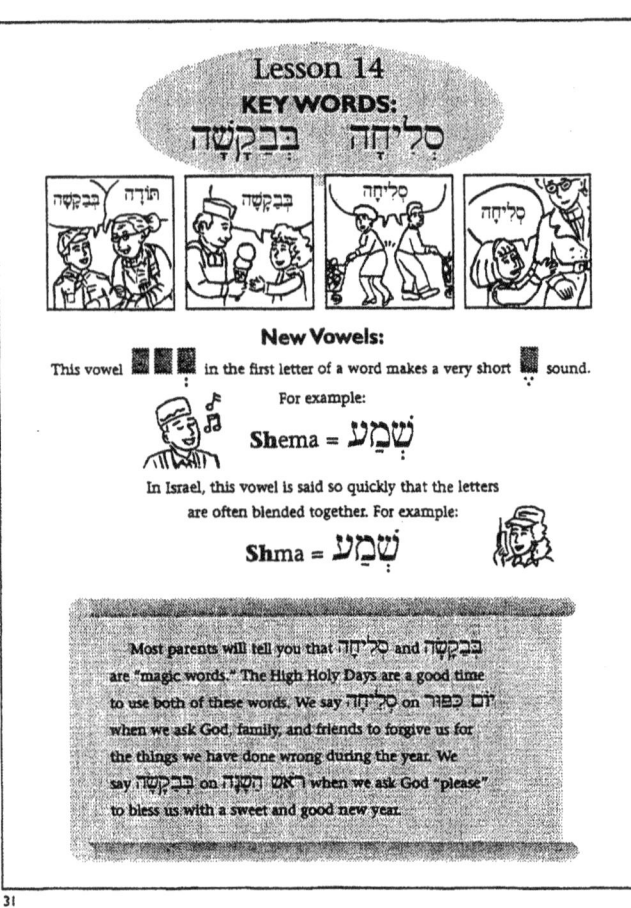

3. Introduce New Letters and Vowels

This lesson introduces only the initial *Shva*. Note that according to grammar rules, the initial *Shva* is always voiced (as it is a שְׁוָא נָע). However, in spoken Hebrew, the first two letters are often blended. A good example of this is the word שְׁמַע. Technically, the word should be pronounced as: "Sh'ma." However, in spoken Hebrew, the first two letters and the *Shva* are blended to form a one syllable pronunciation: "Shma." This is shown on the Introduction Page, page 31.

Teach the rule as follows: it is always correct to pronounce the initial *Shva* as a very short "eh" as in bed. However, if the first two letters can be blended to form one syllable, we do so in spoken or modern Hebrew. How do we know in advance that we can blend? For an English speaker, it is nearly impossible to be able to tell, as consonant combinations that are never blended in English are blended in Hebrew. Examples of this include **zm** (as in זְמַן) or **zv** (as in זְבוּב). Thus, it is best to tell your students to make the short "eh" sound if they are in doubt.

4. Using the Reading Page

There is only one Reading Page (page 32) for this lesson.

Line 1 consists of short words in which the *Shva* can either be voiced or unvoiced.

Line 2 contains words associated with the worship service.

Four of the words on line 3 have to do with the sounds of the *shofar*.

Lines 4 and 5 contain feminine numbers from one to ten. (Note that שָׁלוֹשׁ is spelled with a וֹ, since students will not learn the double duty dot until Lesson 20.) Teach the numbers if this fits into your curriculum.

From this lesson on, phrases from our tradition appear at the bottom of many Reading Pages and Prepare for Prayer Pages. Most of these phrases have been set to music, and you may want to take the opportunity to teach students the songs. (See page 149 in this Teacher Guide.)

5. **Using the Worksheets**

Page 33: Use this page to contrast reading the initial voiced *Shva* and silent medial *Shva*. Practice as a class before students begin to work independently. The new vocabulary word צְדָקָה will no doubt be familiar to most students.

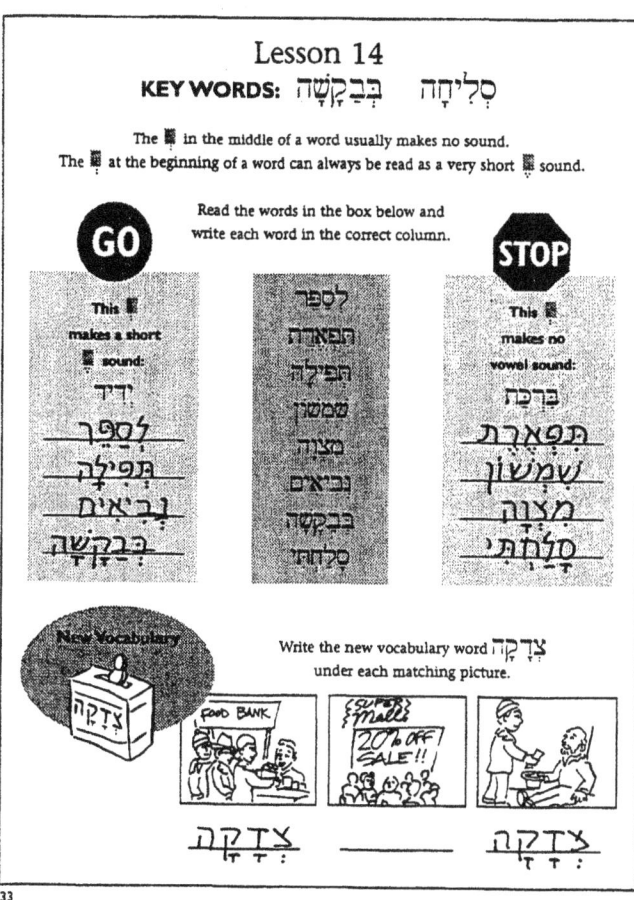

Page 34: This page is for students who are doing the language component of the program. Teach the new verb (אוֹהֵב/אוֹהֶבֶת) before you assign this page.

Page 35: Read the conversation with the entire class. If you are teaching vocabulary, have students fill in the blanks independently. (For purposes of pronunciation, the word "ketchup" is spelled with a פ at the end.)

6. Prepare for Prayer

This page reviews the concept of Hebrew roots and should be read by all students. Pay special attention to the root ש.ל.ם since שָׁלוֹם was a Key Word in Lesson 13, and the root's relationship to the word יְרוּשָׁלַיִם is explored here.

7. Evaluate and Remediate

Accept all short "eh" pronunciations of the initial *Shva* as correct. Make sure students haven't overgeneralized and are still pronouncing the medial *Shva* as the end of a syllable.

Suggested Additional Activities

1. Play *I Like* (see page 149 in this Teacher Guide).

2. *Speed Reading* (see page 142 in this Teacher Guide).

LESSON 15

Key Words: מַזָל טוֹב (congratulations, good luck)
בֵּית־כְּנֶסֶת (synagogue)   חַג שָׂמֵחַ (happy holiday)

New Letter: ז

New Vowel Combinations: חַ   יֵ   אֵ   הֵ

New Vocabulary: נֵר (candle)   זֶבְרָה (zebra)   קָטָן (small)
כִּסֵא (chair)   עִפָּרוֹן (pencil)   לוּחַ (blackboard)   גָדוֹל (big)

Special Points: ו ≠ ז   (in some schools, יֵ = ֵ)

Oral Language Lesson (optional)

In this lesson there are seven new vocabulary words. Three are classroom objects, and two are adjectives. Practice this vocabulary with games that require actually using the objects. For example, show two pencils of unequal size and describe them as עִפָּרוֹן קָטָן and עִפָּרוֹן גָדוֹל. Show other pairs of classroom objects, such as books or notebooks, and give students commands or ask questions using the vocabulary they already know. You can also use the words candle and zebra in this activity, even though they aren't usually found in a classroom. Use a stuffed zebra or a picture. Examples follow.

גִיר גָדוֹל עַל עִפָּרוֹן קָטָן.
עִפָּרוֹן גָדוֹל עַל כִּסֵא.
נֵר תַחַת כִּסֵא?
לוּחַ קָטָן עַל־יַד זֶבְרָה.
דָוִד יֶלֶד גָדוֹל?
עִפָּרוֹן גָדוֹל בַּסֵפֶר.
מִי עַל־יַד הַלוּחַ?
עִפָּרוֹן קָטָן תַחַת מַחְבֶּרֶת.

(See *Listen and Do!* on page 148 in this Teacher Guide.)

The Seven Lesson Steps:

This lesson contains several new concepts, including a vowel combination that students often forget (the חַ) and a letter they often confuse with the ו (the ז). You will need to allot extra time for this lesson, especially if your school teaches that the ֵ and the יֵ make two distinct sounds. A suggested order for introducing the new concepts is given below. You may divide your lesson into two or three parts after introducing any of the new concepts.

1. Review

Begin this lesson with a thorough review of vowels, since in each of the remaining lessons, a new vowel (or vowel combination) is taught. Review the meaning of טוֹב (good).

2. Evoke the New Key Word(s)

Students are likely to know the expression מַזָל טוֹב. Act out or show magazine pictures of different situations when this greeting is appropriate, so that students do not think it is specific solely to a wedding or a Bar Mitzvah.

Students may know the second Key Word, the Hebrew word for synagogue (בֵּית־כְּנֶסֶת). If not, they may have an idea what the two parts of the word mean. Ask:

"Is the first part of the word for synagogue familiar? (בֵּית). It sounds like the Hebrew word for house (בַּיִת) and is actually a form of that word. The second part of the word might also be familiar to you. Do you know what the כְּנֶסֶת in Israel is? It is the Israeli congress, where laws are made, and where the members meet together. כְּנֶסֶת means "meeting." So together the words mean _____" (house of meeting, synagogue).

The third Key Word expression (חַג שָׂמֵחַ) is

more difficult to pronounce and students are less likely to know it. They may be familiar with the "Happy Birthday" song in Hebrew (יוֹם הֻלֶּדֶת שָׂמֵחַ). Point out to them that the word שָׂמֵחַ appears in both expressions. You can sing the song as well. Teach the two words in חַג שָׂמֵחַ separately, and see if students notice that the adjective follows the noun, as it did in בֹּקֶר טוֹב and מַזָּל טוֹב.

3. Introduce New Letters and Vowels
a. Consonant:

If you want to divide this very full lesson, teach and practice the new letter ז as soon as you evoke the Key Word מַזָּל טוֹב. Students can read the first three lines of the Reading Page on page 38, and complete the exercise on the top of page 41. The *Activity Book* also provides practice in reading words with the ז, but not the other new concepts taught in this lesson. Ask students to identify the letter sound in מַזָּל טוֹב, which

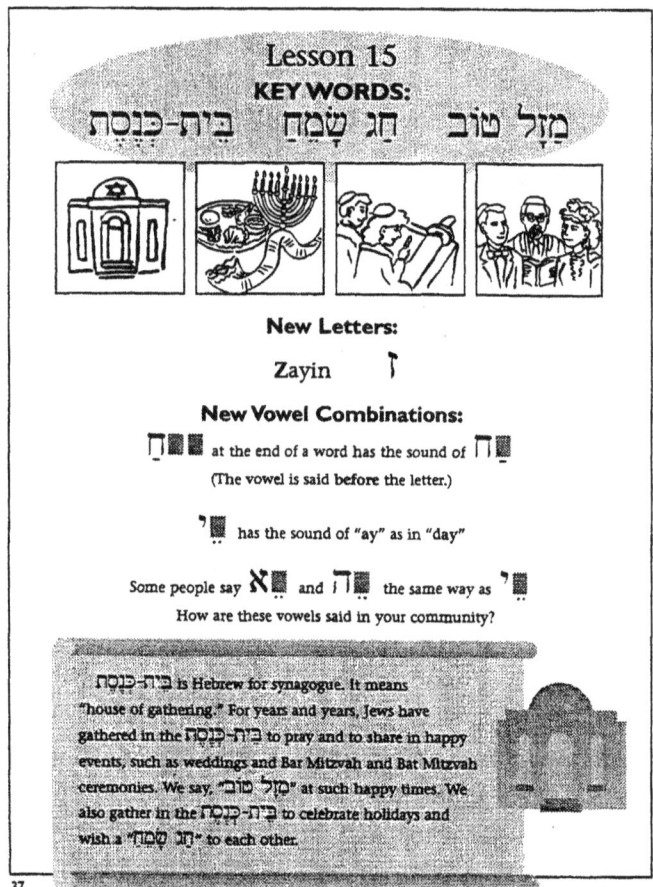

they have not yet learned (z). *Zayin*, the new letter for this lesson, is often confused with letters that sound or look similar. Therefore, the exercises on page 41 are included to help students in discriminating the letter. The top exercise requires students to distinguish the letter's shape, while the bottom one asks them to hear the difference in its sound. You may do these exercises before you read the Reading Page, but the bottom one can be done only after you have introduced the ח sound. (See *Using the Worksheets* below.)

b. Vowel-letter combination:

This lesson introduces the vowel-letter combination יִ◌. If your congregation and students pronounce the ◌ vowel as a long **ay**, then this will be an easy concept to teach. Remind students that any י that is not followed by a vowel makes a vowel sound. Tell students that just like the combination יִ◌ sounds the same as the ◌, the יִ◌ sounds the same as the ◌. Refer back to the discussion of the ◌ pronunciation on page 89 of this Teacher Guide. If the sound is not a new one for your students, you should read all of the Reading Page (on page 38) as soon as you teach the ז and mention the יִ◌, since you really aren't teaching a new concept here. Likewise, the א◌ and ה◌ sounds will not be new to your students, and will only need to be briefly mentioned.

If you have taught the modern Israeli pronunciation of ◌ (eh as in bed), then you are now teaching a new sound. Introduce the א◌ and the ה◌ sound at this time. According to classical Hebrew grammar, these combinations make the same sound as the יִ◌. Again, rely on your Rabbi, Cantor, and Director of Education for guidance as to how these vowels should be taught.

Whether or not the יִ◌ sound is a new sound for your students, DO NOT mention the יִ◌ combination now.

After you introduce the יִ◌, א◌, and ה◌, students should read Reading Page 38 before continuing and learning the *Patach-Gnuvah* (◌◌ח).

c. Vowel-letter combination:

The *Patach-Gnuvah* is one of the more difficult Hebrew vowels. Initially, the concept itself is confusing for children. Later, unless they review it frequently, they simply forget it, as it is an exception to the normal letter-vowel rules in Hebrew. Tell students:

"When you see **this** letter and **this** vowel at the end of the word, pronounce the vowel first. This letter, with this vowel, only when it occurs at the end of the word." It is best to introduce it using a word that is already in the children's repertoire. Ideally, they will have learned the word לוּחַ orally. If so, you can use it. לוּחַ is also good to use because it has only two, rather than the three vowels in שָׂמֵחַ. The *Patach-Gnuvah* is taught in this lesson because when preceded by a ◌ֵ, the ◌ֵ is given the long **ay** sound by those who pronounce the אֵ and הֵ as a long **ay**.

Before proceeding to the Reading Pages, provide additional practice in reading this vowel through the use of felt letters or the chalkboard. Read the entire Introduction Page (page 37) with students at this point.

4. Using the Reading Pages

The first Reading Page (page 38) provides a lot of practice with letters that either look or sound like the ז. Since this letter looks dissimilar in different styles of type, show students what this letter looks like in several other books. Congratulate the students. They can now read the Hebrew title of the Workbook. The יֵ, אֵ, and הֵ are drilled as well. The second Reading Page (page 39) focuses mainly on the *Patach-Gnuvah*.

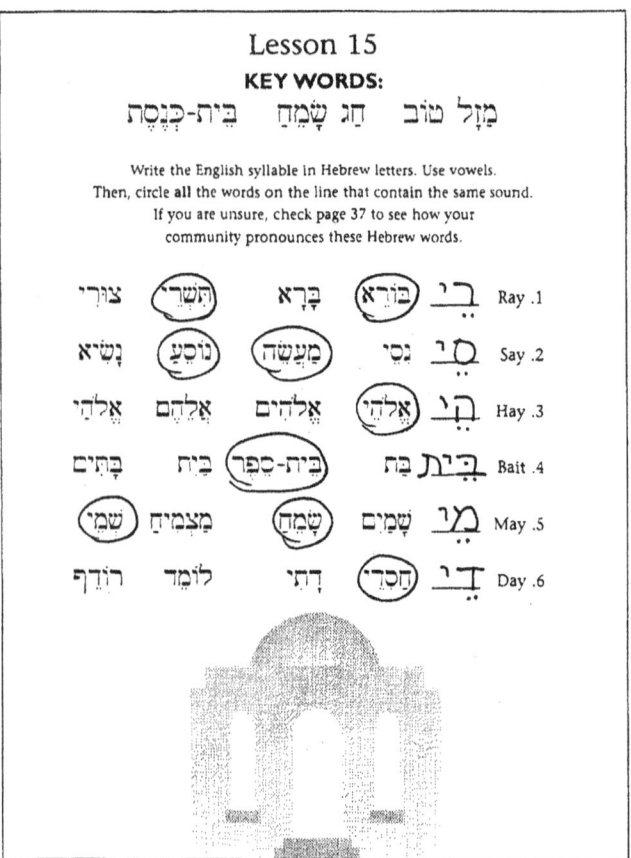

5. Using the Worksheets

Page 40: Students' answers will depend upon your community's pronunciation of the ◼ vowel and vowel combinations. For example, in number 6, "Day" could be written as דָה, דָא, or דָי. Students could circle רוֹדֵף and לוֹמֵד, or might not.

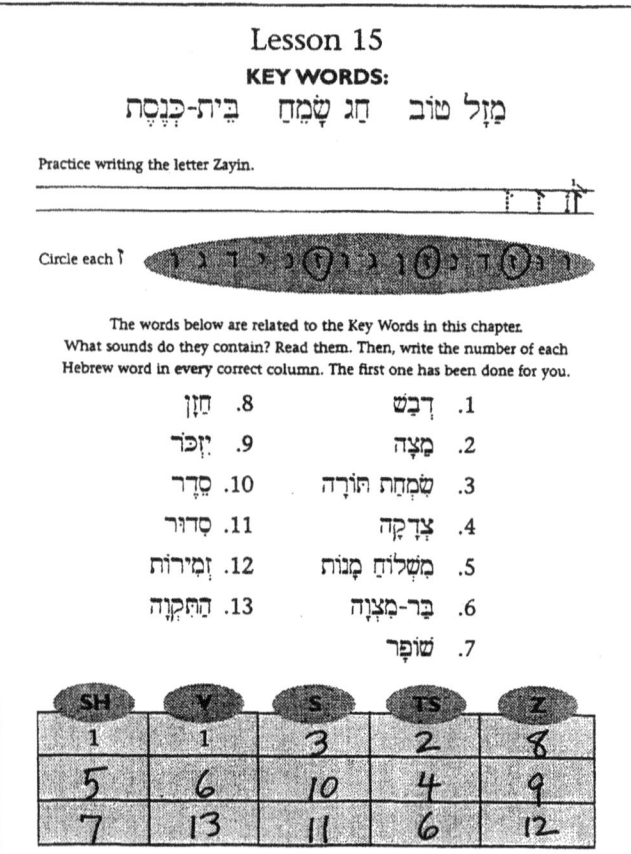

Page 41: Make sure you demonstrate on the board an easy way to write the ז. For the chart exercise at the bottom of the page, insist that students pronounce the words out loud as they read them. Make sure students understand that one word may contain two of the sounds, as in the example. The only other word that actually does this is number 6, בַּר-מִצְוָה.

Page 42: Before doing this exercise, be sure to review instructions with students. Words are considered to be rhyming if they end in the same vowel and consonant. If a student still thinks that ה at the end of a word makes the חָה sound, they will circle the wrong words.

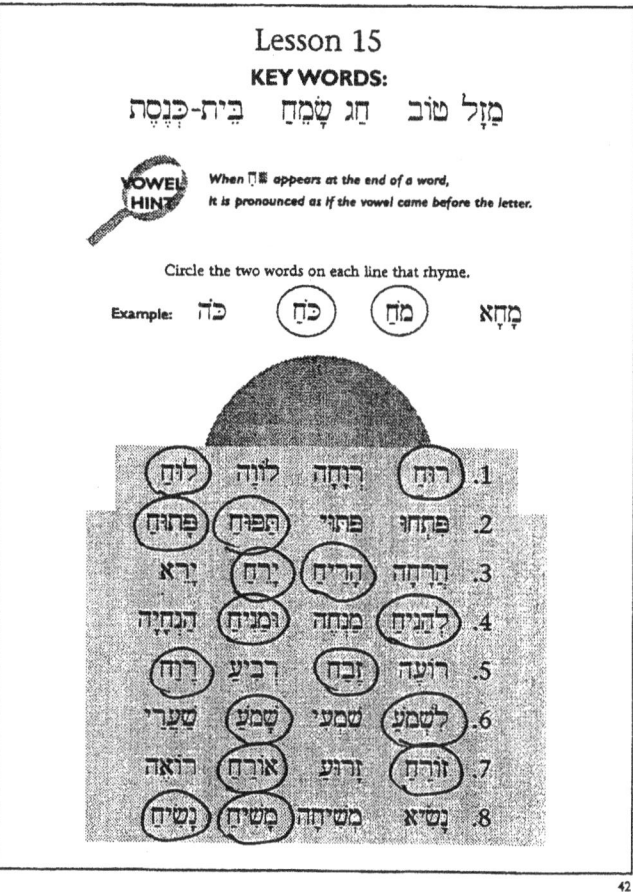

Page 43: Students need to match the greetings with the illustrations. Since all the words are Key Words, all students should complete this page. You can do a review with picture cards and Key Word Poster Cards before having students complete the page independently.

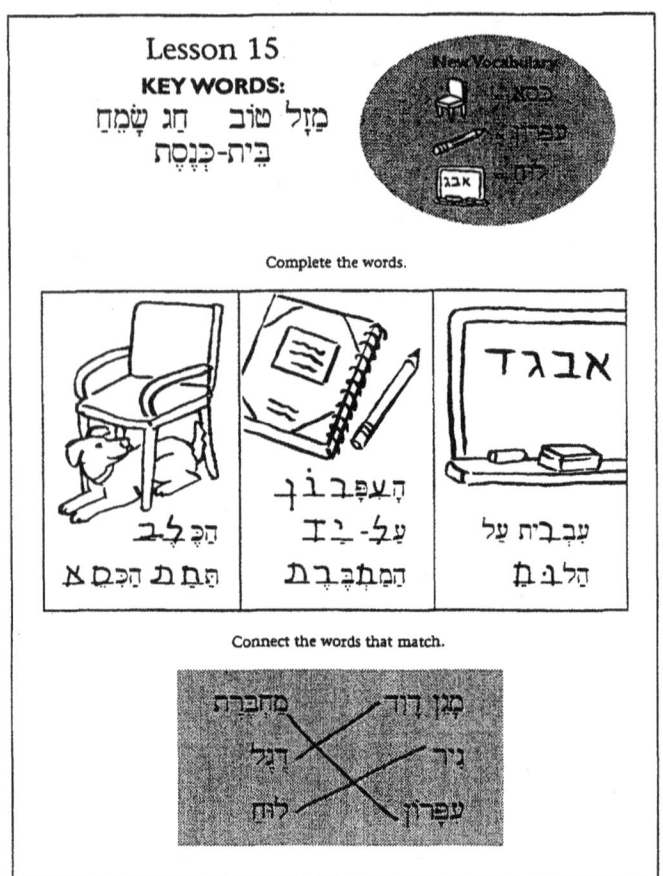

Page 44: This page is for students who are doing the language component of the program. Students complete the pictures as well as the words.

Page 45: This page is for students who are doing the language component of the program. Make sure that students understand the new vocabulary words from the pictures, and don't think they mean "big dog" and "small dog."

Page 46: This conceptually challenging page is for students who are doing the language component of the program. Students are required not only to make classifications, but to deduce the criteria on which their classifications are to be based. Every attempt was made to have only one answer be the logical choice, but if students have a different answer that they can logically justify, accept it.

Page 47: Use the crossword puzzle to review the Key Words and additional vocabulary. Only students who are doing the language component of the program will be able to complete it.

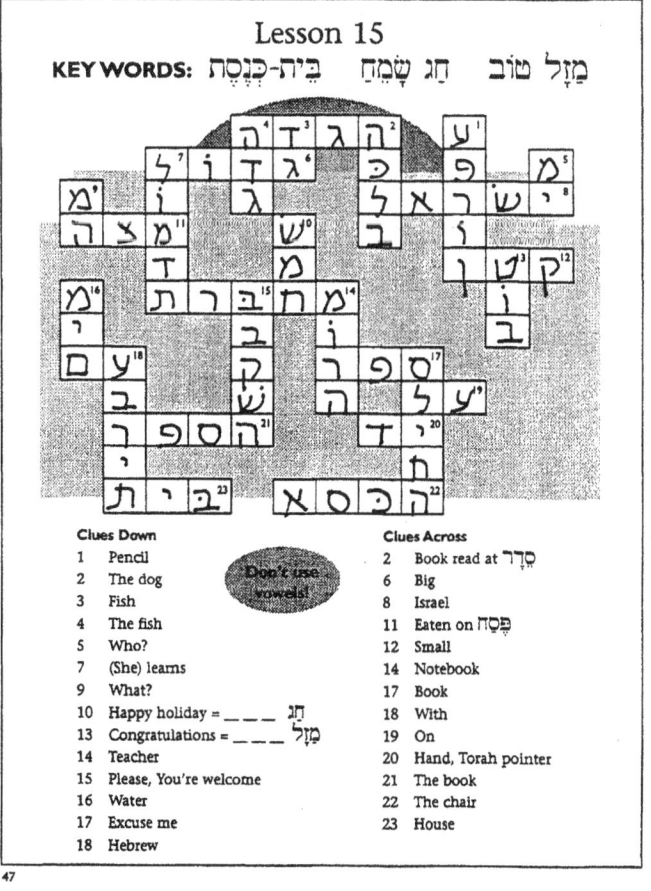

6. Prepare for Prayer

Page 48: This page presents phrases from the *Siddur* that contain the new concepts taught in this lesson. As these concepts were difficult, most students will benefit greatly from the additional drill. Line 1 comes from the beginning of the *Amidah* prayer. Line 2 is a song from the *Kabbalat Shabbat* service. Line 3 is the opening line of the *Alaynu* prayer. Line 4 is part of the Chanukah song "*Ma'oz Tsur*" (Rock of Ages). Lines 5-7 are part of the *V'Shamru*. Line 8 is the first three words of the Torah.

As some students may be feeling discouraged because the reading is getting more complex, tell everyone they should be very proud that they can read so much from original Hebrew texts.

7. Evaluate and Remediate

Make sure every student is correctly reading the *Patach-Gnuvah* and the וֹ. The variations in pronunciation of the ◼ in combination with other letters can be so slight that mispronunciations should not be of concern. As long as students pronounce this vowel combination in a way that is correct in some Jewish community, do not overly correct them. A student who pronounces יִ◼ as "eh-ya," with the י pronounced as a consonant, however, should be corrected.

Suggested Additional Activities

1. Create situations in which students decide which of the greetings they learned in Lessons 13 through 15 would be appropriate. With props, have students mime the situations, and then have the class decide which of the greetings should be used. (See *Guess That Act!* and *Dramatic Play* on page 148 in this Teacher Guide.)

2. Make חַג שָׂמֵחַ cards for any upcoming Jewish holiday. (See "Judaica Arts and Crafts" on page 150 in this Teacher Guide).

3. Play an *Open-ended Board Game* (see page 143 in this Teacher Guide.)

4. Have *Chalkboard Races* (see page 145 in this Teacher Guide). Call out a simple word ending with the ה and have students race to write it first, with vowels.

LESSON 16

Key Words: (tree of life) עֵץ חַיִּים
(commandments) מִצְוֹת
New Letter: ץ
New Vowel Combination: ו followed by a ▨ (vo) וֹ
New Vocabulary: (school) בֵּית־סֵפֶר (where?) אֵיפֹה?
Special Points: ץ ≠ ע   ץ = צ

Oral Language Lesson (optional)

This is the last lesson in which new vocabulary (other than Key Words) is introduced. Review question words learned in previous lessons and teach the new question word, אֵיפֹה. Practice using this word along with vocabulary learned thus far, especially reinforcing the preposition words בְּ_, עַל, תַּחַת, עַל־יַד, and עִם.

The Seven Lesson Steps:

1. **Review**
Review final letters learned thus far and the צ in preparation for the ץ.

2. **Evoke the New Key Words**
The two Key Words in this lesson and most of the Key Words in the remaining lessons are related to synagogue life. Some may know the melody to the prayer עֵץ חַיִּים. You can sing it together, but they will not be able to read it yet. The phrase עֵץ חַיִּים (literally, tree of life) is what we call the wooden Torah roller, and figuratively, the Torah itself.

Tell students that the second Key Word is the plural form of a Key Word they already know, מִצְוָה. If they are unfamiliar with the term, explain that plural means "more than one." Ask them to guess how we say it. Some may know, being previously familiar with the word, but don't expect them to know that וֹת is a plural ending in Hebrew.

The pictures used on the Introduction Page (page 49) to illustrate מִצְוֹת are the same pictures previously used to depict מִצְוָה. The pictures for עֵץ חַיִּים show both figurative meanings of the expression.

3. **Introduce New Letters and Vowels**
a. Consonant:
Emphasize that the ץ is shaped like a צ but the base has been extended, or stretched out, below the line. Use this opportunity to review the other final letters learned thus far, especially ן and ף that also extend below the line.

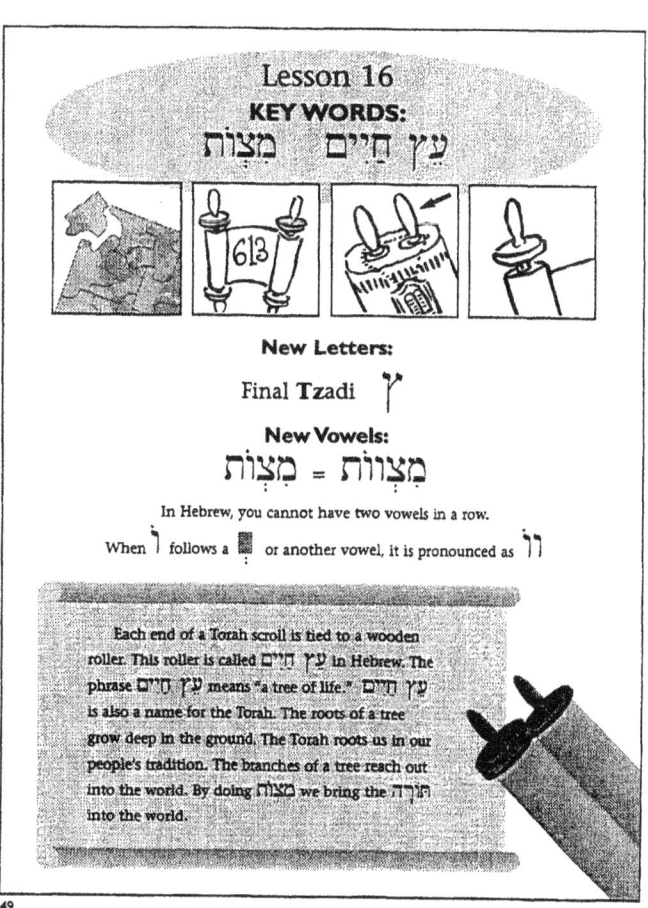

b. Vowel Combination:
Tell students:

"When you see the ו and there is another vowel before it, the ו is not just going to make a vowel sound. Why wouldn't it?" See if students can articulate that, in Hebrew, we never write two vowels in a row. When we want to make two vowel sounds in a row, we put a silent letter in between them. This may be a hard idea for them to realize on their own, in which case you say:

"In Hebrew, we usually can't write two vowels in a row. So, if you see the symbol ו after any vowel, even the ▒, you have to realize it can't be a vowel. It must be the **letter** ו followed by the ▒ vowel."

Teach the rule from page 49, the Introduction Page. Then, show many sample words that both follow and don't follow the rule. This combination is not very prevalent in Hebrew, and מִצְוֹת is really the only word they will read with any frequency that contains it.

Read the entire Introduction Page with students. Ask students to give examples of how doing מִצְוֹת brings Torah into the world.

4. Using the Reading Page

This is a short lesson, with only one Reading Page (page 50), and two concepts that appear fairly infrequently in Hebrew.

The Reading Page reinforces the ץ and reviews the other finals. Notice that the ע, which often gets confused with the ץ, is found on lines 3, 5, and 7, but not in the final position. Remind students that if the letter isn't at the end of the word, it can't possibly be a ץ.

The **vo** sound is drilled on lines 1 and 2, and later lines contain words that look as though they might have the sound, but do not. Remind students of the rule that appears on page 49, the Introduction Page.

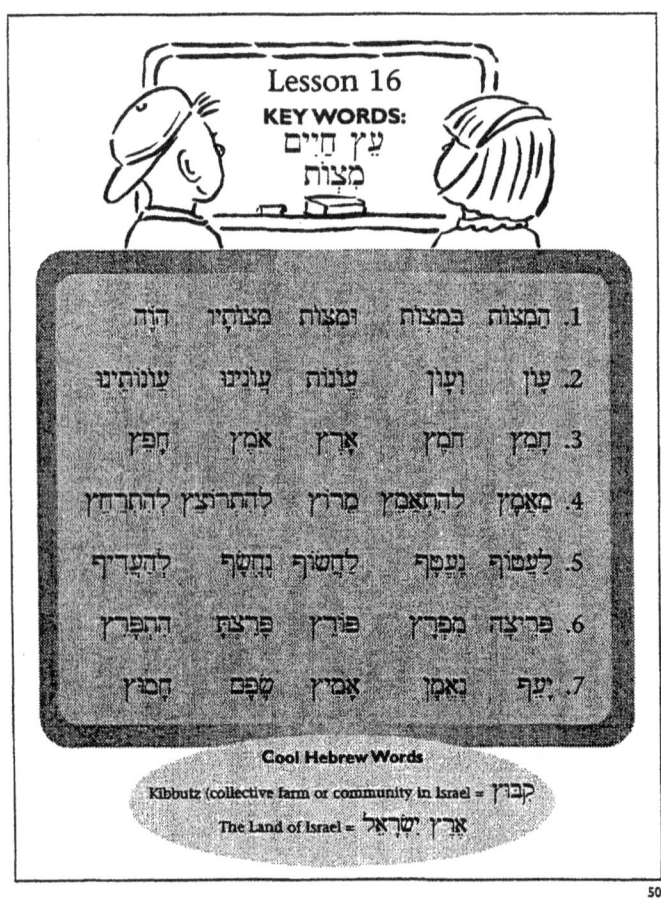

5. Using the Worksheets

Page 51: This page focuses directly on the new letter-vowel combination of וֹ. Read the rule at the top of the page with students and explain the instructions, as students may find the point values confusing.

Students must read the words to determine which of the two on each line has the **vo** sound. Note that on one line the letter and vowel בוֹ make the **vo** sound. All the words on this page are real Hebrew words spelled correctly, though many of them, such as עֵדוֹת (which appears in I Kings 2:3), are obscure. If a student manages correctly to complete the page without actually reading the words, this would demonstrate that he or she has correctly understood the vowel rule.

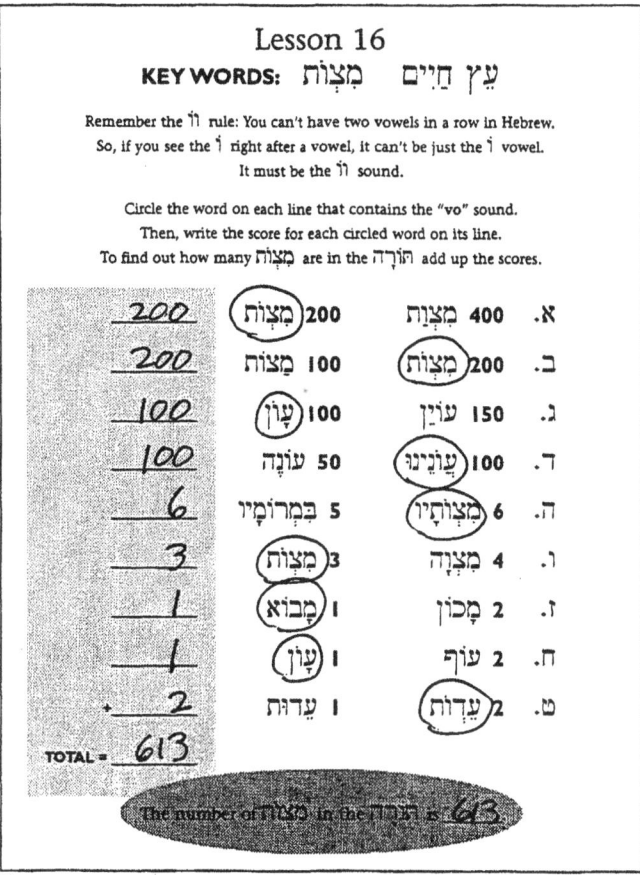

Page 52: Students complete the worksheet. Directions and answers are self-explanatory.

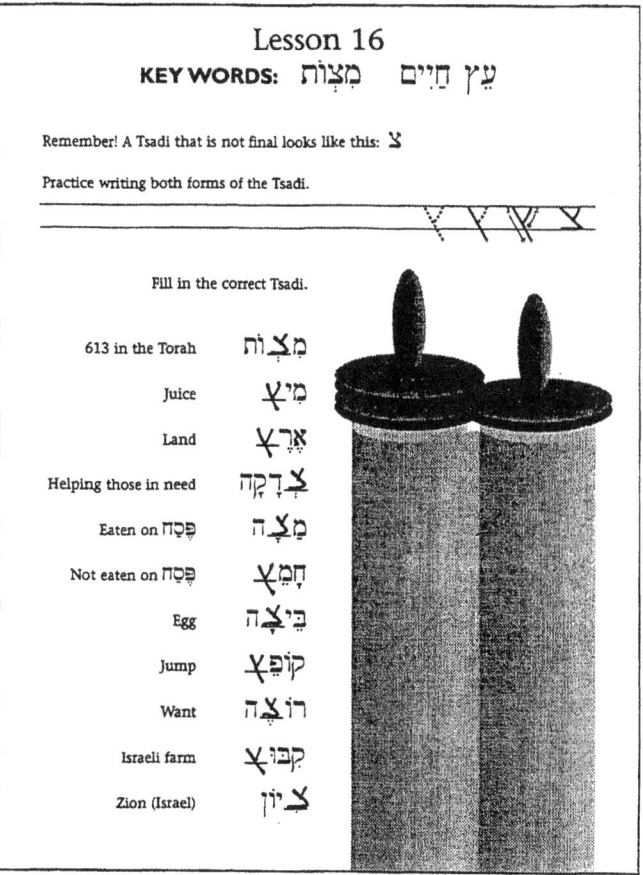

121

Page 53: This page is for students who are doing the language component of the program. Notice that the answers to the questions are not complete sentences. You can have students do a similar activity orally before completing the page independently. Draw an outline of each of the three buildings on the chalkboard. Ask each question as you hold up a picture with the person or object on it. Student volunteers answer each question and stick the picture into the correct building. Back the pictures with double sided tape, blue tack (sticky stuff), or magnetic strips (if your board is magnetic).

Page 54: This page is for students who are doing the language component of the program. This is one of the more challenging vocabulary pages in the Workbook. Before you assign this page, give students practice doing a similar exercise in English. An example in English:

Fill in the blank with who, what, or where.
_____ is the pencil? The pencil is on the desk.

Review the Hebrew question words before you assign this page. Note that מִי was taught in Lesson 5 and מָה in Lesson 6.

6. Prepare for Prayer

This page provides practice in reading phrases from the prayer book and Torah. Line 1 is from the blessing for fruit that grows on trees. Line 2, "from the land of Egypt," appears in many places, as does line 3, "Torah and Mitzvot." Line 4, "a land flowing with milk and honey," comes from the Torah. Lines 5 and 6 are from the "Grace after Meals." Line 7 is from the Yom Kippur service. Line 8 is from the *Adon Olam* prayer.

At the bottom of the page, students are asked to give their own interpretation of the figurative meaning of עֵץ חַיִּים. You can have students make more elaborate drawings on separate pieces of paper and create a bulletin board using as a title the Cool Hebrew Phrase.

7. Evaluate and Remediate

Students can proceed to the next lesson if they are reading accurately in general. The new concepts of this lesson are not found frequently in Hebrew texts.

Suggested Additional Activities

1. Using page 54 in the Workbook, make the following two games:

a. Paste each of the ten questions and answers onto separate index cards, omitting the question word. On a game board, write each question word several times in different boxes, in no particular order. Leave blank spaces between these question words. Place the index cards upside down in a pile. A student takes a card and has to decide which of the question words applies. Student then advances to the first box that contains that word.

b. Use these same cards for a relay game, but back the cards so that they will stick to the chalkboard. Divide the class into two groups. Write the three question words on the board twice (once for each group). Give each group a set of cards, shuffled. Each student goes up to the board and places a card in the correct column.

2. Make *File Folder Houses* (see page 147 in this Teacher Guide). Write the name of each building on each of the envelopes. (Omit the fourth envelope.) Decorate each envelope appropriately. Sort into the proper envelope the questions found on page 48 in the Workbook.

3. *Break the Chain* (see page 142 in this Teacher Guide).

LESSON 17

Key Words: (blessing) בְּרָכָה
(table) שֻׁלְחָן
New Letter: כ
New Vowel: ֻ
Special Points: ֻ = וּ

Oral Language Lesson (optional)

No new vocabulary is introduced. Review the vocabulary that has already been taught and elaborate on it. For this lesson, a review of classroom objects and prepositions would be useful, as they are drilled in the exercise on page 61. Holiday words are used on page 62, so these would also be beneficial to review.

The Seven Lesson Steps:

1. Review
Review the וּ vowel (avoiding the וֹ) as well as the ח, because you will be teaching their sound-alikes in this lesson.

2. Evoke the New Key Words
The first Key Word, בְּרָכָה, will be familiar to most students, possibly in the form בָּרוּךְ. Discuss the concept of blessing.

Students may remember the second Key Word, שֻׁלְחָן, from an earlier lesson, if you taught it orally when students learned classroom vocabulary.

Use the pictures on the Introduction Page, page 56, to introduce the Key Words. Ask students what the children are saying as they prepare to eat, and why.

3. Introduce New Letters and Vowels
Students already know the sounds for this lesson, but need to learn the correct symbols.

a. Consonant:
Only one new letter is taught in this lesson. This letter needs to be reinforced sufficiently, even though it appears infrequently. Students sometimes confuse the כ with the ב and the ם. Therefore, when first introducing it on the felt board, avoid those letters.

A convenient mnemonic for this letter is to take the letter ח and turn it on its side to get a כ. Provide sufficient practice interchanging the two letters that make the **ch** sound. Since students have had so much practice with the ח, they will tend to remember only it, forgetting that there are two letters that make the **ch** sound.

b. Vowel:

The *Kubutz* (ֻ) is used less frequently than other vowels. Teach it in association with the *Shuruk* (וּ), as they both make the same sound. Like the כ and the ח, you want students to associate the two symbols with one sound. Avoid similar looking vowels such as the ִ, ֵ, and the ֶ when first introducing the ֻ. Read the entire Introduction Page with students. Ask students to give examples of celebrations when Jews gather around the שֻׁלְחָן and recite a בְּרָכָה. Students should mention Passover, Shabbat, and perhaps Chanukah.

4. Using the Reading Pages

The first Reading Page (page 57) focuses only on the כ. Initially, the two letters with which כ is most likely to be confused (the ם and the ב) are avoided.

The second Reading Page (page 58) introduces the vowel ֻ and reinforces the וּ. On lines 1-3, ֻ does not appear.

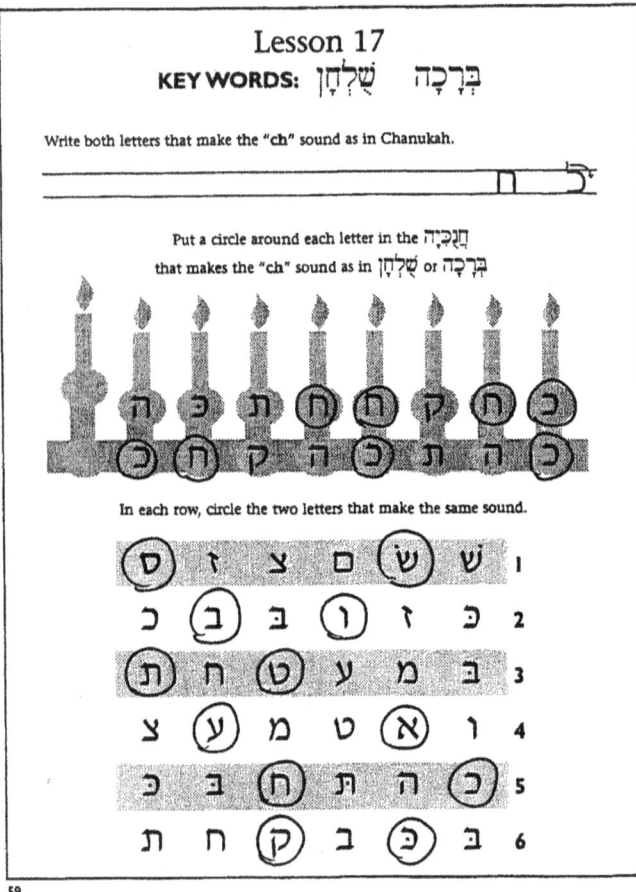

5. Using the Worksheets

Page 59: Students write both letters that make the **ch** sound, to reinforce the association between the two sound-alike symbols. In the חֲנֻכִּיָה, students circle any ח or כ they see. The exercises on this page require students to make fine distinctions between similar sounds and similar letter shapes.

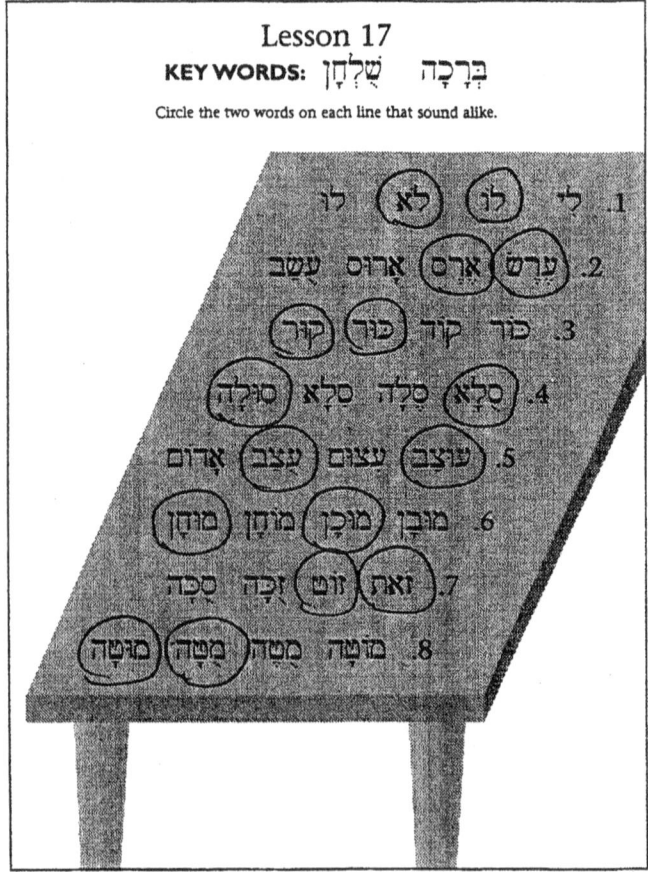

Page 60: This page drills the new vowel, contrasting it with the sound-alike vowel וֹ. All the words on the page are real Hebrew words, though some of them are very obscure. Since students are not reading for meaning, it is only important that what they see conforms to the rules of Hebrew orthography, not that the words are commonly used.

Page 61: This page is for students who are doing the language component of the program. The top of the page requires only knowledge of vocabulary. However, the bottom exercise requires good comprehension. If the page seems too difficult for your students, work on it in small groups or together with the whole class.

Page 62: Review the names of the holidays and their symbols before you assign this page. Students who don't enjoy word searches do not need to complete the puzzle.

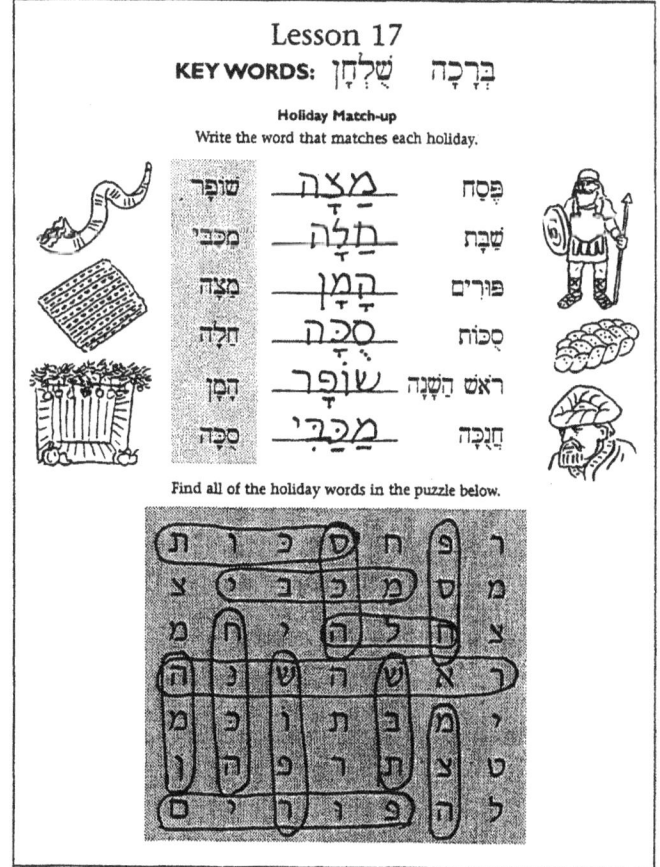

6. Prepare for Prayer

Page 63: If your students are reading without errors and you are concerned about finishing the program by the end of the school year, you may want to read only part of this page. In this case, have students read line 7 only. Ask them to find each of this lesson's Key Words in the sentence. Students doing the language component of this program will also know the word בַּבַּיִת (in the house) and may be able to recognize וְעַל (and on). The sentence is from the "Grace after Meals" and means, "May the Merciful One send us abundant blessing in this house and on this table upon which we have eaten."

7. Evaluate and Remediate

Make sure students are not confusing the כ with the ס or the ב.

Suggested Additional Activities

1. *Connect-4* (see page 142 in this Teacher Guide).

2. Play *Go Fish* (see page 144 in this Teacher Guide) using the holiday words on page 62 and an additional two words for each holiday.

3. Play *Charades* (see page 145 in this Teacher Guide). Use the classroom vocabulary from page 61 in the Workbook.

LESSON 18

Key Words: (king, ruler) מֶלֶךְ
                                (alive) חַי

New Letter: ךְ

New Vowel Combination: יִ   יַ

Special Points: יִ ≠ יֵ ≠ יַ   ךְ = כ   ךְ ≠ ך

Oral Language Lesson (optional)

Review the vocabulary that appears on page 70. Other than ‎_ו, which means "and," all the words on page 70 are nouns. Since students are learning their last Hebrew letter in this lesson, do an activity with the alphabet. Starting with א, have students see if they know a word that begins with each letter. With some letters, they may know many words; you can keep track of the letter for which they remember the most words. Allow them to look in the dictionary in the back of the Workbook before you start the game, but not while you are playing.

The Seven Lesson Steps:

1. **Review**
Review the כ, as you will be teaching its final form in this lesson.

2. **Evoke the New Key Words**
Students may know this lesson's Key Words from a variety of sources. Many students may be familiar with the song that appears at the bottom of the Reading Page on page 66, "דָּוִד מֶלֶךְ יִשְׂרָאֵל, חַי וְקַיָּם." Play a tape of the song or sing it to the class. Focus on the meaning of the words, as both of this lesson's Key Words, and the Key Word יִשְׂרָאֵל from Lesson 11, are in the song. Students may also know מֶלֶךְ from blessings they can say. Tell them that after this lesson, they will finally know enough Hebrew to be able to read most blessings. They may know the word חַי from the חַי necklaces that are worn, or some students may make the connection to the Key Word עֵץ חַיִּים. Another connection is the word לְחַיִּים, although this is an association adults are more likely to make.

3. **Introduce New Letters and Vowels**
a. Consonant:
In the last lesson you taught the regular כ. Now teach its final form. Reinforce the visual similarity between the two forms of the letters. Try the following: Tell students that כ has a final form. Ask: "How do you think the final form of כ may look?" By now, they may be able to generalize that most final letters are basically just extended versions of the regular letter.

b. Vowel Combination:
In this lesson you will be teaching two vowel-letter combinations. The first is the יַ combination. Give students the following hint for pronunciation: Start pronouncing this combination as if it is just a ַ sound, and then elongate it by adding the y sound as in "my." (Clearly this is an oversimplified technique). Note that in Hebrew this combination is problematic only at the end of a word. When students read the יַ combination in the middle of a word, as in the words בַּיִת or חַיִּים, they quite naturally make the **eye** sound; it is only at the end of the word that the correct pronunciation is not intuitive. Thus, without instruction, students might read the word סִינַי as "**See-nah**," or "**See-nay**." When initially introducing the יַ combination, avoid the יֵ and יִ combinations, as they can be confused.

The יִ combination is also taught in this lesson. Logically, this combination should have been introduced when the ִ was introduced,

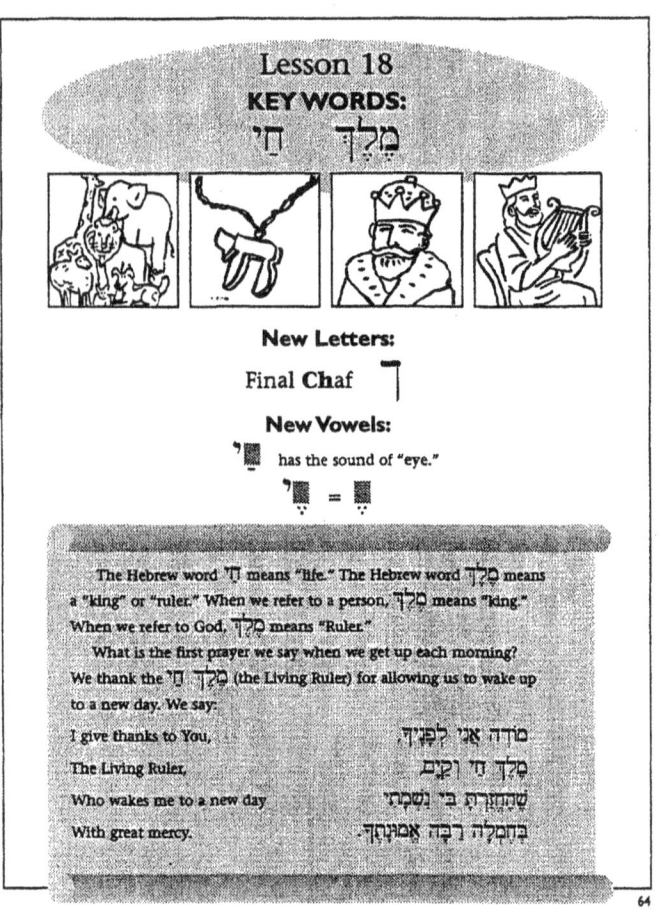

since it makes the **exact** same sound as the ◌ֶ and the ◌ַ. However, the ◌ֶי combination most often appears before the ךָ, which is introduced now in Lesson 18. To have introduced the ◌ֶי without ever practicing it would have been pointless; thus the introduction takes place now. So as to prevent students from confusing the ◌ֶי with the ◌ַי, it is recommended that you only casually mention the ◌ֶי sound. Tell students:

"The ◌ֶי sounds just like the ◌ַ." Then, devote most of your drilling to the ◌ַי sound.

4. Using the Reading Pages

The first Reading Page (page 65) offers practice in reading the ךָ and the ◌ַי. The first line has words with the ךְ, while the second line has the same words spelled with a ךָ. Tell students that these are by far the most common forms in which this final letter appears.

Line 4 provides practice with all of the extended final letters. Note that both the regular and final forms appear in each of these words. Lines 5 through 7 are forms of words from the same root.

The second Reading Page (page 66) begins with three lines that feature the י◌ combination, without drilling the ׳◌. Line 4 has samples of the ׳◌ combination only, and by the end of the page, all the vowel combinations are reintroduced and used together.

Lines 6 and 7 contain mostly names of God. Call students' attention to the pronunciation of אֲדֹנָי and יְיָ.

5. Using the Worksheets

Page 67: Students write three forms of the כ, to reinforce the association between the final and non-final forms. The exercise below directly focuses on vowel sounds, especially the vowel combinations. Students check the column that lists the ending sound of each Hebrew word.

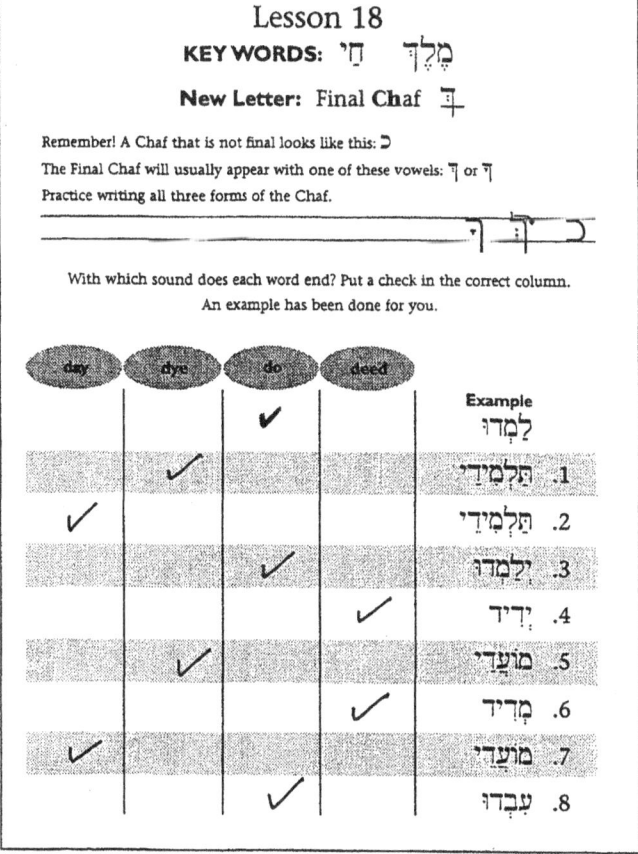

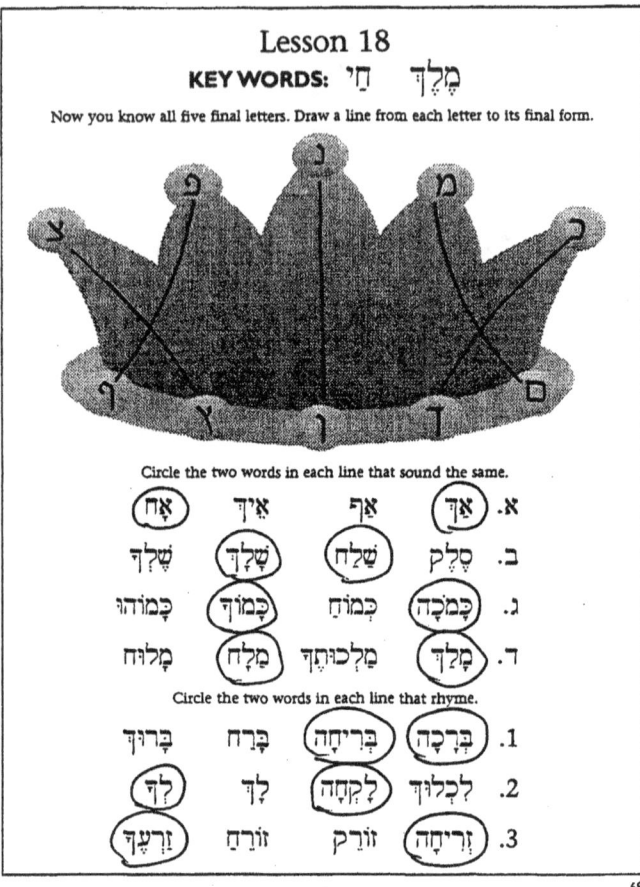

Page 68: The exercise at the top of the page reviews the five final letter forms, as students have now learned all final letters. The exercise at the bottom of the page requires students to pay close attention to pronunciation. Note that the first four questions ask students to find words that sound exactly the same, while the last three require students to find the rhyming words. Two words are considered to rhyme if they end in the same vowel and consonant sounds.

Page 69: This page provides practice filling in either the regular or final form of letters that have both forms.

Page 70: Students now know every Hebrew letter in every form (the last two lessons introduce only vowels). Congratulate them! Hang an *alef-bet* chart in the class and teach an *alef-bet* song. Students completing the language component of the program will complete the top half of the activity, but all students can fill in the chart at the bottom. Note that final forms and letters with and without a *dagesh* are all considered to be one letter. For example, פ, פ, and ף are one letter, not three.

6. Text Reading

Page 71: Now that students have learned the ךּ, they can read these Shabbat blessings. Bring into class the objects required for the blessings: candles, grape juice, and bread or *challah*. Conduct a short *Kabbalat Shabbat* ceremony.

7. Evaluate and Remediate

If students are reading accurately, but without fluency, use ideas found in "Games and Other Activities" on pages 142 and 143 in this Teacher Guide.

Suggested Additional Activities

1. *Illustrated Letter Cards* (see page 150 in this Teacher Guide). If you have not been preparing these cards all along, assign each student a letter to prepare now.

2. Show students prayers that are written as acrostics with lines in alphabetical order, e.g., אֵשֶׁת חַיִל or אַשְׁרֵי.

3. *Speed Reading* (see page 142 in this Teacher Guide).

4. Play *Bingo* to review vocabulary (see page 144 in this Teacher Guide).

5. *Human Tic-tac-toe* (see page 146 in this Teacher Guide).

133

LESSON 19

Key Words: (with all your soul) בְּכָל נַפְשְׁךָ
New Vowels: ָ ְָ = וֹ = ָ (Kamatz Katan as in כָּל)
Special Points: כָּל = כּוֹל

Oral Language Lesson (optional)

This step is not necessary in this lesson.

The Seven Lesson Steps:

1. Review
Review the silent medial *Shva* (Lesson 9) and initial voiced *Shva* (Lesson 14) before you teach the two *Shvas* in a row.

2. Evoke the New Key Word(s)
Students who know how to chant the prayer וְאָהַבְתָּ will have heard these Key Words. To put these words in context, say the prayer. Discuss the meaning of the prayer and its place in the worship service. Read the story on the Introduction Page, page 72.

3. Introduce New Letters and Vowels
When teaching the *Kamatz Katan* (as in כָּל) do not explain any rule governing its pronunciation, just provide practice reading words in which it appears. Tell students that whenever they see these words, they will have to remember how to read them. For extra practice read the וְאָהַבְתָּ prayer in a *Siddur* after you have taught the double *Shva*. Have students read those words which have a *Kamatz Katan*. In some prayer books the *Kamatz Katan* looks different from the regular *Kamatz*, as is explained on the Introduction Page.

By this time, students may intuit how to pronounce the double *Shva*. They might apply the rule that a *Shva* after a consonant is silent and then realize that the second one must be voiced just like the initial *Shva*. See if students can figure this out themselves. Use an easy word, such as נִגְמְרוּ or נִשְׁמְרוּ.

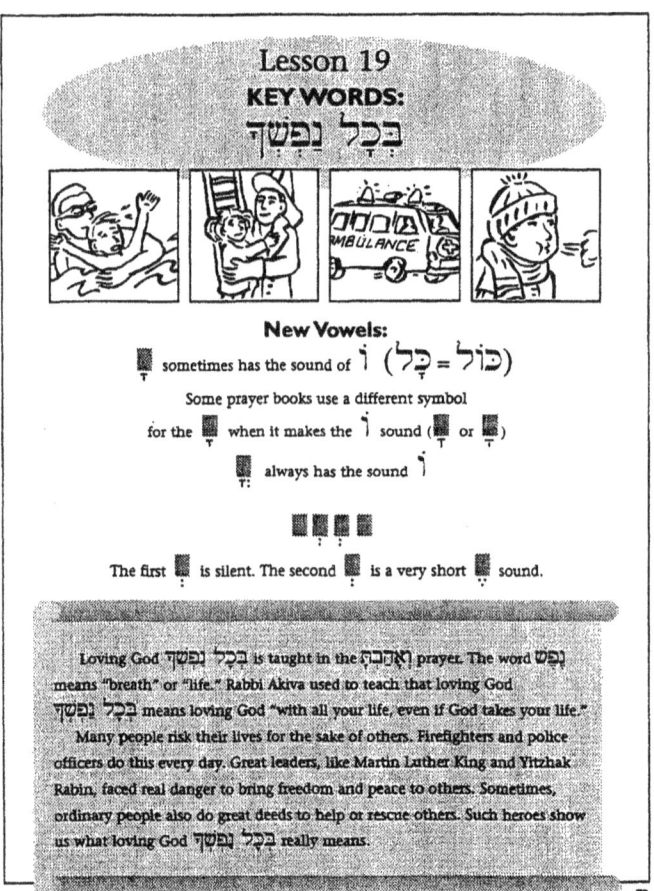

4. Using the Reading Page

On the Reading Page (page 73), every *Kamatz* is a *Kamatz Katan* and pronounced similar to וֹ.

5. Using the Worksheets

Page 74: This page reviews the *Kamatz Katan* sound. Remind students that the instructions state that each word contains only one vowel that makes the וֹ sound. Thus, in a word containing both the וֹ and the ָ, the ָ must make the **ah** sound.

Page 75: This page requires students to classify cognates.

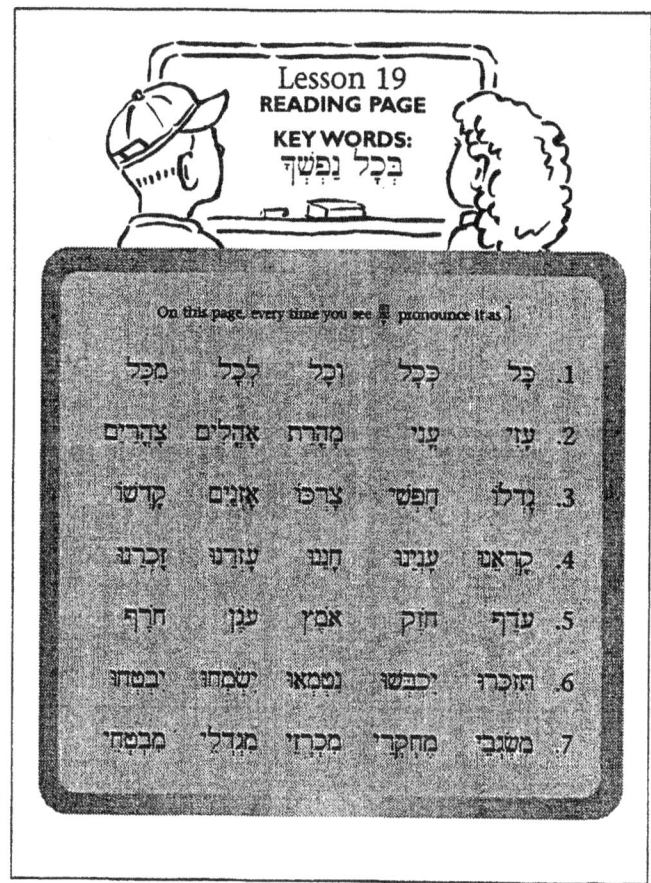

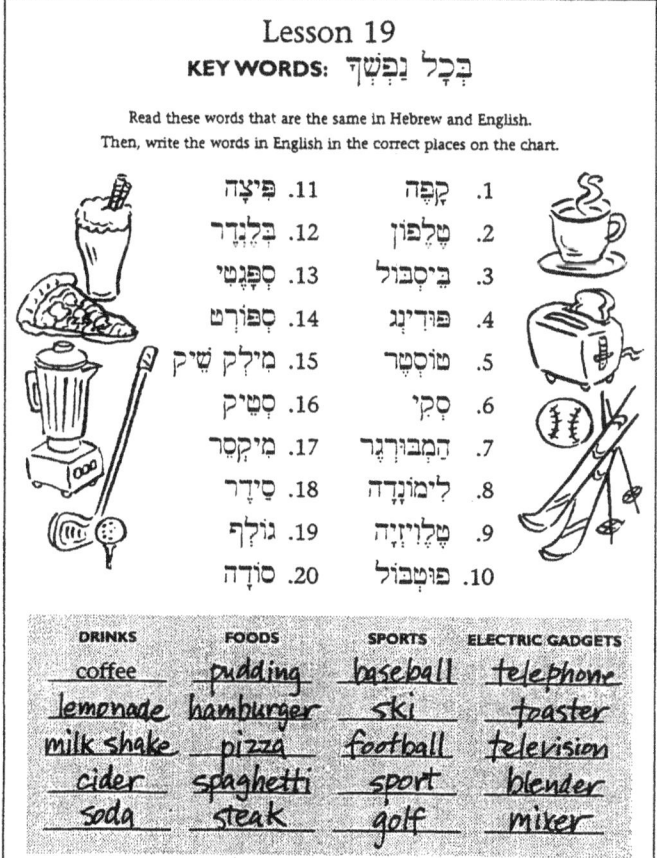

Page 76: This page is for students completing the language component of the program. Students must write a caption for the seventh picture.

6. Text Reading

Page 77: Rather than a prayer passage, this lesson concludes with Israel's National Anthem, הַתִּקְוָה. The text was included in this lesson because it includes two examples of the *Kamatz Katan*.

7. Evaluate and Remediate

Do not be overly concerned with mispronunciation of the *Kamatz Katan*, since it does not appear in many words.

If the students are having difficulty with the double *Shva*, it is probably because they have not yet internalized the rules about reading the *Shva* in other combinations. In this case, first review the silent medial *Shva*, then the voiced initial *Shva*. For some of your students this may be their last evaluation, since the material evaluated in Lesson 20 is very sophisticated. If you feel you need a more comprehensive evaluation in order to pinpoint special problems from all of these lessons, use the Placement Test on page 163 in this Teacher Guide.

Suggested Additional Activities

1. Students should now be ready to read almost any text. Choose an unfamiliar, short, but important prayer to read from the *Siddur*. Explain that there are extra markings in the *Siddur* that should be ignored for now.

2. *Climb the Ladder* (see page 143 in this Teacher Guide).

3. *Floor Board Game* (see page 146 in the Teacher Guide). Play just for fun.

LESSON 20

Key Words: (nation) גוֹי (Moses) מֹשֶׁה
New Vowel Combination: וֹי   שׁ ("double-duty dot")

Oral Language Lesson (optional)

This step is not necessary in this lesson.

The Seven Lesson Steps:

1. **Review**
Use review time to go over any remaining trouble spots.

2. **Evoke the New Key Word(s)**
Students may know the name of Moses in Hebrew from Lesson 4, in which the two Key Words were related to Passover. If they know the second Key Word, גוֹי, it may have a negative connotation as a word for a non-Jew. As the story on page 78, the Introduction Page, explains, the word actually means "nation." Sing the song "לֹא יִשָּׂא גוֹי" as part of the introduction to this lesson, as the song appears on the Reading Page.

3. **Introduce New Letters and Vowels**
The word מֹשֶׁה has a dot which serves a dual purpose. However, students by now are pretty sophisticated Hebrew decoders and can often figure such nuances out for themselves. See the Reading Page on page 79, lines 1 and 2, for other such words.
וֹי, which occurs infrequently, is easy to pronounce.

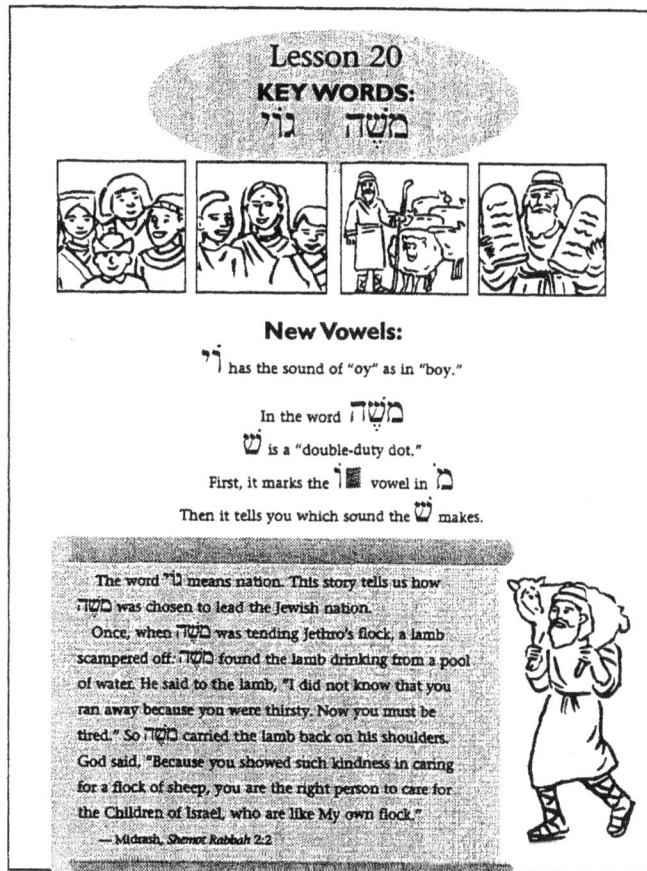

4. Using the Reading Pages

This Reading Page (page 79) has fewer individual words than usual, but two lengthy phrases which contain the Key Words.

Lines 1 and 2 focus on the dual purpose dot, lines 3 and 4 on the וֹ combination.

The next to last word on line 5 has the distinction of being the longest word in the Torah, while the last word on line 5 is the longest word in the Workbook. Neither of these words is particularly difficult to read. Students get a big kick out of reading them.

5. Using the Worksheets

Page 80: This is a challenging page that tests student mastery of the vowels. You may need to complete the page together with your students.

Page 81: This page drills the double duty dot. Remind students that the only purpose of the letter they circle is to help them answer the riddle at the bottom of the page; the letters have no relationship to the words they read.

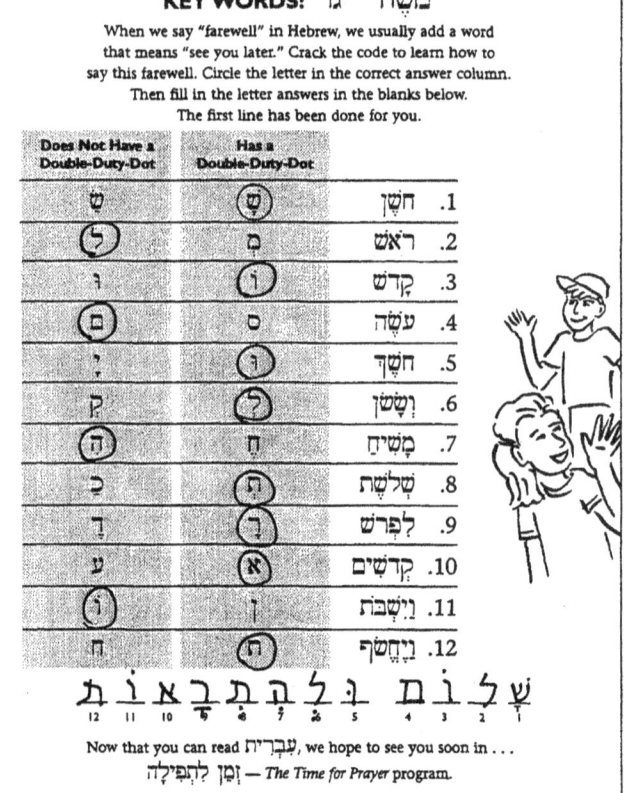

Pages 82, 83, and 88: All students should complete these worksheets as a review of the entire program.

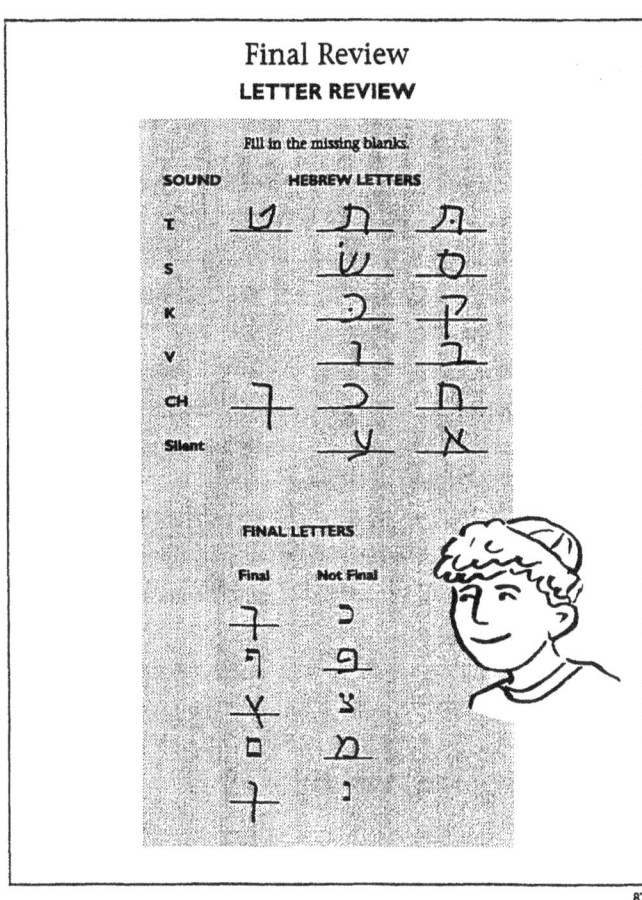

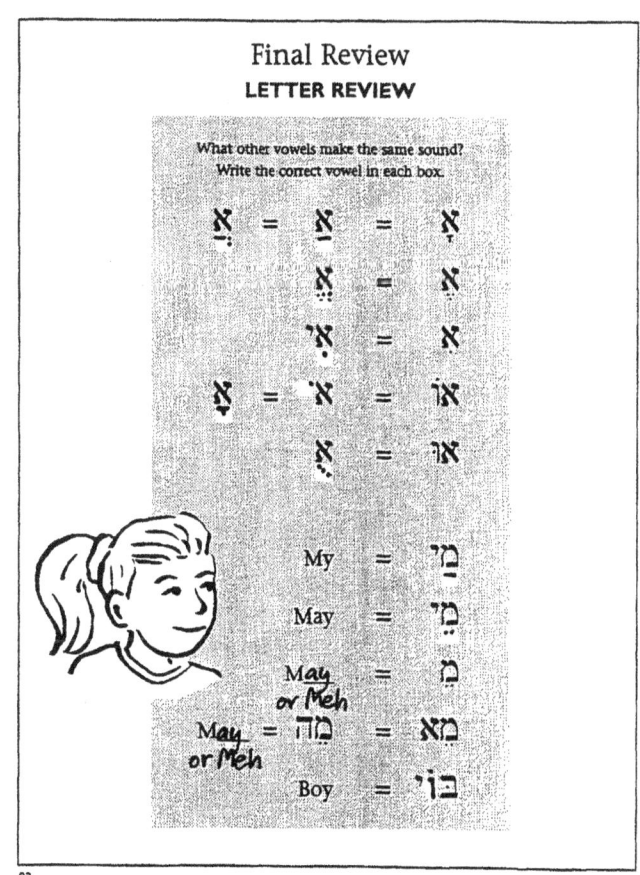

6. **Prepare for Prayer**

The Prepare for Prayer activity appears on the Reading Page, page 79. Explain the context of each quote to students.

The first phrase is one of the best known visions of a messianic age. Written by the prophet Isaiah, who lived in Jerusalem during the Assyrian conquest in the eighth century B.C.E., it gives us hope that one day people will neither learn nor experience war. Rather, they will live together in peace. It is interesting to note that in Akkadian, an ancient language related to Hebrew, the word *lamadu* means "experience." Thus, Isaiah's prophecy is all the more profound, as he envisions a world in which people will never suffer the consequences of armed conflict.

The second quote comes from the book of Leviticus and serves as the introduction to the "Holiness Code," a list of the מִצְוֹת that define living a truly sanctified life.

7. **Evaluate and Remediate**

The evaluation for this lesson primarily tests the most difficult and infrequent combinations. Students who can pass this evaluation are very sophisticated Hebrew decoders. Test only students who can read the Reading Page accurately.

Suggested Additional Activities

1. Use the dictionary (on pages 86 and 87 in the Workbook) as review or as a quiz for advanced students. (The numbers in parentheses correspond to the lesson in which the word first appears.)

2. *Illustrated Dictionary* (see page 150 in this Teacher Guide). If your class has been working on this group project, photocopy it and send it home with students.

3. Congratulations! You have now completed זְמַן לִקְרֹא and your students should be able to open any Hebrew text with vowels and read to you. Have a wonderful party!

GAMES AND OTHER ACTIVITIES

Games, dramatic play, arts and crafts, and other like activities are very effective for learning and review. Such activities can make the necessary repetition of words, sentences, and Reading Pages enjoyable for students. Reciting Hebrew aloud to others is less embarrassing in the context of a game.

Most of the games suggested here can be adapted to teach a variety of concepts, and can also be adapted to involve students who have differing levels of ability. You will find that certain of these games are recommended for particular lessons. These recommendations are merely suggestions. Try out several kinds of games with your students to find out which work best in your class and which your students like most. Use most often the games that are effective for your students. Competitive games with winners and losers can be exciting and keep interest high. But if winning becomes too important, the anxiety level will be also very high. Create situations in which everyone feels they have a chance to win, and in which each student's participation makes a difference. This can be accomplished by having teams play rather than individuals.

Whenever possible, have students participate in both the planning and the making of a game. This will increase students' personal involvement, and is in itself often a learning experience. Keep a supply of game making materials on hand and monitor legibility and neatness. Game making is a good enrichment activity for students who have completed their work.

Basic Materials

The following materials can be used in many games and activities that will be described in this section.

Flash Cards

3" high poster cards printed on card stock are available through A.R.E. Publishing, Inc., for both the Key Words and the Vocabulary Words. If you have two sets, children can play *Concentration*.

You can also make your own cards, if you need cards of a different size or want to include cards with the English translations of the words. In this case, make sure that the letters are large and clear and that cards are thick enough so that writing cannot be seen from the back. You can photocopy the words from the book and enlarge them several times. Or, use large rub-on letters. Or, carefully draw the letters freehand or with a stencil using a dark marker. You can also make sets for each student on index cards. These can be stored on a ring or in a file box.

Kadimah Cards

These cards, available through A.R.E. Publishing, Inc., feature each letter taught in the pre-primer *Kadimah!* and a picture of its corresponding Key Word. Each of these Key Words also appears in this program, either as a Key Word, as vocabulary, or as a cognate. The set includes only initial consonants.

Use the cards to drill the entire class or individuals. Each picture is hidden by a flap. Hold the card closed and have students guess what the picture hidden inside is. Run through the entire set of cards for the letters students have learned. This activity reinforces both the new vocabulary and the new letter sounds.

Hebrew/English Letter Cards

Make several sets of cards with Hebrew letters on them. These can be used for games and by individual students who are having difficulty remembering letter sounds. At the end of this Teacher Guide, you will find a complete set of Hebrew letters and vowels. These may be duplicated onto card stock. Write the English letter equivalent on the back of each card, or have each student do this. You can send these cards home with students who are not retaining letter sounds. They can be used by the student even if no one at home knows Hebrew. In the classroom use the letter cards for drilling, for *Open-Ended Board Games* (see page 143), or for *Around the World* (see page 146).

Picture File

Develop a file of magazine pictures that illustrate Key Words, vocabulary, or cognates taught in this program. Mount and laminate the pictures to protect them. Look for colorful and humorous pictures and file them by lesson or by topic. (See page 9 in this Teacher Guide for the Sequence Chart.)

Reading Games

The following games are for phonetic reading. No vocabulary knowledge is required.

Connect-4
Materials: A few blank overhead transparencies or laminated Reading Pages, several non-permanent markers.
Number of Players: 2 or more
Purpose: Reading review
Instructions: When two are playing, place a blank overhead transparency over a Reading Page or laminate the sheet. Each student has a non-permanent marker in a different color. The object is to read four words in a straight line correctly, somewhat like *Tic-tac-toe*. Students take turns reading single words starting anywhere on the page and circle their word after it is read correctly. A good strategy is to start from the middle, and try to get three in a row correct, with the option of adding another word at either end. The student who can "Connect-4" is the winner. Wipe off the plastic with a damp sponge or paper towel and start over.

When the entire class is playing, project onto a screen a Reading Page that was photocopied on a transparency. Divide the class into two teams and have them take turns responding. This game allows you to have children reread the identical Reading Page several times without becoming bored. Notice that you cannot play this game with Lessons 1, 9, and 20, since you need Reading Pages with five columns of words.

Speed Reading
Materials: Stop watch
Number of Players: Any number
Purpose: Fluency (once accuracy is acquired)
Instructions: There are basically two ways to play. You can set the amount of time (preferably 30 seconds) and have student(s) read as many words as possible within that time. It is best to assign line numbers for this version of the game. You can also have students read a certain column, row, or section in the least amount of time possible. Reading by columns gives students an opportunity to read words of different levels of difficulty. This method of reading is also more fair when groups are competing, since the columns are generally of equal difficulty. When working with groups, number the columns 1 to 5 and divide the class into 2 to 5 groups (depending on class size). Each group reads one column, and each student should have at least one word to read. Through working in groups, more skilled readers can help those who are less skilled. Encourage groups to beat their own record, as well as the record of the other groups.

Break the Chain
Materials: None
Number of Players: 2 or more
Purpose: Reading accuracy and listening skills
Instructions: Seat students so that they can hear each other well. Decide on a particular order in which they will read. Each student plays "teacher" for the student who will be reading next, and earns a point by detecting an error. Decide who reads the first word, and make sure students know who their "teacher" is. If the word is read correctly (or an error is not detected), no points are awarded, unless a third student detects the error. Thus, students are encouraged to listen carefully and to pay atten-

tion while other children are reading. Furthermore, since points are given for detecting errors, less skilled students have an opportunity to be winners. Continue reading until one student gets a predetermined number of points.

Climb the Ladder
Materials: Seven rung ladder drawn on the chalkboard (or paper), marker for each student or team (use game token, magnet, or paper stick figure)
Number of Players: 2 or more
Purpose: Reading accuracy
Instructions: On the board or on paper, draw a ladder with seven rungs. Assign each child a column to read. A marker is used to indicate the highest level reached. The goal is for students to read correctly as many words as possible, and to try to beat their own record. Each child reads in turn. For each word read correctly, the child advances one rung. His/her marker remains in place until his/her next turn. For each successive round, students begin at the bottom of the ladder and try to climb higher than they did during the previous rounds. In large groups play with two teams.

Hot Potato
Materials: Stopwatch that beeps or kitchen timer
Number of Players: 5 or more
Purpose: Reading accuracy, fluency, attention to task
Instructions: Seat students in a circle. Set the timer for at least one minute. Going around the circle, students take turns reading one word at a time. A student's turn is over only when the word has been read correctly. When the timer goes off, the student who is reading is out. Continue until one student remains. Vary the length of time on the timer each round. It is to the students' advantage to read quickly and not lose their place on the page. But winning also involves luck.

Shva Cubes (for Lesson 9)
Materials: 2 cubes 1" x 1" in 2 different colors, a 3 minute egg timer, glue to paste on the following word parts:

Cube Two		Cube One	
מָר	חָל	מֹשׁ	פּוּנ
קָן	מָד	גַּל	נִל
וָד	תָּם	קוֹל	צִנ

Number of players: 2–4
Purpose: Practice reading silent medial *Shva* words
Making the game: Paste all the word Hebrew parts for Cube One, above, onto the first cube and word Hebrew parts for Cube Two, above, onto the second cube.
Instructions: The object of the game is to read as many words as possible formed from the two cubes in three minutes (shorten to one minute if necessary). One student tosses the cubes, reads the combinations, and continues to do so until time runs out. The "winner" is the student who reads the most words correctly during the allotted time. Make sure students read the syllable ending in a *Shva* first.

Card and Board Games

The games in this section can be adapted to review either phonics or vocabulary. All involve some advance preparation.

Open-ended Board Game
Materials: Game board (teacher/student made or purchased at a teachers' supply store), question cards, markers, and rules for advancing
Number of Players: 2 or more
Making the game: If you are preparing your own

board, laminate or cover it with clear Contact Paper. Mark the board with colors, Hebrew letters, etc., to match the method of advancing on the board. Questions can be letter recognition, phonetic reading, vocabulary translation, etc. The board is "open-ended" because any subject matter can be drilled. If you want children to be able to play the game without the teacher, fold index cards, write the questions on the outside and the answers inside. Place the cards in a pile with the question side face down. Students take turns selecting cards.

Students especially enjoy playing games they have made themselves. Encourage them to incorporate Hebrew or Judaica for the themes of their game boards (for example, a *Flying To Israel* game with the starting point as the city in which they live and the final destination Ben-Gurion airport). The board can have illustrations of the students' city and of Israel.

Instructions: The object of these games is to reach the end of the path. Children advance, after responding correctly to a question card, by spinning an arrow, throwing dice, or picking a Hebrew letter card.

Bingo

Materials: Bingo boards, markers (dry beans, buttons, colored chips), 16 3" x 5" index cards
Number of Players: 2 or more
Making the game: Give students a piece of paper with 16 blank squares, four to a row. On each of 16 index cards, write a vocabulary word in Hebrew. Each student prepares his/her own board, drawing in pictures (or pasting a photocopy) of the 16 vocabulary items. Pictures should be placed in different positions on the boards.
Instructions: The teacher or a student picks an index card and reads the item. Each student places a marker on his/her board in the matching spot. The winner is the first one with a complete line of markers running in any direction. The winner can then read the index cards for the next round.

Go Fish

Materials: 28-40 Teacher prepared cards
Number of Players: 2 to 3
Preparing the Game: The teacher should prepare the cards for this game, as it involves a lot of writing. For vocabulary review, prepare a deck of cards with vocabulary words divided into up to ten categories (e.g., people, foods, classroom objects, etc.), so that for each category there are four cards. Each card should have on the top the category name (usually in English) and four words in that particular category. Highlight a different word on each card and, if desired, illustrate it with a drawing or picture. The זְמַן לִקְרֹא *Activity Book* contains a complete game set of *Go Fish* cards which can be cut out and used to play.
Instructions: Each player is dealt seven cards. The object of the game is to be left without any cards by putting down all your cards on the table in complete sets of four. The game begins with all players laying down any sets of four they already have. The player with a complete set of four must accurately read the four words on his/her cards. One player begins by asking the other for a certain card, beginning with the category and then indicating the specific item within the category. If the other player has it, he/she gets it and can take another turn, if not the player must "go fish," i.e., draw a card from the deck. If this card is what the player asked for, he/she gets another turn. If this card completes the set, it is laid down and the first player goes again.

When the first player does not get what he/she asks for or does not complete a set, the second player has a turn. The game continues until one of the players is left with no cards. Advanced students can play the game in Hebrew by asking יֵשׁ לְךָ? or יֵשׁ לְךְ?.

Memory/Concentration

Materials: Teacher or student prepared cards
Number of Players: 2 to 3
Preparing the game: Prepare six to 12 pairs of cards. A pair consists of two items that are to be matched. Examples of matches: a cognate card and a Hebrew letter (corresponding to the initial sound), or a Hebrew vocabulary word and its

English translation. Make sure the cards are of the same size and color and that the writing cannot be seen through them.
Instructions: Place the cards face down on the table in neat rows. The first player turns over one card and then turns over another to find its match. If a match is found, the player takes both cards off the table and gets another turn. If not, the cards are turned face down again in the same spots, and the next player gets to turn two cards over. The game continues until all the cards have been matched. The winner is the player with the most matches. This game format allows you to review practically any content and, in addition, strengthens memory and attention.

Charades
Materials: Cards with instructions
Number of Players: Small or large groups
Preparing the game: Prepare two sets of eight to twelve cards with a sentence that can be acted out, for example, sentences with prepositions. The following is a list of sentences that are appropriate for Lesson 17:

הַמַחְבֶּרֶת עַל הַסֵפֶר.
הָעִפָּרוֹן עַל הַכִּסֵא.
הַכֶּלֶב תַחַת הַשֻלְחָן.
הַסֵפֶר עַל-יַד הָעִפָּרוֹן.
הָעִפָּרוֹן בַּמַחְבֶּרֶת.
הָעִפָּרוֹן תַחַת הַסֵפֶר.
הַמַחְבֶּרֶת וְהָעִפָּרוֹן בַּסֵפֶר.
הָעִפָּרוֹן וְהַסֵפֶר עַל הַכִּסֵא.
הַסֵפֶר עַל-יַד הַשֻלְחָן.
הַנֵר בַּסֵפֶר.

Instructions: Turn one set of cards upside down. One student picks a card and, without showing anyone, acts out the sentence on the card. The other students look through the other set of cards and have to guess which card was acted out.

Chalkboard Games

The games in this section are played using the chalkboard or wipeboard. They can be used to practice phonics or language.

Chalkboard Races
Materials: זְמַן לִקְרֹא *Key Word Poster Cards* or *Vocabulary Poster Cards*
Number of Players: 2 or more
Purpose: Vocabulary review, practice writing the Key Words
Instructions: Divide the class into two teams. Pick one student from each team, making sure to pick two children who are evenly matched in ability. Ask one question to both students. The first student who correctly writes or draws the answer wins that round. Students can be asked to spell a Key Word or a vocabulary word, or to illustrate a word or phrase from a flash card that you show to both students. Award a point to the student who answers the question first, then choose another pair of students to compete.

Chalkboard Tic-tac-toe
Materials: זְמַן לִקְרֹא *Key Word Poster Cards* or *Vocabulary Poster Cards*
Number of Players: 2 or more
Purpose: Vocabulary review, reading practice
Instructions: Draw a large *Tic-tac-toe* board on the blackboard. This version of the game provides you with many options. You can tape letters, words, sentence cards, or pictures onto the chalkboard. To qualify to place an "X" or an "O" on a spot, students may be asked to read, translate, act out, use a word in a sentence, etc.

Jeopardy
Materials: Prepared questions
Number of Players: 2 students, or teams of 2 or more
Purpose: Vocabulary or reading review
Instructions: Create four to six categories: Foods (*challah, matzah,* wine, fish); Greetings (*mazal tov, shalom,* excuse me, please); Religious Objects (*Torah, yad, aytz chayim, kipah*); Words with medial *Shva*; Words with unusual vowel combinations, etc.

For each category write four questions, each of increasing difficulty, and each worth 1, 2, 5, or 10 points. For example, for a Jewish vocabulary category, use the following statements.

(1 point) The special day that begins every Friday night

(2 points) The special bread we eat on Shabbat

(5 points) What we call the blessing over the wine

(10 points) The four Hebrew letters on a *dreidel*

Preparing the Jeopardy board: Write the categories across the board with possible points listed underneath. For example:

Shva Words	Food	Holidays	בַּבַּיִת	בַּכִּתָּה
1	1	1	1	1
2	2	2	2	2
5	5	5	5	5
10	10	10	10	10

Divide students into two teams. Each student chooses a category and point value and the teacher asks a question. As each point value is chosen and answered, erase it. Continue until all questions have been chosen.

Action Games

The games in this section involve the entire class and include physical activity. They provide a welcome alternative to being chair bound after a long school day. These games can be adapted for any content.

Around the World
Materials: זְמַן לִקְרֹא *Key Word Poster Cards* or *Vocabulary Poster Cards*
Number of Players: Entire class
Purpose: Vocabulary review
Instructions: Seat all students in a circle facing in. One student stands outside the circle facing the center, behind a seated student. The object of the game is for one student to move around the circle completely (i.e., move "around the world").

The teacher flashes a card to both the seated and standing student or asks a question of them. If the standing student answers first, he/she moves to stand behind the next student, while the sitting student remains seated. If the sitting student answers first, he/she gets up and starts traveling "around the world," and the standing student sits. The game is over when one student is able to make his/her way around the entire circle ("around the world"). Flash cards can have Hebrew letters, words, sentences, or pictures.

Human Tic-tac-toe
Materials: Masking tape, 5 "X's" and 5 "O's" drawn on construction paper
Number of Players: 10 or more
Purpose: Vocabulary or reading review
Instructions: Place masking tape on the floor in the shape of a *Tic-tac-toe* grid. Prepare "X's" and "O's" on construction paper. Divide the class into two teams and ask questions (reading, vocabulary, etc.). A player who answers correctly chooses the square on which to place an "X" or an "O" and stands in the square holding up the card.

Baseball
Materials: Prepared questions at four levels of difficulty
Number of Players: 8 or more
Purpose: Vocabulary or reading review
Instructions: Each corner of the room becomes a base. Students request a single, double, triple, or home run, which determines the difficulty of the question you ask. Students move around the bases. There are no balls or strikes; three wrong answers and the second team is up. To keep both teams involved, have students prepare questions themselves in advance to "pitch" to the other team. Check the questions to determine their level of difficulty.

Floor Board Game
Materials: Prepared questions or זְמַן לִקְרֹא *Key Word Poster Cards* or *Vocabulary Poster Cards*, 8½" x 11" sheets of paper or card stock
Number of Players: 2 or more
Purpose: Vocabulary or reading review
Instructions: Play an open-ended board game on the floor. For the squares, tape 8½" x 11" sheets of paper or card stock to the floor. Play the game with the entire class divided into teams. One student from each team moves around the board. Let students who need some extra attention be the markers.

Games for Individuals

The following games are designed to be played by individual students. They are all self-checking and require some advance preparation.

File Folder Puzzle

Materials: A file folder, magazine picture, 1 piece 8½" x 11" light colored card stock, scissors, glue
Number of Players: 1 or 2
Purpose: Reading or vocabulary review
Instructions: Find a large amusing or interesting magazine picture (preferably 8½" x 11"). Glue the picture onto a light colored card stock of equal size. Cut the picture into ten pieces each the same size. On the blank side of each piece, write a question (or an item to match). Questions can require reading, translation, or writing.

Take a blank file folder, open it, and reassemble the magazine puzzle (picture upside down). Trace the outline of each piece onto the file folder. Remove the puzzle. On each space you have traced, write the answer to the question asked on the corresponding puzzle piece. Write a game title on the outside of the folder relating to the magazine picture. Inside the folder, staple a Ziploc plastic bag with the puzzle pieces in it. Write the following instructions to students inside the folder:

1. Match each puzzle piece to its correct answer.
2. Close the folder.
3. Carefully turn the folder over.
4. Open the folder and discover . . . (add something that relates to your magazine picture).

File Folder Houses

Materials: 3 or 4 envelopes, file folder
Number of Players: 1 or 2
Purpose: Reading or vocabulary review
Instructions: Open a file folder and glue three or four small envelopes so that index cards can be placed in them. Decorate the envelopes to look like houses (the flaps can become peaked roofs). Write words on index cards for students to sort, and label each "house" accordingly. Categories can be: items found at home, in class, in the synagogue, or Hebrew words with specific letter sounds. Staple a Ziploc plastic bag inside the file folder and write the instruction: "Put each card in its right house."

For variety cut the cards into fish shapes and decorate the envelopes to look like fish bowls, or cut the cards in *challah* shapes and decorate the envelopes as Shabbat tables. To make this a self-checking activity, put a colored dot on the back of each card and write the answer key on the outside back cover of the folder.

Two Piece Puzzles

Materials: Index cards, scissors
Number of Players: 1 or 2
Purpose: Practice in letter sounds, vocabulary or reading review
Instructions: Cut about ten index cards into two pieces. Make the cut shapes unusual. On each piece write items that need to be matched. An example follows:

Students have to find the matching pieces. As an enrichment activity, students can make their own cards.

Computer Index Cards
Materials: Index cards, metal rings, hole punch, notebook reinforcements
Number of Players: 1 or 2
Purpose: Reading practice or vocabulary review
Instructions: On an index card, write a multiple choice question. Below it, punch four holes and write an answer next to each hole. On the back of the card, stick a colored notebook reinforcer around the hole that is next to the correct answer (or just circle the hole with a marker). Prepare a pile of these cards and put them together on a ring (punch another hole in a corner). A student takes a card, reads the question, and places his/her pencil in the hole next to the answer he/she thinks is correct. Then the student turns the card over to see if his/her answer is right. Students play alone or in pairs. The activity does not require a teacher's help. Advanced students may make their own cards.

Spoken Language

While the primary goal of this program is to teach phonetic Hebrew reading, a secondary goal is to teach Hebrew vocabulary. Vocabulary practice should be held in a low-stress environment. Do not force anyone to speak, and instead of correcting errors, repeat what a student says in the correct form.

Listen and Do! (TPR)
For Introducing New Vocabulary:
Materials: Props for vocabulary words you are teaching (i.e., book, notebook, pencil, table, etc.)
Number of Players: Any number
Purpose: Acquiring listening comprehension and oral language skill
Instructions: TPR (Total Physical Response) is a very effective system of foreign language acquisition that can be applied to Hebrew. The teacher describes a situation in Hebrew (without translating) and students demonstrate it. At first, the teacher demonstrates so that the students need only watch, listen, and mimic. As the class becomes familiar with the game, the teacher stops modeling, asks smaller groups to respond, and adds variety and humor. Once students become used to TPR and realize how much fun it can be, they often ask to lead the game themselves, e.g., כִּסֵא עַל גִיר, הַמוֹרָה תַּחַת הַשֻׁלְחָן.

For Reviewing Vocabulary:
Materials: Props for vocabulary words you are teaching
Number of Players: Any number
Purpose: Reviewing vocabulary
Instructions: This is a variation of TPR. It should be used for review of previously learned vocabulary, not for teaching new words. Divide the class into two teams. Have a volunteer from each team come to the front of the room. Give an instruction to both students. The first to complete the instruction earns a point for that team. Then pick two more volunteers. Alternatively, instead of dividing the class into teams, let the student who wins the round compete against a challenger.

Guess That Act!
Materials: Props for vocabulary words
Number of Players: 2 or more
Purpose: Understanding and using oral language
Instructions: This is an advanced language game. Divide the class into two teams. A volunteer from one of the teams comes to the front of the room and the teacher whispers a sentence. The student has to demonstrate the sentence and the other students have to guess what the Hebrew sentence is. The team that guesses correctly first sends another volunteer to act out the next sentence.

Dramatic Play
Materials: Puppets, costumes, props
Number of Players: Any number
Purpose: Understanding and using vocabulary orally
Instructions: There are several conversations in the Workbook (in Lessons 7, 8, 13, and 14) that can be acted out. In addition, you can write other skits using vocabulary that the students have learned. Public speaking, particularly in a foreign language, is less stressful and more amusing when puppets are used. You can either purchase several puppets or have students make them. Use a variety of materials, such as socks, paper bags, cardboard, or Styrofoam. Encourage,

but never force, students to speak. Allow less skilled students to watch and try to understand the Hebrew spoken by more skilled students.

What's Missing?
Materials: 6 to 8 vocabulary objects
Number of Players: Any number
Purpose: Reviewing vocabulary orally
Instructions: Put out on a table six to eight objects that students can name in Hebrew. Review the names of the items. One student goes out of the classroom (or covers his/her eyes). Then remove an object. Call the student back into class and ask, "What's missing?" Make the game more demanding by removing two objects.

What's in That Bag?
Materials: A paper bag, 6 to 8 objects
Number of Players: Any number
Purpose: Reviewing vocabulary orally
Instructions: Place in a paper bag six to eight objects that students can name in Hebrew. A student reaches in the bag and has to name the object in Hebrew after touching it and feeling it.

I Study (for Lesson 13)
Materials: None
Number of Players: Group or class
Purpose: Practice sentences using לוֹמֵד/לוֹמֶדֶת
Instructions: Write the following phrases on the blackboard:

אֲנִי לוֹמֵד.

אֲנִי לוֹמֶדֶת.

מָה אַתָּה לוֹמֵד?

מָה אַתְּ לוֹמֶדֶת?

Play this game in small groups. A volunteer comes up to the chalkboard and illustrates a subject they like to study. For example, a student who likes music might draw a musical note. Other members of the group have to guess what that subject is by asking:

אַתְּ לוֹמֶדֶת מוּסִיקָה?

After three incorrect guesses, the fourth child asks:

מָה אַתְּ לוֹמֶדֶת?

I Like (for Lesson 14)
Materials: None
Number of Players: Group or class
Purpose: Practice sentences using אוֹהֵב/אוֹהֶבֶת
Instructions: Seat all students in a circle. Write the following phrases on the chalkboard:

אֲנִי אוֹהֵב.

אֲנִי אוֹהֶבֶת.

Practice until students can read and understand the phrases. Ask students to think of something they like (preferably that starts with the first sound in their name). The first student (Sharon) says in Hebrew:

אֲנִי אוֹהֶבֶת שׁוֹקוֹלָד.

The second student (Miriam) says:

שָׁרוֹן אוֹהֶבֶת שׁוֹקוֹלָד.

אֲנִי אוֹהֶבֶת מִילְק שֵׁיק.

The third student (a boy) says:

שָׁרוֹן אוֹהֶבֶת שׁוֹקוֹלָד.

מִרְיָם אוֹהֶבֶת מִילְק שֵׁיק.

אֲנִי אוֹהֵב פִּיצָה.

Continue in this manner. If a student forgets, provide the correct response and continue until all students have had a chance.

Songs

It is easy and enjoyable to learn new vocabulary through songs. Children often come to class with a repertoire of Hebrew songs they know by heart, but do not understand. Sing with your students or use a tape recorder. Teach the meaning of select words from the songs that fit in with your curriculum. You do not need to teach the meaning of every word. Teach the songs on the bottom of the Reading Pages for Lessons 15 to 20. You can put your own words to familiar melodies to reinforce vocabulary. The songs on the זְמַן לָשִׁיר *Time to Sing Hebrew* tape (available from A.R.E. Publishing, Inc.) were specifically written to teach the Hebrew language presented in this program. See the section on using the זְמַן לָשִׁיר songs beginning on page 152 of this Teacher Guide.

Arts and Crafts

Arts and crafts provide an opportunity to reinforce learning in a different sensory modality. Students will also enjoy expressing their creativity. Keep an accessible supply of magazine pictures, construction paper, crayons, markers, scissors, and glue.

Little Books
Materials: Paper, ribbon or string, hole punch, pictures, crayons or felt markers, scissors, glue
Number of Players: Individuals
Purpose: Vocabulary review and writing of Key Words and vocabulary words
Instructions: Fold and cut paper (or card stock) to make little books. Punch two holes on the right side and tie with ribbon or string to keep the book together. (Do not tie until the book is completed, enabling students to add or remove pages.) Students can write and illustrate Key Words, vocabulary, sentences, conversations from the Workbook, etc. Provide students with magazine pictures, as well as crayons and markers for illustrations. When books are completed, host a "Book Fair" and have students share their books.

Illustrated Letter Cards
Materials: Card stock, felt markers, or crayons
Number of Players: Any number
Purpose: Letter sound review, vocabulary review, and teaching the order of the *alef-bet*.
Instructions: Each time a new letter is learned, assign a student to make a decorated card showing the new letter along with one or more Hebrew words that begin with that letter. (You will need to use some cognates.) If you want to teach the order of letters in the alphabet in Lesson 18 after all the letters have been learned, stretch a clothesline across the classroom and hang the cards with clothespins. Remove some of the cards and see if students can replace them in the correct order.

Illustrated Dictionary
Materials: Card stock, felt markers, crayons
Number of Players: Any number
Purpose: Vocabulary and Key Word review
Instructions: Paste onto individual pieces of card stock the Key Words and vocabulary words from the program (see page 9 in this Teacher Guide for a list of these words). Ask for a volunteer or assign a student to illustrate a word as it comes up during a lesson. Use the opportunity to give a student special attention or to encourage a particularly artistic student. Place the expanding dictionary in a special place where students can come to check a word when necessary.

Judaica Arts and Crafts
Many of the Key Words in the text are Jewish objects or concepts that students can either make or illustrate. For example, students can make covers for *challah*, *matzah*, and the *Haggadah*, *Kiddush* cups, write Hebrew letters on *dreidels*, write and illustrate Hebrew greeting cards, etc. Students can also actually bake *matzah* and *challah*. For further ideas, consult Jewish crafts books such as *100+ Jewish Art Projects for Children* by Nina Streisand Sher and Margaret Feldman, and *Creative Puppetry for Jewish Kids* by Gale Solotar Warshawsky, both published by A.R.E. Publishing, Inc.

Jigsaw Method
The Jigsaw Method is a cooperative learning technique that utilizes two different types of groupings. First, students are assigned to heterogeneously grouped teams of four or five. Each team should contain one of the top students in the class as well as one of the weakest students in the class, with the average students divided equally among all the teams. Each member of the team is given a unique piece of information on a topic that the entire group is studying.

After receiving their unique pieces of information, representatives of each team meet in "expert groups." These groups are composed of those members of each team who are responsible for mastering the same piece of information. In the expert group meetings, the students discuss their piece of the puzzle, making certain that every member of the group understands the information completely.

Students then return to their teams and teach their teammates the information that they have learned. Teams work together to make sure that every member masters the information as well as possible. The entire class is then tested for individual grades or overall team scores. The latter has the advantage of reinforcing the premise that the team as a whole is responsible for helping its weakest members to become more successful.

For example, in using this method with Lesson 11, the teacher might divide the information into these five pieces: (1) how the ◼ is pronounced in your school's community; (2) reviewing the Hebrew letters and vowels studied so far that make the same sound; (3) exploring the Key Word פֶּסַח; (4) exploring the Key Word יִשְׂרָאֵל; (5) creative ways of practicing the Reading Pages. Each group would complete a task together in order to master their unique piece of information. For example, the first group might be asked to meet with the Rabbi, Cantor, or Director of Education. They would ask their interviewee to read the first four lines on page 3 (the first Reading Page in Lesson 11). By listening to a community leader's reading, the students must then determine how the two new vowels are pronounced within the school or community.

USING זְמַן לָשִׁיר IN THE CLASSROOM

The זְמַן לָשִׁיר *Time to Sing Hebrew* song curriculum consists of a songbook and cassette tape. It is available from A.R.E. Publishing, Inc. Although its songs can be an integral part of any Hebrew language program, they specifically reinforce the vocabulary of קָדִימָה! and זְמַן לִקְרֹא. זְמַן לָשִׁיר is designed to introduce a core vocabulary of basic Hebrew terms in small incremental steps, with much of the vocabulary repeated and reinforced in several of the songs.

Music can be a powerful tool for teaching foreign language vocabulary. Rhythm and melody enhance retention and enjoyment, and the lyrics provide opportunities to act out situations and concretize abstract concepts. Because repetition of speech is a necessary part of learning a second language, practicing language elements through song can be a very enjoyable replacement for tedious language drill. Students who may be reticent about speaking Hebrew words will often feel much more comfortable about singing them in a song.

Many current language acquisition theorists suggest that the manner of learning a second language should be similar to the way one acquires a first language, with oral language preceding written language. This appears to be a particularly effective second language learning strategy for children. Similarly, in a naturalistic second language program, receptive language should precede expressive language. This is how children acquire their native language — comprehension comes before speech, and speech comes before reading and writing.

By using זְמַן לָשִׁיר, students are provided with the opportunity to acquire an oral language base (albeit a limited one) before they are confronted with print. Teachers can begin teaching the songs before students are taught to read Hebrew words. Conversely, some of the songs are also appropriate for use as reading texts in a reading comprehension component during the later stages of the זְמַן לִקְרֹא program. This kind of reading comprehension activity can be a very positive experience for beginning Hebrew readers, and one that is highly motivating for them as well. To facilitate this approach, some of the recommendations for teaching specific songs include suggestions for reading comprehension questions and activities. For quick reference, an "Oral Language Level" is provided for each song; a "Reading Level" indication is also included where appropriate.

In a naturalistic language learning environment, comprehension precedes speech. For this reason it is advisable to work on developing comprehension of the vocabulary before expecting students to use it actively. זְמַן לָשִׁיר readily facilitates aural comprehension. Allow students time just to listen to the tape before asking them to join in a song. You can also play the tape as "background music" while students are completing independent tasks at their seats. Gradually, they will realize that they can understand the words they are hearing.

When you are actually ready to teach the songs, the enthusiasm you project is much more important than the musical talents either you or your students possess. Rely on the tape to learn and teach the melodies. If you play an instrument, you can later accompany yourself and your students. If your school has a music specialist, these songs can be integrated into the music curriculum once students master the vocabulary. As your students learn to read Hebrew, you can distribute song sheets or use an overhead projector to show the words to the songs.

Here are several guidelines for teaching the זְמַן לָשִׁיר songs:

1. Pre-teach the most essential vocabulary needed to understand the song, especially any words in the songs that are taught in זְמַן לִקְרֹא.

2. Much of the זְמַן לָשִׁיר vocabulary is presented in זְמַן לִקְרֹא. You may want to teach these songs before you teach student to read those words. In this way the vocabulary will be familiar and already part of the child's oral Hebrew language. The chart on page 160 of this Teacher Guide summarizes the type of vocabulary taught in זְמַן לָשִׁיר organized according to language function.

3. Whenever possible, use pantomime, body movement, hand motions, puppets, pictures, and/or actual objects to act out the meaning of different words and phrases. This kind of "direct instruction" is especially suited for teaching concrete language items, and should be employed for teaching whenever possible.

4. By the same token, it is not essential to teach all of the vocabulary in the songs. Some of the more abstract phrases such as הַכֹּל מוּכָן ("everything's ready") can be quickly translated as you are singing the songs and don't need to be specifically taught. It is not necessary for students to understand each and every word of a song, as long as they understand the important words and the basic theme.

5. Once the students have mastered a song, provide them with rhythm instruments and encourage them to use these as they sing.

6. If you incorporate the songs from זְמַן לָשִׁיר into a reading comprehension component, be sure to prepare song sheets for the students. These sheets should contain the lyrics in Hebrew only (without translation or transliteration). You can illustrate them using *The Big Book of Jewish Clip Art* or *Computer Jewish Clip Art* (both available from A.R.E. Publishing, Inc.). You can test students' comprehension using worksheets that ask them to match the Hebrew words with the pictures that illustrate them, or that ask students to answer questions about what takes place in a specific song. Sample comprehension questions have been included for the nine songs whose lyrics are all in Hebrew.

Following are specific recommendations for teaching each of the songs of זְמַן לָשִׁיר along with the זְמַן לִקְרֹא lesson relevant to most of the central vocabulary items of each song. Where appropriate, the lesson necessary for reading the Hebrew lyrics is also cited, and sample comprehension questions and activities are provided.

Side A

1. "Time To Read Hebrew"/"זְמַן לִקְרֹא"
Oral Vocabulary: Lesson 15 (students will have learned all the letter names).

This is an *alef-bet* song that teaches the names of the letters of the Hebrew alphabet in order, omitting the letters שׂ, פ, כ, ב. Three of these letters (פ, כ, and ב) are actually not separate letters, but simply secondary pronunciations of the letters פ, כ, and ב. If you have a Hebrew letter wall chart that excludes these (and the final letters), point to the letters as you sing the song. You can also ask students to point along to the letters on the chart that they created by completing the activity on page 70 of Volume Two (Lesson 18). The melody is very similar to the one used in the well-known ABC song.

The title of both קָדִימָה! and זְמַן לִקְרֹא are mentioned in the song. Explain to students that קָדִימָה means "Forward" and that זְמַן לִקְרֹא means "Time to Read." Note the ticking clock sound in the background which reinforces the meaning of "זְמַן" (time).

2. "Good-Getting-Up-Morning Song"/ "בֹּקֶר טוֹב"
Oral Vocabulary: Lesson 13.

This song has an upbeat, morning feel to it. Use pictures to illustrate the important words in the song: יַלְדָה קְטַנָה (little girl), יֶלֶד קָטָן (little boy). If your students have already acquired other vocabulary you can substitute אִמָא אוֹמֶרֶת (Mom says) with אַבָּא אוֹמֵר (Dad says).

Explain the difference between הַמוֹרָה אוֹמֶרֶת (the female teacher says) and הַמוֹרֶה אוֹמֵר (the male teacher says).

3. "Feline Felicity"/"חֲתוּלִים בַּחֲתֻנָה"
   Oral Vocabulary: Lesson 8.
   Reading Level: Lesson 17.

   Have fun with this one. The concept of a wedding of two cats is quite comical. Hopefully, the humorous aspect of this song will attract students to it, and give them ample practice in making the *Chet* sound. For native English speakers, this is one of the most difficult Hebrew sounds to pronounce, as there is not an equivalent sound in English, and learners often substitute the **h** or **k** sounds for ח. This makes the song quite fun and challenging to sing. The sound is repeated often — beginning with the laughing חָה, חָה, חָה to the repetition of חָתוּל וַחֲתוּלָה מִתַּחַת לַחֻפָּה. Show students pictures of חֻפָּה (wedding canopy), חֲתֻנָה (wedding), חֲתוּלָה (female cat) and חָתוּל (male cat), חָתָן (bridegroom) and כַּלָה (bride), and name them.

   Distribute cut-out magazine photos of two cats to each student, and have them paste these onto a piece of paper and dress them up as חָתָן and כַּלָה using crayons and/or markers. Help students distinguish between the words חָתוּל and חָתָן, חֲתוּלָה and כַּלָה. When they complete this, have them draw a חֻפָּה above the cats. You can also have volunteers act out the "cats' wedding," using a טַלִית for the חֻפָּה and masks for the cats.

   Use pantomime to illustrate the verb עוֹמְדִים (stand, pl.). You can play the game *Simon Says* if you also teach יוֹשְׁבִים/יוֹשֵׁב (sit). If students have not been introduced to verbs yet, you do not need to explain that עוֹמְדִים is in plural form. Note, however, that עוֹמֵד is used in the Purim song "לֹא כָּל יוֹם פּוּרִים." Also, you should teach the vocabulary קוֹל שָׂשׂוֹן (the voice of joy) since the word שָׂשׂוֹן appears in other songs in זְמַן לָשִׁיר.

   By Lesson 17, students will have been introduced to all the letters and vowels they need to read the lyrics of this song in Hebrew.

   Sample reading comprehension questions include:

   מִי הֶחָתָן?
   מִי הַכַּלָה?
   אֵיפֹה הַחֲתוּלִים?
   מִי תַּחַת הַחֻפָּה?
   מִי בַּחֲתֻנָה?

4. "Congratulations Are in Order"/"מַזָל טוֹב"
   Oral Vocabulary: Lesson 15.
   Reading Level: Lesson 17.

   Discuss the different occasions on which we would wish someone *Mazal Tov*. Use pictures to illustrate the occasions mentioned in the song (Bar-Mitzvah, Bat-Mitzvah, wedding). Make sure students are pronouncing the expression as it is said in Hebrew, מַזָל טוֹב (accent on "zal") rather than the Yiddish *Mazel Tov*.

   By Lesson 17, students will have been introduced to all the letters and vowels they need to read the lyrics of this song in Hebrew. To facilitate their comprehension, ask students to create "מַזָל טוֹב" cards that they could give to someone celebrating a Bar-Mitzvah, Bat-Mitzvah, or wedding.

   Sample reading comprehension questions include:

   מָה יֵשׁ לְדָנִי הַיוֹם?
   מָה יֵשׁ לְרוּתִי הַיוֹם?
   מָה רוּתִי אוֹמֶרֶת בַּחֲתֻנָה?
   מָה דָנִי אוֹמֵר בַּחֲתֻנָה?

5. "Classroom Capers"/"בַּכִּתָּה"
   Oral Vocabulary: Lesson 10 or 15.
   Reading Level: Lesson 17.

   This song is designed to teach classroom words, the question word אֵיפֹה (where) and two prepositions: עַל (on) and בְּ___ (in).
   The objects mentioned in the song are: לוּחַ (chalkboard), גִיר (chalk), מַחְבֶּרֶת (notebook), עִפָּרוֹן (pencil), שֻׁלְחָן (table), כִּסֵא (chair), and סֵפֶר (book).

   The vocabulary in this song lends itself to acting out. After teaching the word כִּתָּה (classroom) you can demonstrate the word בַּכִּתָּה by making motions to indicate "inside" the room. Translate only if absolutely necessary. Teach the classroom vocabulary by pointing to the objects. For example, point to a pencil and say עִפָּרוֹן, then point to a book and say סֵפֶר. Repeat several times until all students can point to the new words.

When the new nouns are mastered, demonstrate (one at a time) the prepositions עַל and תַּחַת. Teach all of the vocabulary before you sing the song. As you sing, have students point to the objects in the refrain:

לוּחַ וְגִיר מַחְבֶּרֶת וְעִפָּרוֹן שֻׁלְחָן וְכִסֵּא

This technique can be used with other songs as well. When you are singing the verses, have students hold up their hands in a questioning position as they ask each question. As you sing the responses, act them out. When students have mastered the vocabulary, sing the song slowly and ask students to act out the responses. Make sure that they have all the objects needed. You can also play the games מֶה חָסֵר (*What's Missing?*) and חַם וְקַר (*Hot and Cold*). In מֶה חָסֵר the teacher arranges several items on a table. You will need a miniature chair and table for playing this game as part of this lesson. Ask one student to leave the room. Remove one of the items from the group. When the student returns to the room, he or she must identify מֶה חָסֵר (what is missing).

In חַם וְקַר a student is asked to leave the room. The teacher names one object in Hebrew. The student is invited back into the room, and must guess what item the teacher selected by walking around the room. As the student gets closer to the item, the class shouts out "חַם" ("hot"). As the student moves away from the object, the class calls out "קַר" ("cold").

By Lesson 17, students will have been introduced to all the letters and vowels they need to read the lyrics of this song in Hebrew. To foster their reading comprehension, ask students to create labels for items in the classroom. You can also give them a picture of a classroom and ask them to label all the items they know in Hebrew.

Sample reading comprehension questions include:

אֵיפֹה הַגִּיר?
אֵיפֹה הָעִפָּרוֹן?
אֵיפֹה הַלּוּחַ?
מָה עַל הַמַּחְבֶּרֶת?
מָה עַל הַכִּסֵּא?
אֵיפֹה הַכִּתָּה?

6. **"Who Is Learning What?"/ "מִי לוֹמֵד עִבְרִית"**

Oral Vocabulary: Lesson 13.
Reading Level: Lesson 15.

This song directly drills the singular masculine form of the verb לוֹמֵד (learns). The subjects being studied are mostly cognates, i.e., foreign words used in Hebrew, but some of these are pronounced slightly differently in Hebrew. Pay attention to the pronunciation.

Ask students to guess what the "subjects" are: גּוֹלְף (golf), טֶנִיס (tennis), הִיסְטוֹרְיָה (history), בֵּיְס-בּוֹל (baseball). Students will be amused by this, and you may wish to have them guess other words that are not used in the song, such as גִּיאוֹגְרַפְיָה (geography) and בִּיוֹלוֹגְיָה (biology).

Prepare pictures (or objects) that illustrate what each child in the song is learning, and corresponding English and/or Hebrew name cards for each of the children in the song. Pass out name cards to individual students. Display the pictures or objects illustrating what each child in the song is learning. Redistribute the name cards and sing the song again. After students have heard the song several times, play various games that require them to respond to each of the questions either by singing the response or demonstrating it with a picture or movement.

Explain that we ask, "מִי לוֹמֵד?" ("Who learns?") in the masculine singular form, since we do not know if the answer is going to be singular or plural, masculine or feminine. But, in the final lines of the song, when the questions ask what each specific child is learning, we do know the gender of the child about whom the question is being asked, so we do use לוֹמֵד for a boy and לוֹמֶדֶת for a girl.

When you sing the line containing the words אֲנִי אַתְּ וְאַתָּה (I, you fem. and you masc.), point to yourself, then to a girl, and finally to a boy in the correct order. Practice the verb in the masculine (לוֹמֵד) and feminine (לוֹמֶדֶת) form using students in the classroom and/or puppets.

a. Point to a child and ask the students if you say לוֹמֶדֶת or לוֹמֵד.

b. After the students can do this reliably,

have them say a complete sentence together: (דָנִי לוֹמֵד עִבְרִית).

Initially use one subject (e.g., דָנִי) and then alternate by using the pictures or objects you used to teach the song. Other regular verbs used in זְמַן לָשִׁיר are: אוֹהֵב (love/like), אוֹמֵר (say), שׁוֹאֵל (ask) and עוֹמֵד (stand). Notice that the verbs לוֹמֵד and עוֹמֵד sound much alike and can easily be confused. Do not teach these together.

By Lesson 15, students will have been introduced to all the letters and vowels they need to read the lyrics of this song in Hebrew. Show students a picture of a classroom and ask them to write Hebrew sentences to describe what is going on. The best examples can be used with the classroom picture to create a bulletin board entitled "בְּכִתָּה."

Sample reading comprehension questions include:

מִי לוֹמֵד עִבְרִית?
מָה לוֹמֶדֶת גִילָה?
מִי לוֹמֵד תּוֹרָה?
מָה אַתָּה לוֹמֵד?/מָה אַתְּ לוֹמֶדֶת?

7. "Water Play"/"הֵיפוֹ בַּמַיִם"
   Oral Vocabulary: Lesson 8 or 11.
   Reading Level: Lesson 20.

In addition to the names of animals the song teaches the word בַּמַיִם and the plural masculine form of אוֹהֲבִים (love/like).

The song lends itself to acting out, using costume pieces or puppets. Note that each character has an accompanying sound on the tape, from the whistling of the children to the tinkling sound of the fish.

By Lesson 20, students will have been introduced to all the letters and vowels they need to read the lyrics of this song in Hebrew.

Sample reading comprehension questions include:

מִי בַּמַיִם?
מָה בַּמַיִם?
אֵיפֹה הַהִיפוֹ?
אֵיפֹה הַדָג?
מָה חֲתוּלִים לֹא אוֹהֲבִים?

8. "Good Night — Sleepy Time"/"לַיְלָה טוֹב"
   Oral Vocabulary: Lesson 13 or 15.

This song has both Hebrew and English text. The major phrase לַיְלָה טוֹב is translated. This song features the changing of adjectives (קָטָן or קְטַנָה) to match the nouns (יֶלֶד or יַלְדָה). This concept is also reinforced in the Pesach song "מִי בַּסֵדֶר פֶּסַח?" In זְמַן לִקְרֹא the masculine form of big (גָדוֹל) and small (קָטָן) are taught. The animals in the song all appear in קָדִימָה *Kadimah!*, and except for חָתוּל/חֲתוּלִים they are all cognates.

The mood of the song is that of a lullaby. Choose students to play the parts of the characters in the song using props or puppets and act out falling asleep. You can contrast this song with the song "בֹּקֶר טוֹב", and its peppy, lively rhythm.

Side B

1. "I Love Holidays — Foody Blues"/"אֲנִי אוֹהֶבֶת אֶת הַחַגִים"
   Oral Vocabulary: Lesson 15.
   Reading Level: Lesson 19.

This song uses the verb אוֹהֵב (loves/likes) and reviews the different foods we eat (or don't eat!) on the Jewish holidays. Have pictures of the foods or, even better, samples of the foods available. Point to each food as you sing the song.

The song is sung in feminine singular on the cassette tape because the singer is a woman. Once students know the song, they can change the form of the verb. Take turns having the boys sing "אוֹהֵב" and girls sing "אוֹהֶבֶת." Tell them that the word אֶת is just a connecting word without meaning, not to be confused with the feminine verb ending ת.

Note that the melody changes for each different holiday. This does make the song harder to learn initially. However, the melody changes can enhance the learning experience if students are asked to associate the holiday with its melody.

By Lesson 19, students will have been introduced to all the letters and vowels they need to read the lyrics of this song in Hebrew. To foster their reading comprehension, provide them with a Holiday Food Menu, which lists the foods mentioned in the song in one column and the holidays (not directly matching the foods) in another column. The students must first match each food to its correct holiday, then order from the menu. If you use real food items as part of the oral presentation, allow the students to eat the foods only after they "order" them from their menu in Hebrew. You can also have students create holiday food mobiles using cards that illustrate the food item on one side with its matching holiday written on the other side.

Sample reading comprehension questions include:

מָה אוֹכְלִים בְּפוּרִים?

מָה אוֹכְלִים בַּחֲנֻכָּה?

מָה אוֹכְלִים בְּשַׁבָּת?

מָה אוֹכְלִים בְּיוֹם הַכִּפּוּרִים?

מָה אוֹכְלִים בְּרֹאשׁ הַשָּׁנָה?

2. **"Ready for Shabbat"**/"שַׁבָּת שָׁלוֹם"
   Oral Vocabulary: Lesson 1 or 10.
   Reading Level: Lesson 19.

   This is a beautiful song with which to begin any child's study of Hebrew! As an alternative, after Lesson 10, students will know a great deal of the vocabulary contained in this song. Only the family members סָבָא (grandfather), סָבְתָא (grandmother), בֵּן, (son), בַּת (daughter), and a couple of simple nouns — מַפָּה לְבָנָה (white tablecloth), שֻׁלְחָן (table), and נֵרוֹת (candles) — will be new words for them at that point. The ability to read and understand so many of its lyrics makes learning this wonderful song a special treat for students as they complete the first volume, and a motivational tool as they begin the second half of the program. Have a photograph or picture of an extended family on hand or ask students to bring in photographs of their parents, grandparents, and siblings. As you sing the song with your students, point to the different family members mentioned in it, and use a sweeping motion to explain כָּל הַמִּשְׁפָּחָה. Explain the meaning of the phrase הַכֹּל מוּכָן by translating it into English.

In your classroom, set a Shabbat table using a white tablecloth. Demonstrate the meaning of the preposition עַל (on) by placing different Shabbat objects on your table as the song is read or sung. You can demonstrate the movement used while kindling the lights of Shabbat and remind students of the appropriate blessing. After you have sung the song several times, have students point to pictures of different family members and the Shabbat objects on the table as they are mentioned in the song.

By Lesson 19, students will have been introduced to all the letters and vowels they need to read the lyrics of this song in Hebrew. To facilitate their mastery of Hebrew reading, ask students to create "שַׁבָּת שָׁלוֹם" placecards for a family Shabbat dinner. They can include any family member who might attend such a dinner. Parents can be encouraged to use these placecards for Shabbat dinner at home (or for a class Shabbat dinner if your school hosts them).

Sample reading comprehension questions include:

מָה עַל הַשֻּׁלְחָן?

מִי בַּמִּשְׁפָּחָה?

מִי אוֹמֵר שַׁבָּת שָׁלוֹם?

3. **"Happy Holidays"**/"חַג שָׂמֵחַ"
   Oral Vocabulary: Lesson 15.

   To demonstrate the meaning of the expression חַג שָׂמֵחַ (happy holiday), create a poster that illustrates the different holiday celebrations mentioned in the song. Note that the holidays are named in correct chronological order. Thus, once the words of the song are memorized, students will have learned the correct order of the major holidays. Point to each holiday picture as the song mentions it.

4. **"Purim Comes but Once a Year"**/"לֹא כָּל יוֹם פּוּרִים"
   Oral Vocabulary: Lesson 15.
   Reading Level: Lesson 19.

   This song presents a delightful contrast between the playful spirit of Purim and the more serious feeling of Shabbat. Begin your presentation with a review of Purim and its major symbols: the *Megillah*, noisemakers, masks, and costumes. Bring in props to dress up a student as a Rabbi with a mask on and another as the Cantor reading from the *Megillah*. Give the remaining students noisemakers. Have the students act out the words of the song as the tape is played (or as you sing the song). Specific words to act out are: עוֹמֵד (stands, masc. sing.), מַסֵּכָה (mask), קוֹרֵא (reads, masc. sing.), מִתְפַּלְלִים (pray, pl.), כִּפָּה (yarmulke), טַלִּית (tallit), and רַעֲשָׁנִים (graggers).

Notice how the melody shifts when the scene changes from the rowdy Purim to the peaceful Shabbat. (This melody is a variation of that used in the song "שַׁבָּת שָׁלוֹם" on the cassette tape.) Have the appropriate props here for the Rabbi — a כִּפָּה and טַלִּית. The punchline "לֹא כָּל יוֹם פּוּרִים" is a common Israeli expression that means special events or circumstances do not occur every day. It is often used as a gentle reminder for children that they need to stop behaving in a rowdy manner.

By Lesson 19, students will have been introduced to all the letters and vowels they need to read the lyrics of this song in Hebrew. If Purim is late (or you are pretty far along in the program), allow students to create מִשְׁלוֹחַ מָנוֹת plates that illustrate some of the lines about Purim from the song. Students can then fill these plates with goodies, and give them to each other or to students in the younger grades.

Sample reading comprehension questions include:

אֵיפֹה הָרַבִּי בְּחַג פּוּרִים?
אֵיפֹה הָרַבִּי בְּשַׁבָּת?
אֵיפֹה הַחַזָּן בְּחַג פּוּרִים?
אֵיפֹה הַחַזָּן בְּשַׁבָּת?
מַה יֵּשׁ לָרַבִּי בְּחַג פּוּרִים?
מַה יֵּשׁ לָרַבִּי בְּשַׁבָּת?
מַה יֵּשׁ לְכָל הַיְלָדִים בְּחַג פּוּרִים?
מַה קוֹרֵא הַחַזָּן בְּחַג פּוּרִים?
מַה קוֹרֵא הַחַזָּן בְּשַׁבָּת?

5. "Four New Questions for the Seder"/ "מִי בְּסֵדֶר פֶּסַח?"

Oral Vocabulary: Lesson 11 or 16.
Reading Level: Lesson 19.

This delightful song teaches the question words: מִי (who), מָה (what), and אֵיפֹה (where), as well as Passover vocabulary. It provides four creative new questions about Passover, a play on the Four Questions that are likely to be a familiar part of the Passover experience for many students.

For teaching the vocabulary, prepare two separate posters: one which illustrates who is at the *Seder* table and the other to show what is on it. All of the words in this song are taught in זְמַן לִקְרֹא except for the following: שׁוֹאֵל (asks), מַה נִּשְׁתַּנָּה (the Four Questions), סָבָּא (grandpa), סָבְתָא (grandma), כַּרְפַּס (green vegetable), חֲרֹסֶת (charoset), מָרוֹר (bitter herb), גַם (also), זְרוֹעַ (shankbone), בֵּיצָה (egg), אֲפִיקוֹמָן (afikoman), and הִנֵּה הוּא כָּאן (here it is). Most of these are already familiar terms to many Jewish students. Others, such as the Hebrew terms for grandparents, may also be familiar since they were introduced in previous songs. Go over each of the vocabulary words to introduce or review them. Act out the final question, "אֵיפֹה הָאֲפִיקוֹמָן?" (Where is the *afikoman*?) The first time you present the vocabulary from the song, demonstrate searching for the *afikoman* in the places mentioned in the song. Once students have mastered the vocabulary, ask for a volunteer to conduct the search.

By Lesson 19, students will have been introduced to all the letters and vowels they need to read the lyrics of this song in Hebrew. To help them with comprehension, you can assign them to make Passover decorations that illustrate the song's lyrics. These decorations can then be donated to the Jewish patients at a local hospital or to a neighborhood nursing home for their Jewish residents. All the questions in this song are reading comprehension questions that can be used to test each student's mastery of the concepts.

6. **"Hello, Goodbye"**/"שָׁלוֹם, שָׁלוֹם"
   Oral Vocabulary: Lessons 13.

   This song introduces the most common meaning of the word שָׁלוֹם, and its use as a greeting and a farewell. שָׁלוֹם is probably the best known and most commonly used Hebrew word. Ask students if they know what the word means. Use picture illustrations to introduce its most common meaning (peace), and use pantomime to demonstrate its use as two different salutations (hello and goodbye). Since the song lyrics describe saying שָׁלוֹם in virtually every place, have students draw pictures of people saying "שָׁלוֹם" to each other in the house, on the street, at school, and so on. Similarly, since שָׁלוֹם is a universal Jewish expression, students can illustrate Jews from various countries saying "שָׁלוֹם" to one another. These can be used to make a class bulletin board entitled "תָּמִיד אוֹמְרִים שָׁלוֹם." Similarly, if the situation warrants it, students can make "שָׁלוֹם עַל יִשְׂרָאֵל" cards to express their support for Israel, or for Jews that are in danger anywhere. These cards can be sent to people in Israel or a Jewish community in need.

7. **"Time to Read Hebrew"**/"זְמַן לִקְרֹא"
   Reprise.

זְמַן לָשִׁיר Vocabulary Chart

Greetings	Animals	Jewish Ritual	Life Cycle	Jewish Celebrations			
				Purim	Pesach	Shabbat	
שָׁלוֹם	חָתוּל (חֲתוּלִים)	בֵּית-כְּנֶסֶת	מִשְׁפָּחָה	הָמָן	חַג הַפֶּסַח	שַׁבָּת	
בֹּקֶר טוֹב	כֶּלֶב	מְזוּזָה	חֲתֻנָּה	מְגִלָּה	מַצָּה	יוֹם	
לַיְלָה טוֹב	צִפּוֹר	נֵר	חָג	מִסְכָּה	הַגָּדָה, סֵדֶר	נֵר	
אֵיךְ שְׁלוֹמְךָ	חַיּוֹת/חַיָּה	תַּלִּית	מַתָּנָה		חָרוֹסֶת, מָרוֹר	מוֹתָר	
לְהִתְרָאוֹת	דָּג	סִדּוּר	שָׁלוֹם		כַּרְפַּס	חַלָּה (חַלּוֹת)	

Classroom	Question Words	Adjectives	Prepositions, Adverbs	Verbs	Pronouns	Family/People
סֵפֶר	מִי	טוֹבִים	עַל	אוֹכֵל/אוֹכְלִים	אֲנִי	אַבָּא, אִמָּא
כֶּסֶא	מַה	גְּדוֹלָה	בְּתוֹךְ	מְהַלֵּל/מְהַלְּלִים	אַתָּה	הוֹרִים, הוֹרֶה
שֻׁלְחָן	אֵיפֹה	קְטַנָּה/קְטַנָּה	מִן	רוֹצִים/רוֹצִים	אַתְּ	אָח
חַלּוֹן			בַּ–	אוֹמְרִים	הוּא	אִשָּׁה
דֶּלֶת			בְּ–	אוֹמֵר/אוֹמֶרֶת	הִיא	יֶלֶד
לוּחַ			לְפְנֵי, אַחֲרֵי	בָּא		סָבָא, סַבְתָּא
תַּלְמִיד			אֶל, אִם	אוֹהֶבֶת		דּוֹד, דּוֹדָה
יֶלֶד				אוֹכְלָה		
מוֹרֶה				עוֹמְדִים/עוֹמְדִים		
מְנַהֵל(ת)						

CLASS EVALUATION FORM

LESSONS	1	2	3	4	5	6	7	8	9	10	COMMENTS
STUDENT NAMES											
1.											
2.											
3.											
4.											
5.											
6.											
7.											
8.											
9.											
10.											
11.											
12.											
13.											
14.											
15.											
16.											
17.											
18.											
19.											
20.											

CLASS EVALUATION FORM

LESSONS	11	12	13	14	15	16	17	18	19	20	COMMENTS
STUDENT NAMES											
1.											
2.											
3.											
4.											
5.											
6.											
7.											
8.											
9.											
10.											
11.											
12.											
13.											
14.											
15.											
16.											
17.											
18.											
19.											
20.											

PLACEMENT TEST

Name _____ Date _____

Lesson			Lesson			Lesson		
1	1.	בֶּטֶשׁ	9	11.	צִבְתָּן	14	21.	קֶטֶף
2	2.	שָׁגַד		12.	שַׁלְוָה	15	22.	עֲלִיזִי
3	3.	אֱמֶת	10	13.	יַשְׁכִּיבוּ		23.	זוֹרֵחַ
4	4.	הַצַּד		14.	עֱוִית	16	24.	פּוֹצֵץ
	5.	בַּמֶּה	11	15.	מִשְׁתַּכֵּר		25.	מִצְווֹתָיו
5	6.	אֲגָדָה		16.	הֶעֱמִיס	17	26.	מְכֻוָּץ
	7.	יָנִי	12	17.	סִפְרָם	18	27.	אֵינֵךְ
6	8.	תִּקּוּן		18.	שִׁפְשֵׁף		28.	לְכֻלָּךְ
7	9.	פְּרָם	13	19.	כָּבוֹד		29.	חוֹזַי
8	10.	תָּחוּל		20.	טֹפֶס	19	30.	קָדְשְׁךָ

Comments _____

Using the Placement Test

This test is designed to be a tool for quickly asssessing an individual student's skills in Hebrew decoding. Unlike the evaluations that appear at the end of each student Workbook, which give a basis for determining mastery, this test will give you a snapshot of the individual's overall level of skill. It is also very easy to use.

This Placement Test can be used with students who are in need of some extra support by indentifying the point at which the student began to develop difficulties in Hebrew decoding. It can also be used to assess the skills of a student who enters the school either mid-year or in a year following the primer. Finally, it can be administered to entire classes or grades of students to ascertain their decoding skills as a whole.

Administering the Placement Test

1. As with all tools for evaluating a student's oral reading, it is important to test students individually. Give the student a clean copy of the Placement Test. You may want to laminate your student copy so that it can be reused many times. On your clean copy, write the student's name and the date in the appropriate spaces.

2. Tell the student to ignore the numbers in the shaded boxes in the margins, and to look only at the regular numbers. Ask the student to read straight down the column starting with number 1.

3. As the student reads, put a check by each word that is read correctly. Write down on your copy of the test any mistakes that the student makes. You should write these notes phonetically, preferably in Hebrew script just as you do on the individual lesson evaluations (see examples on page 34, 63, and 82 in this Teacher Guide).

4. If a student begins to make errors on every word, you should stop the test.

5. Accept self-corrections, but do not give feedback until the student has read all 30 words (or as many as he or she can read).

Analyzing the Placement Test

1. Examine the completed test for any pattern of errors (e.g., the student confuses several pairs of visually similar letters, or pronounces every *Shva* as a vowel). Note these patterns in the comments section at the bottom of the test.

2. The numbers in the shaded boxes in the margins correspond to the lessons in זְמַן לִקְרֹא. They tell you where any new items in a test word are taught. This can give you an indication of where remediation should begin. For example, if the student begins to make consistent errors with number 16, you should begin remediation with Lesson 11 in זְמַן לִקְרֹא.

3. You should also record other impressions of the student's performance in the comments section. For example, you will want to note that a student reads fluently, or that the student was hesitant or read so softly that it was difficult to hear. Fluency combined with a satisfactory performance overall on basic skills indicates full mastery, while a hesitant reader or one who is unsure may benefit greatly from a little additional support.

DICTIONARY מִלּוֹן Lessons 1-20

א
father	(3)	אַבָּא
mother	(3)	אִמָּא
love/like (m.)	(14)	אוֹהֵב
love/like (f.)	(14)	אוֹהֶבֶת
where?	(16)	אֵיפֹה?
alef	(12)	אָלֶף
I	(5)	אֲנִי
you (f.)	(9)	אַתְּ
you (m.)	(8)	אַתָּה

ב
in the	(5)	בַּ__
you're welcome, please	(14)	בְּבַקָּשָׁה
house	(5)	בַּיִת
synagogue	(15)	בֵּית-כְּנֶסֶת
school	(16)	בֵּית-סֵפֶר
with all your soul	(19)	בְּכָל נַפְשְׁךָ
good morning	(13)	בֹּקֶר טוֹב
blessing	(17)	בְּרָכָה
Bar-Mitzvah	(9)	בַּר-מִצְוָה
Bat-Mitzvah	(9)	בַּת-מִצְוָה

ג
chalk	(7)	גִּיר
big	(15)	גָּדוֹל
nation	(20)	גּוֹי

ד
fish	(2)	דָּג
flag	(11)	דֶּגֶל

ה
the	(4)	הַ__
Havdalah	(9)	הַבְדָּלָה
Haggadah	(4)	הַגָּדָה

ו
and	(14)	וְ__

ז
zebra	(15)	זֶבְרָה

ח
happy holiday	(15)	חַג שָׂמֵחַ
alive	(18)	חַי
challah	(8)	חַלָּה
cat	(8)	חָתוּל

י
hand, Torah pointer	(5)	יָד
wine	(6)	יַיִן
boy	(11)	יֶלֶד
girl	(11)	יַלְדָּה
Israel	(11)	יִשְׂרָאֵל

כ			ס		
כֶּלֶב	(12)	dog	סְלִיחָה	(14)	excuse me
כֵּן	(13)	yes	סֵפֶר	(12)	book
כִּסֵּא	(15)	chair	**ע**		
כִּתָּה	(10)	class	עִבְרִית	(10)	Hebrew
ל			עַל	(10)	on
לֹא	(13)	no	עַל-יַד	(10)	next to
לוּחַ	(15)	chalkboard	עִם	(14)	with
לוֹמֵד	(13)	learn (m.)	עִפָּרוֹן	(15)	pencil
לוֹמֶדֶת	(13)	learn (f.)	עֵץ חַיִּים	(16)	tree of life
מ			**פ**		
מָגֵן דָּוִד	(11)	Star of David	פּוּרִים	(7)	Purim
מָה?	(6)	what?	פֶּסַח	(11)	Pesach
מוֹרֶה	(13)	teacher (m.)	**ק**		
מוֹרָה	(13)	teacher (f.)	קִדּוּשׁ	(6)	Kiddush
מַזָּל טוֹב	(15)	congratulations	קָטָן	(15)	small
מַחְבֶּרֶת	(11)	notebook	**ר**		
מִי?	(5)	who?	רַבִּי	(7)	Rabbi
מַיִם	(7)	water	**ש**		
מֶלֶךְ	(18)	king	שַׁבָּת	(1)	Sabbath
מַצָּה	(4)	matzah	שָׁלוֹם	(13)	peace, hello, goodbye
מִצְוָה	(9)	commandment	שֻׁלְחָן	(17)	table
מִצְווֹת	(16)	commandments	**ת**		
מֹשֶׁה	(20)	Moses	תּוֹרָה	(13)	Torah
מִשְׁפָּחָה	(9)	family	תַּחַת	(8)	under
נ					
נֵר	(15)	candle			

COGNATE PICTURE CARDS

Beginning on the next page, you will find pictures of cognates (words that are used in both English and Hebrew — banana, baseball, etc.). Occasionally the Hebrew pronunciation is a little different from the English. There is one cognate picture card for every Hebrew consonant except for כ and ב and the final letters. There are also cards for two of the Hebrew vowel sounds. Using cognates allows children to utilize their previous knowledge and is a quick way to add to their Hebrew vocabulary.

Reproduce and cut out the cognate picture cards and use them for the following activities:

1. *Memory/Concentration* (see page 144 in this Teacher Guide) – Match a cognate picture card to its beginning sounds.

2. *Bingo* (see page 144 in this Teacher Guide) – Make a board of 16 Hebrew letters. Instead of reading words from 16 index cards, use the picture cards.

3. Place a cognate picture card on the felt board. Student must find the matching letter.

4. *Chalkboard Races* (see page 145 in this Teacher Guide) – Show a cognate picture card. Students race to write the beginning sound.

5. Mount a cognate picture on construction paper with a Hebrew letter on the reverse side. Show the letter and have student guess the picture. Students must be familiar with the pictures before doing this activity.

Note: When using these cards, students will most often have no way of determining if a picture begins with a ט or ת or with a ס or a שׂ; for example, that טֶלֶפוֹן begins with a ט. Since תּוֹרָה is a vocabulary word in this program, students should know that it begins with a ת, but other errors of this sort should be allowed.

List of Cognates on Cards

Hebrew Letter	Cognate	
בּ	Banana	בָּנָנָה
ג	Guitar	גִּיטָרָה
ד	Dinosaur	דִּינוֹסָאוּרוּס
ה	Hippo	הִיפּוֹ
ו	Video	וִידֵאוֹ
ז	Zebra	זֶבְרָה
ח	Chanukah	חֲנֻכָּה
ט	Telephone	טֶלֶפוֹן
י	Yoyo	יוֹ-יוֹ
כּ	Kipah	כִּפָּה
ל	Lemon	לִימוֹן
מ	Mixer	מִיקְסֶר
נ	Ninja	נִינְגָ'ה
ס	Steak	סְטֵיק
פּ	Popcorn	פּוֹפְּקוֹרְן
פ	Falafel	פָלָפֶל
צ	Tsitsit	צִיצִית
ק	Coca Cola	קוֹקָה קוֹלָה
ר	Robot	רוֹבּוֹט
שׁ	Shofar	שׁוֹפָר
שׂ	Sack	שַׂק
ת	Torah	תּוֹרָה

167

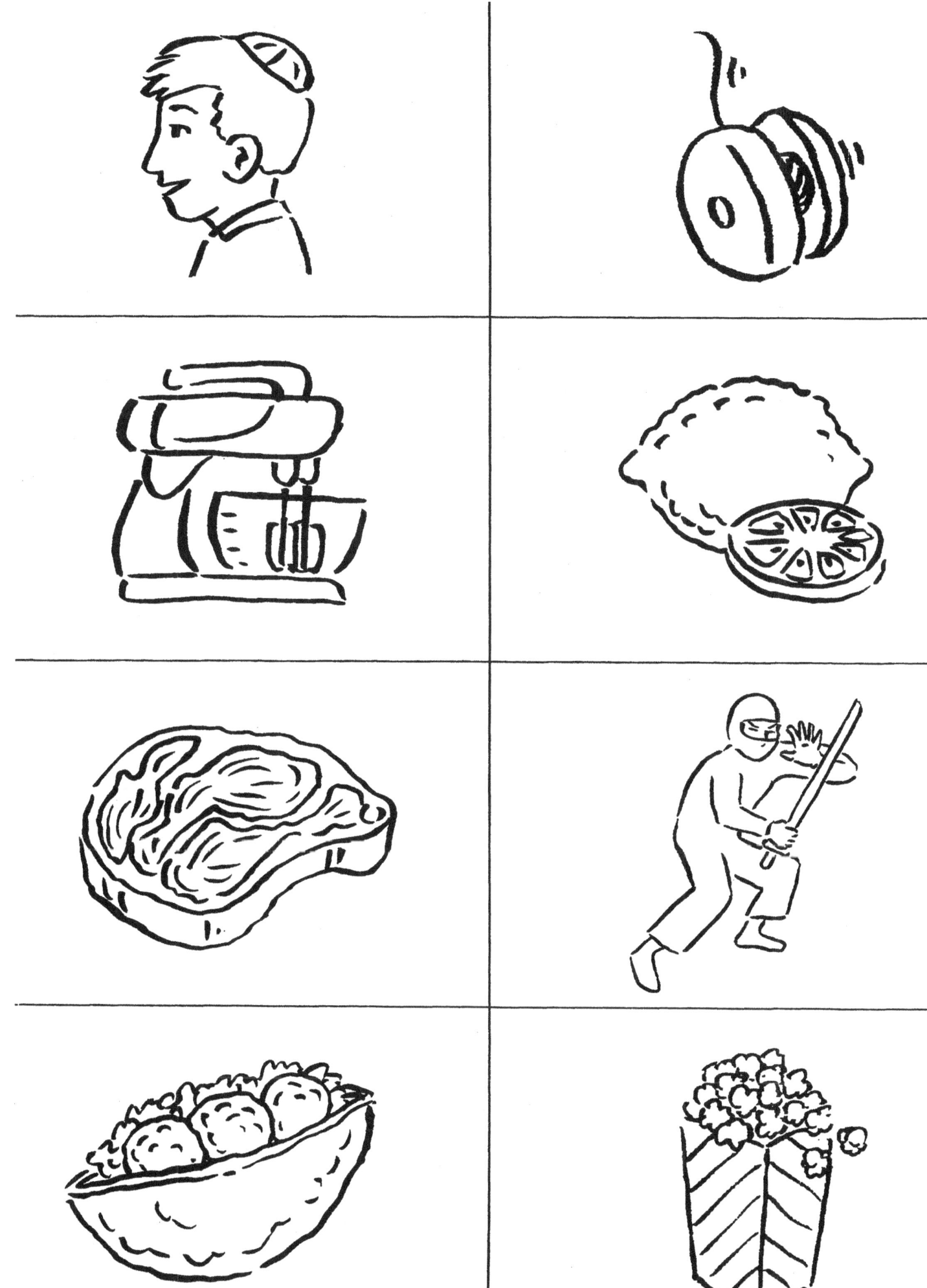

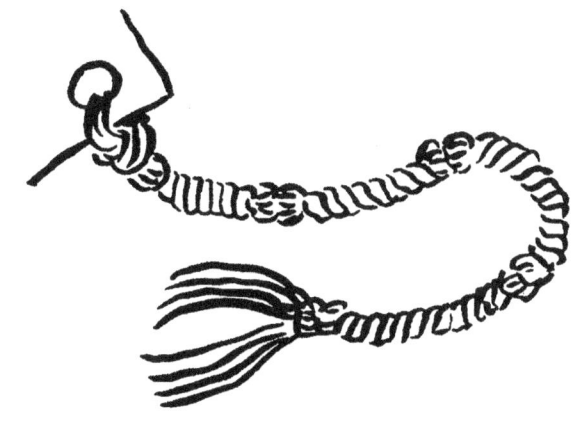

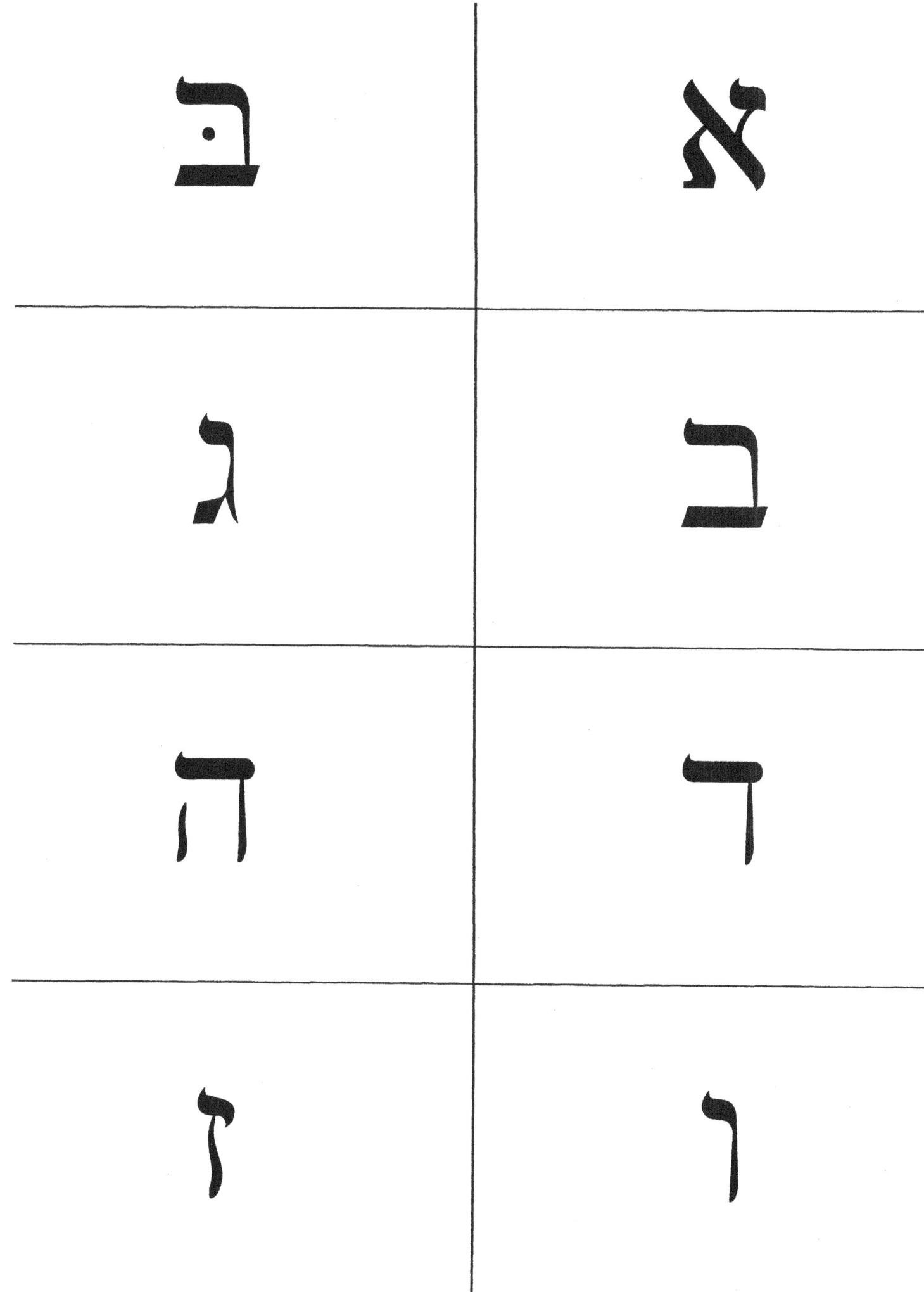

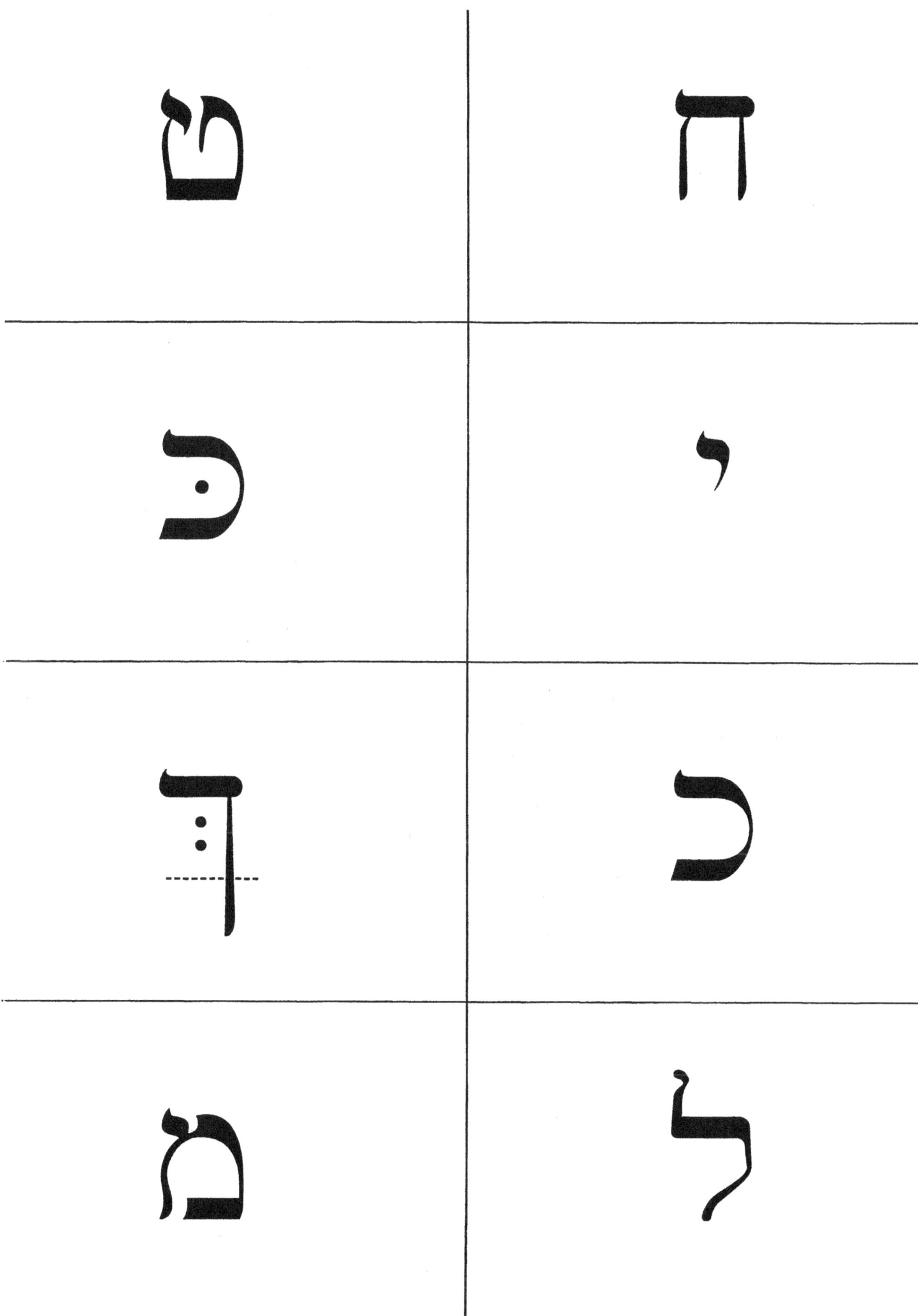

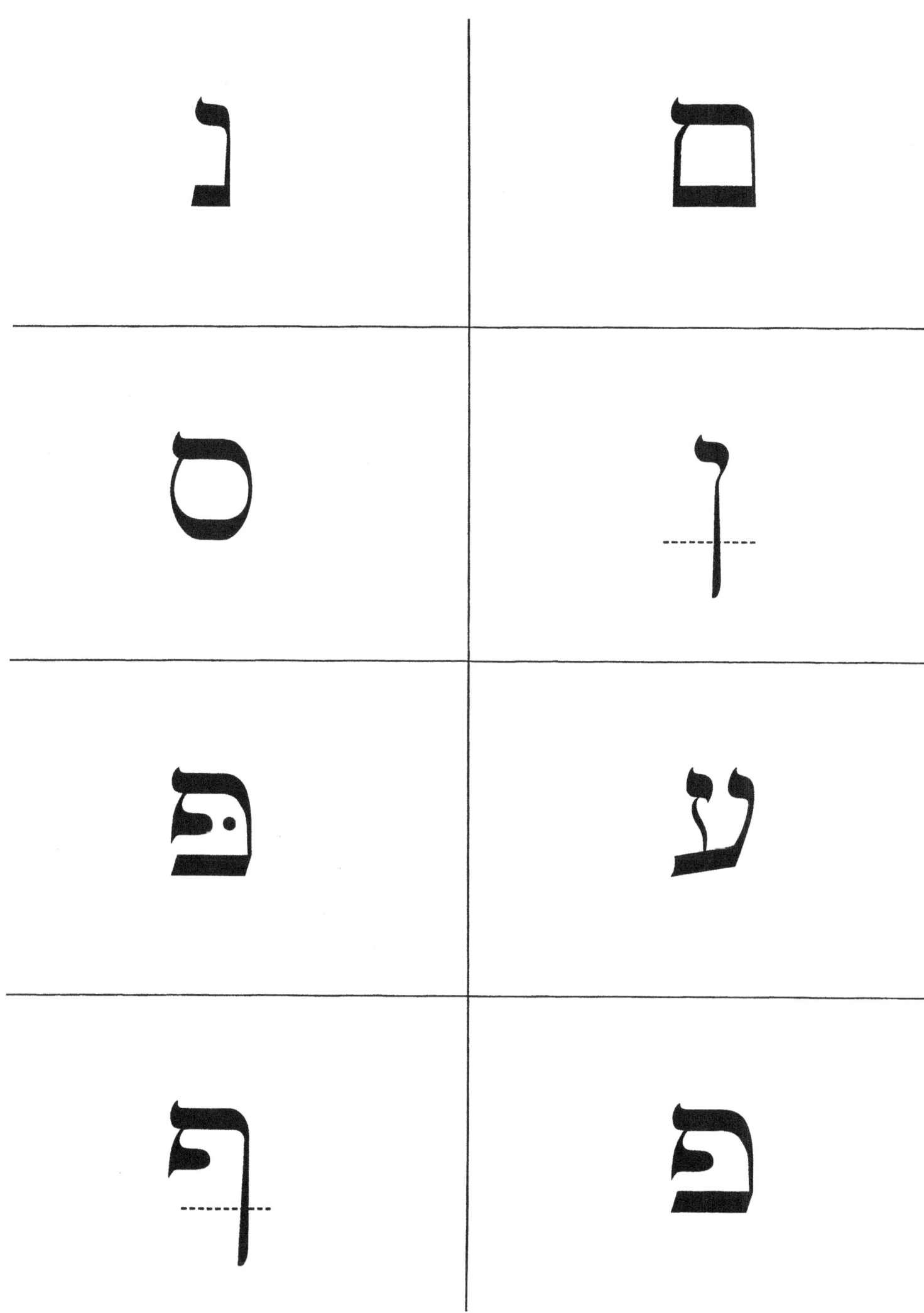

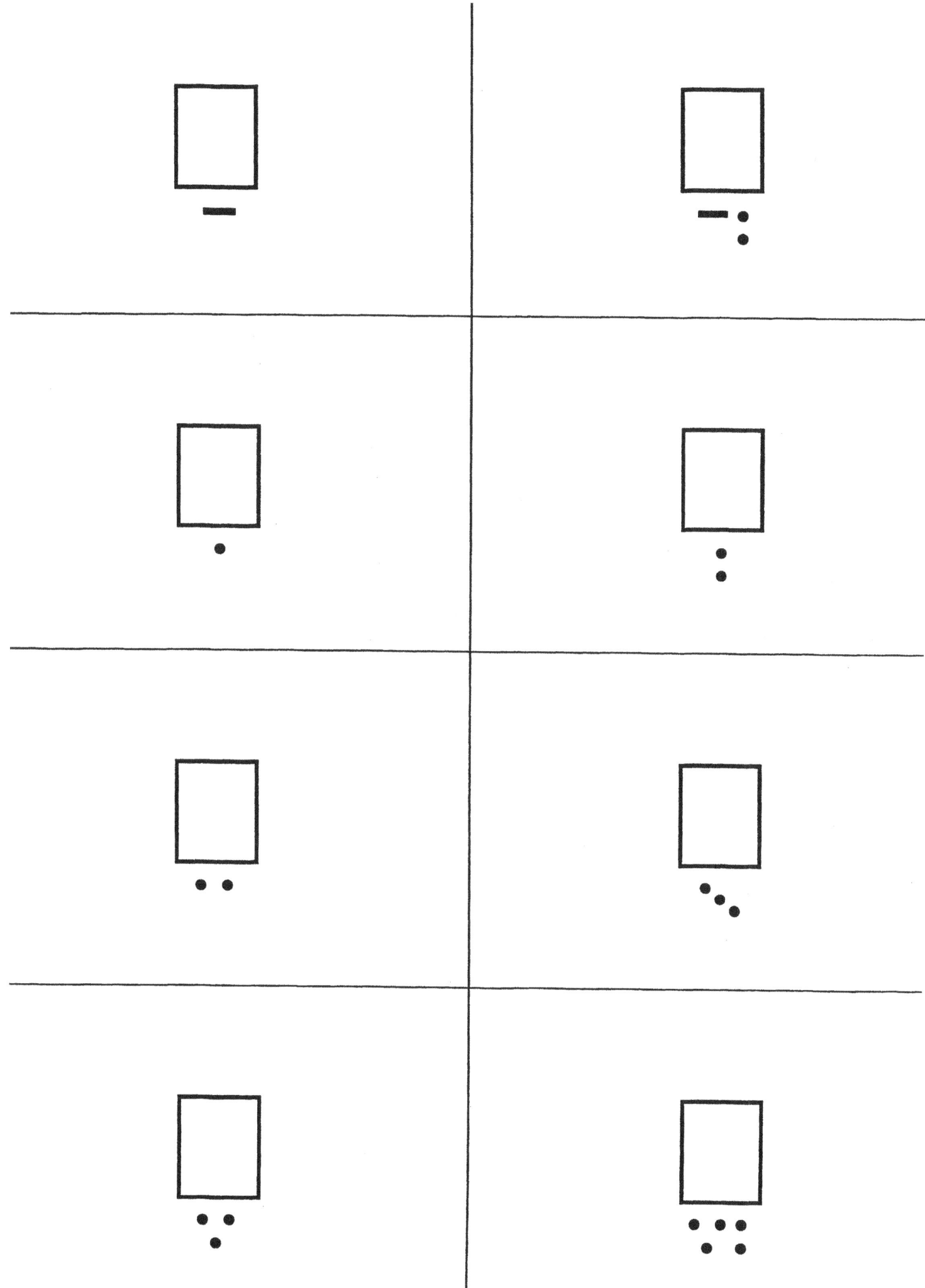

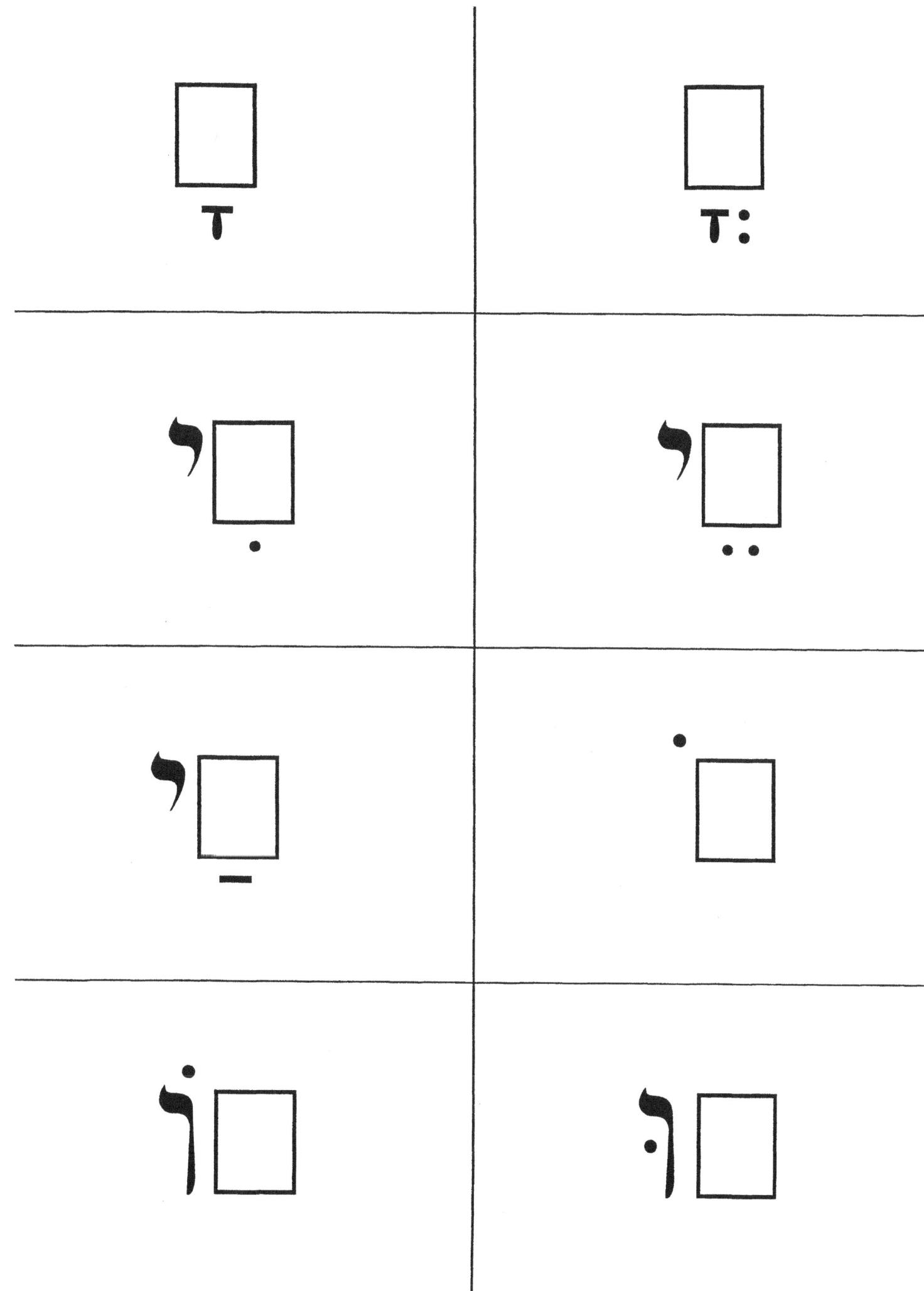